Forgotten Heroes

Royal Asiatic Society Hong Kong Studies Series

Royal Asiatic Society Hong Kong Studies Series is designed to make widely available important contributions on the local history, culture and society of Hong Kong and the surrounding region. Generous support from the Sir Lindsay and Lady May Ride Memorial Fund makes it possible to publish a series of high-quality works that will be of lasting appeal and value to all, both scholars and informed general readers, who share a deeper interest in and enthusiasm for the area.

Other titles in RAS Hong Kong Studies Series:

Ancestral Images: A Hong Kong Collection Hugh Baker

Cantonese Society in Hong Kong and Singapore Marjorie Topley, Jean De Bernardi (ed)

Custom, Land & Livelihood in Rural South China 1750–1950 Patrick Hase

Dragon and the Crown: Hong Kong Memoirs Stanley Kwan with Nicole Kwan

Early China Coast Meteorology: The Role of HK 1882–1912 Kevin MacKeown

East River Column: Hong Kong Guerrillas in the Second World War and After Chan Sui Jeung

Escape from Hong Kong: Admiral Chan Chak's Christmas Day Dash, 1941 Tim Luard

For Gods, Ghosts and Ancestors Janet Scott

Forgotten Souls: The Social History of Hong Kong Cemetery 1845–1918 Patricia Lim

Governors, Politics and the Colonial Office Gavin Ure

Hong Kong Internment 1942–1945: Life in the Japanese Civilian Camp at Stanley Geoff Emerson

Ireland's Imperial Mandarin: Sir Robert Hart. Mark O'Neill

Portugal, China and the Macau Negotiations 1986–1999 Carmen Mendes

Public Success, Private Sorrow: The Life and Times of Charles Henry Brewitt-Taylor Isidore Cyril Cannon

Reluctant Heroes: Rickshaw Pullers in Hong Kong and Canton 1874–1954 Fung Chi Ming

Resist to the End: Hong Kong 1941–1945 Charles Barman, Ray Barman (ed)

Scottish Mandarin: The Life and Times of Sir Reginald Johnston Shiona Airlie

Six Day War of 1899: Hong Kong in the Age of Imperialism Patrick Hase

Southern District Officer Reports: Islands and Villages in Rural Hong Kong John Strickland (ed)

The Lone Flag: Memoir of the British Consul in Macau during World War II John Reeves

Watching Over Hong Kong: Private Policing 1841–1941 Sheila Hamilton

Forgotten Heroes

San On County and its Magistrates
in the Late Ming and Early Qing

Patrick H. Hase

CITY UNIVERSITY OF
HONG KONG PRESS
香港城市大學出版社

Editor	Joanna PIERCE
Editorial Interns	KAN Yuen Yee, CHENG Yu Yuk
Book Design	LAU Wai Chun
Cover Design	Carrie YU

Création
城大創意製作

ISBN: 978-962-937-306-1

Published by
City University of Hong Kong Press
Tat Chee Avenue
Kowloon, Hong Kong
Website: www.cityu.edu.hk/upress
E-mail: upress@cityu.edu.hk

Printed in Hong Kong

This book is for my son

Dr Thomas P.A. Hase

for his constant affection, support and assistance

Contents

List of Maps

List of Plates

Acknowledgements

I would like to thank all those who have helped in the preparation of this book. My grateful thanks go in particular to Dr James Hayes, and Mr Tim Ko Tim-keung, as well as to Dr Thomas Lau, Dr Anthony K.K. Siu and Professor James Watson, for their views and comments on various drafts. I would like to thank them especially for their support at times when serious problems arose in the production of the study. My thanks go also to my son, Dr Thomas Hase, for giving me the views of an educated but non-specialist reader. I would also like to thank Edmund Chan and Joanna Pierce of City University of Hong Kong Press for their forbearance and assistance. I am particularly grateful to Mr Tim Ko Tim-keung, Mrs Rachel Nga-ching Miller, and Dr Joseph Ting for invaluable help with translations. Mr Tim Ko Tim-keung also helped in a major way with the Plates. Plates 26 and 27 are courtesy of the Tai Pang Museum, and Plate 31 is courtesy of Dr Anthony K.K. Siu. As far as possible, suggestions and comments by all these scholars have been included: all remaining errors and infelicities, however, are the author's.

Preface

The counties (縣, yuen, xian) were the lowest level of the Chinese imperial state structure, and the county magistrates, the heads of the county administration, were in a very real sense the foundation which supported the whole of the rest of the administration. Study of the counties and their administrators is, therefore, of great importance, as well as being a study of great fascination. During 40 years of studying the local history of the New Territories of Hong Kong, the relationship between the villagers and the magistracy has frequently caught my attention, and, my interest thus excited, in due course led to the production of this book.

The central role played by the county magistrates in imperial China has inspired a number of English-language books in recent decades. Among others, T'ung-tsu Chü mostly used handbooks for magistrates, prepared by distinguished Qing scholars, to illustrate his work.[1] John R. Watt produced a masterly work on the magistrates, as seen from the centre, relying particularly on the Qing law code and regulations, but also employing some local material to illuminate such questions as tenure, appointment, and dismissal.[2] Philip C.C. Huang has written two books on the activities of the magistrates as judicial officers in the field of inter-personal, "civil", legal disputes.[3] There is also a fine study by Linxia Liang on the magistrates as judicial officers in the field of inter-personal legal disputes.[4]

These studies provide an excellent overview of the magistrates and their work. They do not, however, look primarily at the magistrates from the local viewpoint, and so they do not study in detail the magistrates as they functioned within their counties. Several use those local archives that survive (mostly very late nineteenth-century archives from Ba county, 巴縣, that is, the city of Chongqing, 重興, in Sichuan Province; and from Baodi County, 寶抵縣, in Hebei Province, half-way between Tianjin and Peking),[5] as well as central government archives, and some other local sources here and there. However the main aim of all these works is to illuminate the magistrates as a national administrative and judicial institution, taking China as a whole, and not primarily to look at the work of the magistrates within their counties, nor to clarify how they saw and reacted to local problems in those counties.

Clearly, however, the county magistrates were central to the administration and development of their counties, and, as such, also merit detailed study at the local level, as well as on a nationwide basis.

Bradly Reed has prepared a quite superb book (Clerks and "Runners")[6] which explores the work of magistracy underlings within one particular county (Ba County, the city of Chongqing), at the end of the nineteenth century, but it does not concern itself with the magistrates themselves (except insofar as they managed their underlings), and its setting (a very busy, large, city, a treaty port, at the very end of the imperial period) may well not reflect in its entirety the situation in a small, rural county 250 years earlier.

There were a significant number of handbooks for magistrates written by distinguished scholars in the late Ming and early

Qing. One of these, written by Huang Liu-hung (黃六鴻) in 1694, is a particularly down-to-earth and practical work, and gives a good idea of how competent magistrates viewed their work and the problems they actually faced in this period. It has been published in translation; the introduction to this book by the editor, Djang Chu, is a valuable contribution to the study of the magistrates within their counties in the late Ming and early Qing.[7] This manual looks in great depth (in 32 volumes, 卷), totaling 559 pages in translation)[8] at the work of the magistrate within his county. It concentrates, however, on the practice in the north of China (Huang Liu-hung was magistrate in Shantung and Hebei), and the practices described by Huang Liu-hung do not in every respect illustrate practice in the far south. Most of the other handbooks, from this period and later, while they purport to illuminate the problems magistrates might face, and to give advice on dealing with them, are, in fact, almost all "full of moralistic injunctions, with little practical information",[9] and are of relatively little value in understanding how magistrates in fact operated.

Du Fengzhi (杜鳳治, To Fung-chi) was magistrate of Kwong Ning county (廣寧縣, Guangning), in Kwangtung, in the late Qing; (between 1866 and 1868), and then of Sze Wui county, Kwangtung, (四會, Sehui), and then was once again for a few months in 1870–71 magistrate of Kwong Ning, before being appointed in 1871 as magistrate of the metropolitan county of Nam Hoi (南海, Nanhai: this county covered the western half of Canton city and its western suburbs), where he stayed for some five years, until he was promoted to the prefecture of Law Ting in western Kwangtung (羅定, Luoding). He retired from this post because of ill-health in 1880, at the age of 67.[10] Du Fengzhi left a vast and very detailed diary, (望鳧行館宦粵日記), in 41 volumes, which has recently been published[11] (the second volume of the diary, covering some three months in early 1867, was unfortunately lost during Du Fengzhi's lifetime). It is particularly illuminating for the period Du Fengzhi spent in Kwong Ning, especially in 1866. Cheung Yin (張研, Zhang Yan) and Yau Tsit (邱捷, Qiu Jie) have written a number of important works on the information available in this diary.[12] This material looks at what Du Fengzhi did, in particular within Kwong Ning county. Kwong Ning was, like San On, a generally quiet and rural county, and these essays, therefore, give a fascinating insight into this late Qing magistrate's problems, and how he reacted to them: the information thus discussed clarifies, in some respects, the situation in late Ming and early Qing San On.

This current book, like the essays of Yau Chit and the work of Cheung Yin, aims to look at the magistrates of one particular county, San On, but at an earlier period (essentially the period 1573–1713), primarily to attempt to see how the magistrates viewed themselves and their work within that county, how they viewed the problems of that county, and how they set about dealing with those problems, and secondarily to see how the community of that county viewed them and their work. It aims, therefore, to find out what the magistrates were like as individuals and as officials, and what they did, or failed to do, for that county. The book makes no pretentions to do any more than this. The book's understanding of the general history of China in the late Ming and early Qing is taken from general studies.[13] It likewise takes its understanding of Confucianism and the Confucian "superior man" from general studies.[14]

Apart from the innate fascination of seeing how the San On magistrates functioned when faced with the problems of their county, a major aim of this study is to illuminate part of the pre-British history of the Hong Kong area. Local history, the study of a particular locality, is of great importance. This book is, therefore, intended, at least in part, to throw some light on a vital part of Hong Kong local history and perhaps offer a picture of the magistrates as human figures, struggling with intractable local problems, and, as such, give, it is hoped, a view of them complementary to that given by John R. Watt and Philip C.C. Huang and their colleagues.

The County Gazetteer of San On County (新安縣縣志, Xinan), that is, the county in which the Hong Kong area stood before the coming of the British, with some assistance from the Kwangtung Provincial Gazetteer and the gazetteers of the home counties of the San On magistrates, contains a considerable amount of information which can be used to study the late Ming and early Qing San On magistrates.[15] No archival material from San On is known to survive, and no printed material other than the gazetteers contains anything of marked significance on these officials: almost all that is known of the San On magistrates comes from these publications, without very much in the way of independent supporting evidence. This gives rise to a systemic problem: this study has to use just a tiny handful of sources, and within those sources mostly the writings of the magistrates themselves, along with eulogistic biographies of the magistrates written by scholars of the county, if any such study is to be done. The administrations of these men thus have to be viewed through the eyes of the magistrates themselves, or else through the writings of those who may well have been close to them as community leaders and advisors. Despite these serious problems, however, there seems to be enough evidence to support this study.

The information in the 1688 San On Gazetteer is, in particular, enough to allow a study to be done of the administrations of Zhou Xiyao,[16] who was magistrate between 1640 and 1644, in the late Ming, and Li Kecheng, who was magistrate between 1670 and 1675, in the early Qing, and gives at least some information about some other magistrates in this general period.

This short study of the San On magistrates in the late Ming and early Qing, is intended as a start. Similar studies, such as those of Djang Chu on Huang Liu-hung, and Yau Tsit and Cheung Yin on Du Fengzhi in Kwong Ning, looking at the magistrates in other counties, are desirable, so that a broader-based understanding of these men and their work at the local level can slowly be developed, to put alongside the studies of the magistrates in general as an administrative and judicial national institution. This small book is thus a brick which may one day, together with any other similar studies, form part of a more elaborate and detailed structure.

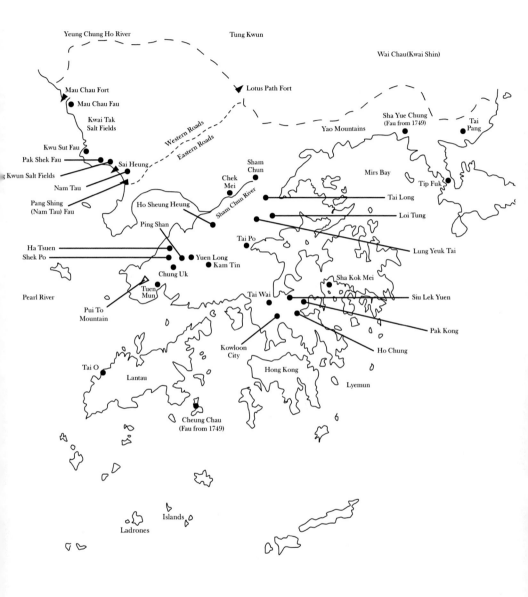

Map 1
San On County: Places Mentioned in Text

Tsing Hong Salt District
靖康鹽場

Tai Ning Salt District
大寧鹽場

Kwai Tak Salt District
歸德鹽場

Tung Kwun County

Border of San On County

Tai Pang City

Territory of the Yao People

Wong Tin Salt District
黃田鹽場

Nam Tau City

Tai Po Pearl
Monopoly Area

Tip Fuk
Salt Sub-District
疊福鹽場
(under Kwun Fu
Salt District)

Tung Kwun
Salt District
東莞鹽場

Au Tau

②

Nai Wai

①

Tuen Mun Naval
Control Point

Hoi Nam Salt Sub-District 海南鹽場
(under Kwun Fu Salt District)

Kwun Fu Salt District 官富鹽場
(Kowloon City) 九龍城

Note: The Kwun Fu Salt District, centred on Kowloon City,
was divided into three sub-districts, Kwun Fu (the Kowloon
Peninsula), Hoi Nam (Lantau Island) and Tip Fuk (the east
Shore of Mirs Bay).

①   The Castle Peak Monastery(青山寺)

②   The Ling To Monastery(靈渡寺)

Map 2
Exclusion Districts: Early Song

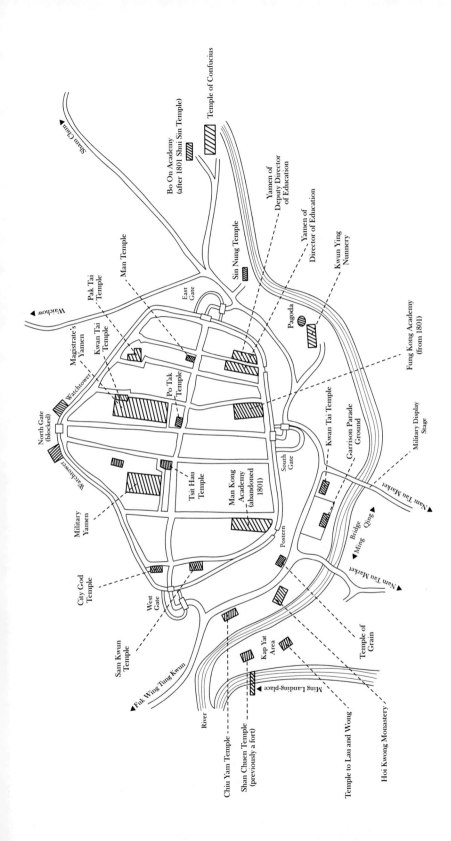

Map 3

Nam Tau City in the Late Ming and Early Qing

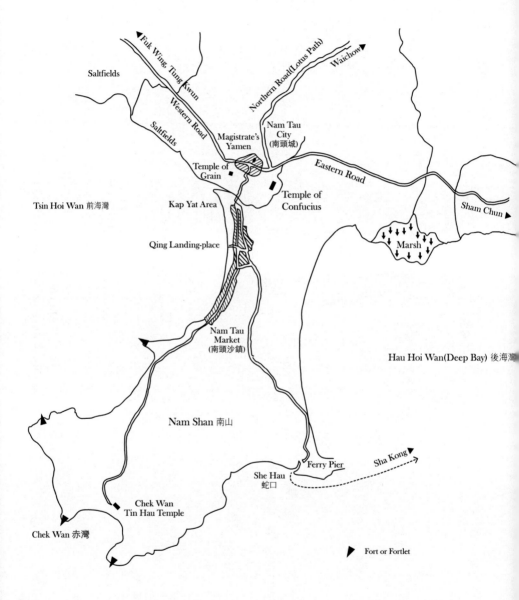

Map 4
The Nam Tau Area in the Late Ming and Early Qing

Saltfields

Fuk Wing, Tung Kwun

Western Road

Saltfields

Northern Road(Lotus Path)

Waichow

Magistrate's Yamen

Nam Tau City
(南頭城)

Temple of Grain

Tsin Hoi Wan 前海灣

Kap Yat Area

Eastern Road

Sham Chun

Temple of Confucius

Qing Landing-place

Marsh

Hau Hoi Wan(Deep Bay) 後海灣

Nam Tau Market
(南頭沙鎮)

Nam Shan 南山

Ferry Pier

Sha Kong

She Hau
蛇口

Chek Wan
Tin Hau Temple

Chek Wan 赤灣

Fort or Fortlet

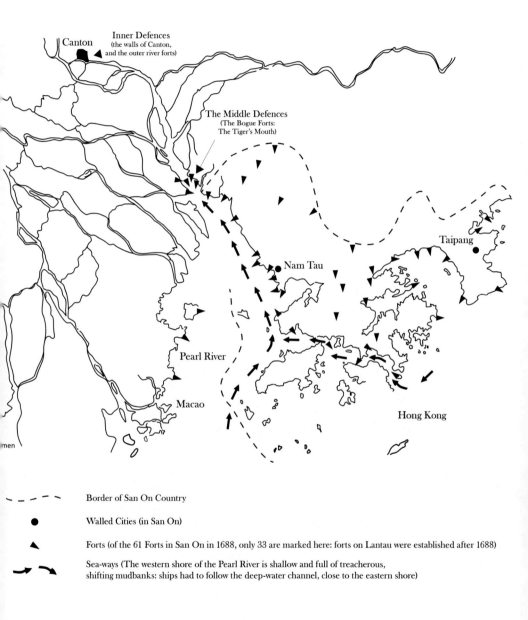

Map 5
San On as the Outer Defence of Canton, 1688

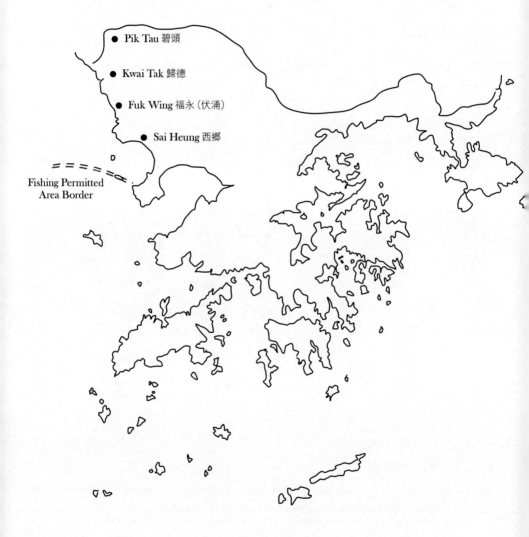

● Pik Tau 碧頭

● Kwai Tak 歸德

● Fuk Wing 福永 (伏涌)

● Sai Heung 西鄉

Fishing Permitted
Area Border

Map 6
Fishermen's Communes, 1573

Forgotten Heroes

San On County and its Magistrates
in the Late Ming and Early Qing

1

Introduction:
The Origins and Early Years
of the County of San On

Before 222 B.C. the Kwangtung (廣東, Guangdong) area was inhabited by unsinicised barbarian peoples, and the southern border of the Chinese Empire lay along the Lingnan Mountains (嶺南, Ling Nam), on the northern border of today's province of Kwangtung. During the fourth and third century B.C., however, merchants from South-East Asia started to arrive to trade at Canton (廣州, Guangzhou), and a thriving mercantile town grew up there. Chinese merchants began to travel south from the empire to Canton to take part in this trade, and a Chinese mercantile community began to establish itself.[1] The first emperor (秦始皇) became concerned that a community of Chinese merchants was growing up outside his control, and he sent his armies across the Lingnan Mountains to bring the Kwangtung area into his empire (234–222 B.C.).[2]

After the Canton area had successfully been absorbed into the empire (222 B.C.), Chinese civilisation slowly spread over the surrounding region. As soon as this happened, counties, to administer this newly Chinese territory, were established. The area to the south and east of Canton, the area centred on the lower East River (東江) valley and the eastern coast of the Pearl River estuary (珠江), was thus divided off to form a new county. This county, at most dates called Tung Kwun (東莞, Dongguan, literally "eastern grasslands"), was originally very large, but was slowly reduced in area until, in 972–973, in the early Song dynasty, it was reduced to the size it was to remain until 1573.[3]

This county of Tung Kwun was centred on the fertile lands along the East River. This was where the county city was established. Between the East River and the Pearl River to the west and between the East River and the southern coast, however, were ranges of hills: in the Song and earlier these ranges were very rough, forest-covered land. Most of the people living in these hills in these early centuries were Yao (猺) people, unsinicised barbarian tribes; the last of these Yao people only disappeared from the area at the time of the Coastal Evacuation in the 1660s.[4]

The coastal strip on the western and southern sides of this range of hills, along the Pearl River and the southern coast, did have some good, flat, and fertile land, but initially it would seem, few if any Han Chinese people lived there.

There are only a few written records of the early history of this riverine and coastal area, and hardly any post-prehistoric archaeological information. In the absence of good written or archaeological records, we are left with assumptions arising from what educated guesses suggest are probabilities, centred on what written records have survived. Nonetheless, it is worth the attempt to sketch these probabilities into a coherent story.

* * *

Taking all this into account, it seems probable that the area to the west and south of the Tung Kwun hills was under military control and martial law in the Northern Song and earlier. The imperial authorities had a number of interests here — salt working, pearl fishing, and ensuring that a naval garrison controlled access into the Pearl River — and these interests meant that the area was required to be kept under close military control. Han Chinese settlement was generally, it would seem, forbidden in the interests of greater security in this period (this was certainly so for the eastern half of today's New Territories, which was, in these early centuries, under the control of the imperial pearl monopoly). At the least, the dates of foundation of the villages in the area today are all quite late, suggesting that establishment of Han Chinese villages was not permitted in early centuries.

The eastern shore of the Pearl River was the closest place to Canton where salt could be made (the water near the western shore, off the delta mouths of the West River, 西江, was too fresh and too laden with silt, for effective salt working). Salt is essential to health, and salt working was usually, throughout the imperial period, a state monopoly, with the salt trade under official supervision and control. The Canton authorities needed direct governance of the salt fields to facilitate state control of the salt trade within Kwangtung. This was especially so during periods when the south of China was independent of north and central China, and thus could not easily access salt from the salt fields in those areas. Long before the Song, therefore, the eastern Pearl River shore below the Bogue (虎口, Hukou, "the tiger's mouth": this is where the Pearl River suddenly broadens out — above it, it is a river, below it, a wide estuary) had been almost entirely turned into salt fields, to provide salt for Canton. A salt superintendency, centred on the fortress at Nam Tau (南頭, Nantou, see Map 1) was established at an early date to control these salt fields. This superintendency was probably established by the Nanyueh (南 越) Kingdom, a southern kingdom covering Kwangtung, Kwangsi (廣西, Guangxi), and the northernmost parts of Vietnam in the second century B.C. Initially there was only one salt field complex here, but, by the early Northern Song there were six salt field complexes under this superintendency (see Map 2).[5]

In 1208, the viceroy, Chen Kuei (經略陳規, Chan Kwai) stated that:

> All the salt fields within the Canton area are in remote and distant areas, they are places without merchants to manage them, and they have low annual income; they cause nothing but harm to the people (廣州所屬鹽場僻遠, 非商賈所經之地, 歲入無幾, 徒為 民害).

He ordered that they be closed (悉行除罷).[6] The editor of the 1464 Tung Kwun County Gazetteer clearly regarded this as a major event in the history of the salt fields in Tung Kwun: it is the only thing recorded in that gazetteer in the "Salt Fields" (鹽 場) section from before the Ming. The implication of this 1208 pronouncement must be that, since the salt fields were "without merchants to manage them", they were, before that date, run directly by the state, implying that the workers were under military discipline, and were thus either convicts or state bond-slaves. Certainly, men from the unsinicised barbarian tribes of the area had been forced into the status of state bond-slaves before the Southern Song period, and tied to the salt fields as labourers, especially in the Kwun Fu (官富, Guanfu) salt fields, centred on the Kowloon (九龍, Jiulong) City area, and with salt fields on the Kowloon peninsula, Lantau island (大嶼山, Dayushan) and in

Mirs Bay (大鵬灣, Dapengwan).[7] It is probable that the salt fields on the Pearl River shore were, before they were closed down in 1208, operated by convict labour.

If these salt fields were worked by convicts or state bond-slaves before 1208, then there was a high risk of the salt workers absconding, to say nothing of the ever-present risk of salt smuggling. These risks would have been very much increased if the salt workers could communicate with Chinese accomplices. As a result, it would seem probable that all the areas immediately inland of the salt fields were closed to ordinary Chinese. There were, it would seem, no Chinese villages permitted in these areas: at the least, the major villages there today claim dates of foundation after this period. Even casual visits were probably forbidden without permits issued by the appropriate authorities in Canton. The area inland of the salt fields was, it would seem, made into a series of exclusion districts, patrolled by soldiers of the salt monopoly, to control the salt works, to check smuggling, and to keep unauthorised Chinese out of the area. Later, the county of San On was divided into districts (都): there were five of these along the Pearl River shore, each with one of the Song salt field complexes in it. It is probable that these five districts represent the pre-1208 exclusion districts of the five salt field complexes there (see Map 2).

There were substantial numbers of these salt troops before 1208. Most is known about the troops attached to the Kwun Fu (官富) salt fields.

In the twelfth century there was a regiment of irregular shock troops, the "sharp attack garrison of water-borne soldiers" (催鋒水軍), headquartered on the coast near Chiu Chau (潮州, Chaozhou). These troops were marines, and had ships: detachments of this garrison could thus be dispatched at short notice to support the regular forces wherever along the coast of eastern Kwangtung they were needed. During this time the islanders living on Lantau, who had been tied to the salt fields there as state bond-slaves, were in an almost constant state of revolt. Detachments of troops of the sharp attack garrison were frequently stationed so as to support the salt troops of the Kwun Fu salt works, and keep the islanders under control. The water-borne soldiers at Kwun Fu in the late twelfth century are referred to as a "half garrison" (半屯 於官富場): since the whole of this sharp attack garrison comprised nominally 1,200 men, this can be taken as implying that 500–600 water-borne soldiers were usually stationed at the Kwun Fu salt works. Some of the unsinicised barbarian men of Lantau were forced to serve as water-borne soldiers: one such conscripted officer mutinied and then led his fellow islanders in a major revolt. Shortly after, in 1197, the authorities decided to massacre the entire population of Lantau to end these constant revolts. The troops used for this massacre were some 300 of the water-borne soldiers (水軍三百) from the garrison at Kwun Fu (官富場屯).[8]

In addition to these soldiers stationed at Kwun Fu, there would have been some land-based regular troops of the salt monopoly there as well. The unsettled situation on Lantau led the authorities (in the years before the decision to massacre them was taken) to gather the population into concentration camps ("stockades", 寨), where they were placed under permanent military guard; the stockade guards were probably land-based salt troops from the Kwun Fu garrison.[9]

It is likely that there were other land-based troops stationed at Nam Tau, who would have patrolled the salt-working areas along the Pearl River shore. Up to 1208, it is probable that almost all the seashore areas of Tung Kwun were controlled by the salt troops, supported by the water-borne soldiers.

The salt superintendent had his offices at Nam Tau on the Pearl River coast, and this was doubtless also where the headquarters of the salt troops were before 1208.

The salt fields were reopened shortly after the viceroy had closed them in 1208 (the 1464 gazetteer says "they were reopened shortly after", 末幾復設), but they were thereafter run by merchants under salt monopoly supervision who employed free salt workers in the same way as elsewhere along the coast of China, and thus could be operated with ordinary Chinese people living nearby, since the risk of the salt workers absconding was much less than before. It is likely that the actions of the viceroy in 1208 thus marked a major change in the operation of the salt fields in this area, and, in consequence, a major change in the management of the coastal areas of Tung Kwun county.

The Tolo Harbour (大埔海) and Sai Kung (西貢, Xigong) areas were, in these early centuries, not under the control of the salt troops, however, but managed by the imperial pearl monopoly. More contemporary documents survive as to how this pearl monopoly area was managed, as compared with contemporary information on the salt monopoly areas. Pearls were found in considerable numbers here, in the Song and earlier. The pearl fishers were men from the local unsinicised barbarian tribes, who were, as with the salt workers in the Kwun Fu salt fields area, forced into the status of state bond-slaves and tied to the pearl fishing grounds as labourers, that is, as pearl fishers. Since pearls are small, but very valuable, the risk of theft and smuggling was clearly very high. The pearl monopoly thus had a large garrison of soldiers (contemporary documents state that there were some

2,000 troops there) to patrol the area behind the pearl-fishing grounds, centred at the local pearl monopoly headquarters at Tai Po (大埔, Dabu). These contemporary documents also state that no Chinese could enter the area without a permit, to reduce the risk. The soldiers of the pearl monopoly also convoyed the pearls gathered up to Canton.[10] The pearl monopoly exclusion district probably extended from the Kowloon Hills to the hills north of Sham Chun (深圳, Shenzhen).

* * *

Sailing ships arriving in China inevitably make landfall at the mouth of the Pearl River: the summer monsoon winds bring all ships from South-East Asia to this landfall (the winter monsoon blows them back to South-East Asia).[11] This made Canton one of the greatest commercial cities of Asia. However, there was always a risk that ships would suddenly appear over the horizon, bringing, not merchants and goods, but brigands seeking to sack the city and make off with its riches. This did, in fact, happen twice, in 404, when the city was captured from the sea by the rebel Lu Xun (盧循), and in 758, when the city was "sacked by Arabs and Persians, who then fled by sea" (波斯與大食同寇廣州劫倉庫焚盧舍浮海而去).[12] The threat of a sea-based bandit attack was, therefore, a real one. The city was sacked once again, in 879, by the rebel Huang Chao (黃巢), but Huang Chao attacked the city by land: his forces approached Canton through the East River Valley.[13]

The response to this threat by the imperial authorities was to establish a strong naval force to patrol the mouth of the Pearl River. This was headquartered at Tuen Mun (屯門, Tunmen), on the eastern, Tung Kwun, shore of the Pearl River. Three naval patrol lines were set up: one at the outer edge of the most seaward of the Ladrones Islands (老萬山, Lao Wenshan), one between Tuen Mun and the Macao area, and the third at the Bogue, where the waterway suddenly narrows. Any ship arriving would be stopped by one of these patrol lines, and brought into Tuen Mun, where the ship would pay duty and be searched for contraband or weapons. It would then be escorted up to Canton under a naval pilot.[14] The threat of smuggling, of offloading valuable material at Tuen Mun to Chinese accomplices, was obviously great, and so the hinterland of Tuen Mun was, again, it would seem, an exclusion district, stretching from Tuen Mun Bay up to at least the Sham Chun River, and so probably covering about half the area of today's New Territories. This area would have been patrolled by the soldiers of the Tuen Mun garrison to prohibit entrance to the area to any person without a permit issued by the Canton authorities, as with the pearl monopoly exclusion district.

In all these areas under martial law, no Chinese villages seem to have been permitted. On Lantau and in the pearl monopoly area the families of the state bond-slave workers grew the food needed, elsewhere food for the salt workers and naval personnel was probably produced by convicts (屯子) working as farmers on the periphery of the salt fields or naval garrison area, hence, probably, the village place name Tuen Tsz Wai (屯子圍), literally "convict stockade", near Tuen Mun.

All of these imperial estates were established well before the Song. The salt fields and the salt superintendency here are mentioned in a document of before 220 A.D., and again in 265, and the salt superintendency also appears in a document from 331.[15] The Eastern Han tomb, at Lei Cheng Uk (李鄭屋, Lizhengwu), dates from before 220, and is quite probably the tomb of a salt official. However, the salt fields were probably established here several hundred years earlier, under the Nanyueh emperors, who established an independent state in the area of Kwangtung, Kwangsi, and north Vietnam, with its capital at Canton, between 196 and 111 B.C. The Nanyueh would not have been able to secure salt from the salt fields further north, which were all under the control of other polities, and would have had to establish salt fields of their own, and this area, the eastern shore of the Pearl River, would have been the obvious choice. The salt field areas would doubtless have been patrolled by salt troops ever since they were first established.

The pearl monopoly garrison at Tai Po is first mentioned in the records of the Nanhan (南漢) dynasty (907–971): this was, again, a separate kingdom, centred on Canton, and ruling the south of China. Pearls were very important to the Nanhan emperors and they certainly greatly extended the work of the pearl monopoly within Kwangtung, but it is possible that the pearl grounds were under imperial control even earlier than this. The pearl monopoly remained in place at Tai Po until 1384, when the local pearl beds were exhausted and the pearl fishing was stopped.[16]

The naval and customs headquarters at Tuen Mun is first specifically mentioned in surviving documents dating from the first years of the Tang (唐) dynasty, about 615, but the naval patrol system is certainly a good deal older. The naval screen across the mouth of the Pearl River, with the Tuen Mun garrison, was probably put in place shortly after the sack of Canton in 404, probably by the Liu Song (劉宋) dynasty (420–478), yet another Southern dynasty.[17] The garrison at Tuen Mun was definitely in place by 424–453, when the monk Pui To (杯渡, Beidu) established a hermitage on the mountain behind the anchorage (the

Castle Peak Monastery, 青山寺), and a monastery (the Ling To Monastery, 靈渡寺), a couple of miles away, to provide religious support to those working in the military there.[18]

Thus, by the later Northern Song it is probable that the coasts of the county of Tung Kwun had been under imperial control, and under martial law, for up to a thousand years and more, although detailed written or archaeological records of this period in this area are unfortunately somewhat few.

This system of military control seems to have started to break down from the later eleventh century, in the late Northern Song and Southern Song period. The Song government was, by that date, in extreme financial difficulties arising from non-stop fighting against the Mongol tribes from the north. The government, it would appear, tried to find some income by releasing military controlled land for development. It would seem that, little by little, the exclusion districts along the Tung Kwun coasts were reduced in size, and eventually done away with altogether.

The exclusion district which is believed to have lain behind the Tuen Mun naval garrison thus seems to have been reduced by half in the last years of the Northern Song (mid-eleventh century), with the border of the exclusion district brought down from the Sham Chun River Valley to the low pass at Au Tau (凹頭, Aotao), just north-east of Yuen Long (元朗, Yuanlang). This was the period when the dominant villages of the area thus released for development were first founded (Kam Tin, 錦田, Jintian, and Ho Sheung Heung, 河上鄉, Heshangxiang). The lands on the northern bank of the Sham Chun River were probably opened for settlement at this date as well: the dominant villages of that area were also, it would seem, first settled in this general period.

The areas behind the salt fields all seem to have been opened for settlement during the Southern Song period (from the mid-twelfth century). The government closed some areas of salt fields in the later twelfth century, probably specifically in order to release land for development. The Kowloon peninsula was thus made available for settlement in the third quarter of the twelfth century, probably in 1163, when the offices of the Kwun Fu salt fields were moved away from Kowloon City (九龍城, Jiulongcheng), to Tip Fuk (疊福, Diefu), on Mirs Bay (大鵬灣, Dapengwan) to the east.[19] The dominant villages of the Kowloon peninsula area, Nga Tsin Wai (衙前圍, Yaqianwei), Ma Tau Wai (馬頭圍, Matouwei), and Po Kong (蒲崗, Pugang), were all founded at this late twelfth century date.[20] Some of the areas along the Pearl River coast near Nam Tau may have been opened for settlement at about this period as well. Following the ending of government management in the San On salt fields in 1208 the risk of salt workers absconding decreased sharply, and the areas inland of the remaining Pearl River salt fields could be settled by Chinese villagers. It is likely that most of the areas behind the salt fields along the shores of the Pearl River — that is, near Nam Tau, and between Nam Tau and the Bogue — were opened for settlement a little after 1208, as the dominant villages of this area seem to have been founded at about this period.

After the governor of Kwangtung, Qian Zhiwang (錢之望, Tsin Chi-mong) sent troops to massacre the population of Lantau in 1197–1200, the now empty island, less the salt fields, was granted to a retired senior Song official, Lei Mau-ying (李昴英, Li Maoying), to develop. The dominant rural villages of the island were all founded at the very end of the Southern Song, or in the Yuan, as tenancies of the Lei Kau Yuen Tong (李久遠堂, Li

Jiuyuantang), the family trust of Lei Mau-ying.[21] After 1208 the salt fields on the island were re-opened using standard free salt workers, employed by merchants.

In the very early Ming, or, perhaps more likely at the very end of the Yuan, the northern border of the Tuen Mun exclusion district was, it would seem, once again moved to the south, from Au Tau down to the watershed at Nai Wai (泥圍, Niwei). The dominant villages of the area thus freed for settlement, Ha Tsuen (廈村, Xiacun) and Ping Shan (屏山, Pingshan), were both founded in the very early Ming, and the smaller villages near them mostly a little later in the Ming. The easternmost part of the Tung Kwun sea coast area, around Tai Pang (大鵬, Dapeng), was probably opened for settlement at about the same date, in the very early Ming, or a little earlier.

The pearl monopoly area was opened for settlement after the pearl monopoly closed down its local operations in 1384, in the early Ming. The dominant village of the area close to Tai Po, Tai Po Tau (大埔頭, Dabutou), was founded at the very end of the fourteenth century, as were Lung Yeuk Tau (龍躍頭, Longyuetou) and Loi Tung (萊洞, Laidong), the dominant villages of the upper reaches of the Sheung Yue Ho River valley (雙魚河, Shuangyuhe), which had probably been within the pearl monopoly exclusion district earlier as well. Settlement was extended as far as Sha Tin (沙田, Shatian) by 1488 (Tai Wai, 大圍, Dawei, the earliest village of that area, was founded in that year), and to Sai Kung by the third quarter of the sixteenth century, when the dominant villages of this area, (Ho Chung, 蠔涌, Haoyong; Pak Kong, 北港, Beigang; and Sha Kok Mei, 沙角尾, Shajiaowei) were all first settled.[22]

Between the last quarter of the eleventh century and the third quarter of the sixteenth century, therefore, everywhere in the coastal area of Tung Kwun County had been opened for settlement, except, probably, for the area immediately around the naval base at Tuen Mun (the area south of Nai Wai, about the same area as today's Tuen Mun District), which may have been opened for settlement only in the early Qing. Settlement had, by the third quarter of the sixteenth century, begun to appear in all the open areas.

At the same time as the coastal areas were opened for settlement and freed of martial law, however, the soldiers who had previously been posted to the area were removed and reassigned elsewhere. The salt troops were probably mostly removed in or shortly after 1208, and the pearl monopoly troops were all removed in 1384. After that date, the only substantial body of state troops remaining in the area seems to have been the troops stationed at Tuen Mun, and these were only just enough to undertake the naval and customs duties they were responsible for.

* * *

Ho Chan (何真, Ke Chen), was a man from Cha Shan (茶山, Chashan), in the north of Tung Kwun. In the late Yuan he became the warlord of Kwangtung. He substantially assisted the first Ming emperor in his takeover of the south, and was greatly honoured by the emperor in consequence, being granted Kwangtung as a private fief, and being appointed as minister of the left (左臣), a high official post. In 1385 he was made earl of Tung Kwun (東莞伯), and, it would seem, was granted the lands of the old imperial pearl monopoly estate at Tai Po, which had been closed down the previous year. Ho Chan retained control of Kwangtung until his death (1388), and his brother succeeded him until his execution for complicity in the Lan Yu (藍玉) conspiracy (1393).[23]

Until 1393, the Ho family had private troops in the area, who doubtless kept bandits at bay. After this, however, these private troops were removed, and the area was at risk of bandit attack. In 1394, therefore, the central Ming authorities established two "bandit suppression garrisons" (備倭寇屯) in the area, with a total of 2,200 troops between them.[24] These were centred on fortresses at Tai Pang and Nam Tau: the walls of Tai Pang were probably first built then, and the walls of Nam Tau were very possibly rebuilt or restored then as well, although they were to be rebuilt again at the establishment of the county of San On in 1573. However, at some date in the following century, these "bandit suppression" troops seem to have been removed. As a result, the area became basically undefended.

By the middle Ming, therefore, the area was full of newly founded villages, still very tiny, or comprising just single, isolated houses standing scattered among the fields, with populations too low to allow the people to join together to defend themselves effectively. The result was that the area became afflicted with bandits and pirates, taking advantage of the defenceless people. The gazetteer thus records, in the "Bandits" (寇盜) section, nine serious bandit attacks in the 78 years 1493–1571 (records of any earlier attacks by bandits have not survived), and mentions at least one other attack which was not included in the "Bandits" section.[25]

The critical period was 1570–1571, when the area was ravaged by the bandit Lam Fung (林鳳, Lin Feng), often known in English as Limahong, a version of his name given him by the Portuguese, who also suffered from his depredations. Limahong is not mentioned by name in the "Bandits" section of the gazetteer, but he was probably the leader of the "Japanese pirates" (倭寇)

mentioned under 1570 and 1571 in that section. He is, however, mentioned by name in the biographies of Tang Sze-mang (鄧師孟, Deng Shimeng) and Tang Hung-lun (鄧孔麟, Deng Konglin).[26]

Limahong was a serious threat. In 1571 the Japanese pirates, probably under his leadership, laid siege to Tai Pang city and were repulsed only with difficulty. Scaling ladders were employed by the pirates in this siege as they tried to break through the walls. The bandits were defeated by a "local resident, Hong Shau-pak" (舍人康壽柏, Kang Shoubai), who took military control of the men of the city, (this strongly suggests that there were few if any soldiers posted there at that date). Limahong captured many residents from the villages of the area, and took them away to hold for ransom: Tang Sze-mang and Tang Hung-lun were both captured for ransom by Limahong. He also sacked the villages very widely, killing many villagers.

In Sha Tin the villagers, hitherto living scattered in isolated houses among their fields, reacting to the ravages of Limahong, somehow found the funds to build two walled villages, Tai Wai, and Tin Sam (田心, Tianxin) with broad moats, guns, and stores of ammunition.[27] Those of the villagers of the Sha Tin area who could not find the cash to move into these defended villages at least moved into tightly nucleated villages for mutual support and defence. Nga Tsin Wai and Ma Tau Wai in Kowloon also built walls around themselves at this same period, as did a number of other villages in the wider area. The walls of Nga Tsin Wai were probably set out in 1573–1574, those of Tai Wai in 1574–1575, and those of Tin Sam "at the same time as Tai Wai".[28] All this strongly suggests that Limahong and his pirates were, indeed, a very serious menace in the early 1570s.

As a result of the devastation caused by Limahong, the residents of the coastal area of Tung Kwun, led by a man named Ng Tso (吳祚, Wu Zuo), petitioned the intendant of the coastal region (巡視海道), Liu Wen (劉穩, Lau Wan), to consider dividing the old county of Tung Kwun and making a new county covering just the coastal strip. Liu Wen, who must have been greatly concerned about how close Tai Pang had come to falling to Limahong, in turn took the matter up with the high provincial authorities, with the result that a new county, San On (新安, Xinan), was established in 1573.[29]

***

The name of the new county, San On (新安, Xinan, "new peace"), was chosen to reflect the security for the local residents that it was hoped the new county would bring. The boundaries of the new county were, to the north, the Yeung Chung Ho (洋涌河, Yangyonghe) River, a tributary of the Pearl River, and then along the crest of the mountains to the sea east of Tai Pang. It is probable that the aim of Ng Tso and the others who petitioned Liu Wen was primarily to get the two "bandit-suppression garrisons" reinstated, and a new county would imply a new county military establishment. In the event, when the new county was established two substantial garrisons were put in place, one at Nam Tau and the other at Tai Pang, with a number of war junks and smaller naval craft to patrol the offshore waters, supported by a dense network of road forts and fortlets.

The new county took the old settlement at Nam Tau as the new county city. It also took over the two assistant magistrates (巡檢) who had previously been posted at Fuk Wing (福永, Fuyong) and (赤尾, Chiwei). Since the areas previously under the supervision of these assistant magistrates now fell within the area of the new county, they were transferred to the new county establishment.

After 1573 the residents of the coastal strip, the new county of San On, thus had a magistrate and a local military command of their own. San On was an entirely typical county, rural, not very heavily populated, and rather remote from the centres of power and, as such, was similar to the great majority of the counties of the empire. The only thing distinguishing it from other rural counties was its unfortunate exposure to bandits and pirates.

The new county was initially very successful in reducing the bandit threat. In the 57 years between 1573 and 1630 only one bandit attack is noted in the gazetteer, in 1580. However, San On County had been established in the first year of the Wanli (萬曆) reign, and it was during this reign that the slide of the Ming state into degeneracy became ever more serious. By 1630 the efficiency of the Ming military had reached dangerously low levels, and there were to be six more very serious bandit attacks on the area of the new county between 1630 and 1644. Furthermore, the lessening of control over the military can be seen to have resulted in an increase in local military corruption. During this same period, shortage of money for the local magistracy also seems to have steadily become more and more of a problem.

The collapse of Ming effectiveness, and difficulties arising from the Qing takeover, meant that Kwangtung Province, and specifically San On County, was in a disturbed and insecure state from about 1630 to about 1713.

The north of China had fallen into civil war in 1644. The last Ming emperor committed suicide. The Qing, who had been ruling Manchuria as an independent kingdom for several decades, invaded and took Peking in 1644, and the Qing king of Manchuria was proclaimed the emperor of China on 4 June, taking the reign title Shunzhi (順治, "smooth rule").

However, the Qing initially only controlled northern China; the south was in the hands of Ming loyalists, who supported various Ming princes all claiming the imperial throne. Kwangtung initially supported two rival southern Ming imperial claimants who fought against each other, while also trying to defend the province from the Qing. It was not until 20 January 1647 that a Qing army, led by generals Tong Yangjia (佟養甲, Tung Yeung-kap) and Li Chengdong (李成東, Lei Shing-tung) was able to capture Canton and to kill one of the two southern Ming claimants. Tong Yangjia started to restructure Kwangtung as a Qing province (including appointment of a man firmly loyal to the Qing as magistrate of San On), but, in May 1648, General Li Chengdong rebelled and declared for the remaining southern Ming claimant, the Yongli (永歷) emperor, and the Qing were thrown out of most of Kwangtung, except for a few enclaves, one of which was San On.

The Qing were only able to retake Canton two years later, after a nine-month siege in 1650: this attack on Canton was led by General Shang Kexi (尚可喜, Sheung Ho-hei).[30] The fall of Canton triggered a terrible massacre, in which some 70,000 people are said to have been killed. After the fall of Canton, General Shang Kexi fought against the southern Ming loyalists throughout the next decade, slowly pushing the Yongli emperor ever further west.

The Shunzhi emperor recognised Shang Kexi's services to the Qing by giving him the title of Pingnan Wang (平南王, "prince who pacified the south") in 1655, and granting him Kwangtung and Kwangsi as a personal fief. Shang Kexi's forces pushed the Yongli emperor into the far south-west (1656) and even, from 1659, over the border into Myanmar where he was later captured and executed. After 1656, Shang Kexi started to rebuild the shattered society of Kwangtung, and to clean up the remaining pockets of anti-Qing feeling. However, the south continued to be unsettled, since there remained significant Ming loyalist forces on Taiwan under Koxinga (國姓爺, "the lord of the imperial surname").[31]

As a first step towards destroying Koxinga, Shang Kexi, with the agreement of the central Qing authorities, decided to drive the population of the coastal areas inland to deny Koxinga any support or assistance from the coastal communities. Huge numbers of those thus displaced died of starvation (see Appendix 2). This Coastal Evacuation edict was rescinded in 1669, and Shang Kexi began to concentrate his efforts on rehabilitation from that year. In 1676 Shang Kexi, by now old (72 years of age), and ill, attempted to retire and surrender his fief. However, his son, Shang Zhixin (尚之信, Sheung Tz-shun) refused to accept this, and put his father under arrest. Then, when his father died (November 1676), he claimed the title of Pingnan Wang for himself and joined the other southern feudatories in the Rebellion of the Three Feudatories (三藩之亂). By 1677, this rebellion had been crushed by the Qing Army and Shang Zhixin was arrested (he was forced to commit suicide in 1680). Kwangtung was thereupon brought back into the Qing fold, although it took some time for the scars caused by the troubles of the previous 50 years to be healed. Taiwan was eventually brought under central government control from 1681.

Thus, between 1644 and the early eighteenth century, Kwangtung was wracked with violence and ravaged by political insecurity. San On, following on from its problems in the late Ming period, 1630–1644, was caught up in this wave of early Qing insecurity: indeed, the county was almost destroyed as a functioning entity. It was only in the early years of the eighteenth century, in fact, that the county can be seen to have achieved a measure of normality again after a half-century and more of devastation.

This short book is an attempt to sketch the way the magistrates of San On, in the decades after 1573, administered the county, how they faced and dealt with the political instability and insecurity of the time, and how the community viewed them and their work.

2

The San On Gazetteer:
The Magistrates and the County Community

Almost everything we know of the county magistrates of San On in the late Ming and early Qing is to be found in the early Qing county gazetteer (新安縣志), with support, in particular, from the early nineteenth-century Kwangtung Provincial Gazetteer (廣東通志), and the gazetteers of the home counties of the San On magistrates.[1] Unfortunately, the information which can be gathered from the gazetteers is somewhat limited. None of the San On County archives are known to survive.

This San On Gazetteer is conventionally dated to 1688 (the date of the introductory preface, written in that year by the then county magistrate, Jin Wenmo, who was magistrate 1687–1694). However, this gazetteer records, in the "Civil Officials: Magistrates" (文官表: 知縣) section of the gazetteer, the arrival as magistrate of Jin Wenmo's successor, Ding Tangfa, who only took up the post as magistrate in 1694, six years after the date given in the preface as the publication date.[2] Furthermore, one of Ding Tangfa's works is included in the "Fine Writings" (藝文) section of this gazetteer.[3] Moreover, Ding Tangfa founded a new school in the San On County city, Nam Tau, the Po On Academy (寶安書院, Baoan Shuyuan), and this is also mentioned in this gazetteer.[4] Presumably, therefore, despite the date of 1688 given in the preface, the final version of the gazetteer was not published and issued until after 1694. The 1688 gazetteer does not refer to Ding Tangfa's successor as magistrate, Jin Qizhen (1700–1713), who is only recorded in the later San On Gazetteer, published in 1819. Jin Qizhen took up the position as magistrate in 1700, and the gazetteer must have been issued, therefore, before that date, that is, in the period 1694–1700, probably quite late in that period. However, the conventional date of 1688 is used in this study for the sake of convenience, since that is the date universally used by scholars, even if it is, undoubtedly, inaccurate.

In the gazetteer, in the "Civil Officials: Magistrates" (文官表, 知縣) section,[5] can be found the dates when each magistrate took up the post and when he handed it on to his successor, together, usually, with details of the official's home province and county, and his examination status.[6] In addition to this formal information, the editor of the 1688 gazetteer, in a number of places, refers to actions of the magistrate.

The editor, Tang Man-wai (鄧文蔚, Deng Wenwei), was a villager of Kam Tin (錦田, Jintian: see Map 1 for places mentioned), and was himself a Kui Yan (舉人, Juren: graduate of the second, provincial, level of the imperial examinations), of 1657. He went on to become a Tsun Sz (進士, Jinshi, graduate of the highest, national, level of the imperial examinations) in

1685, and then became a county magistrate in Zhejiang. Before he graduated as Tsun Sz, however, he was, as the leader of the San On graduates, an unofficial advisor to the San On County magistrate, and he comments in particular on those magistrates he had himself known personally, and especially Li Kecheng.[7]

* * *

There was in San On, as in other counties, a shrine where the tablets of illustrious officials were revered — in the 1688 gazetteer this was called 祀名宦 and 名官祠, and 名宦祠 in the 1819 gazetteer, all meaning "Shrine of Illustrious Officials". This lay within the complex of the county Temple of Confucius, on the east side of the main courtyard, across the courtyard from its sister shrine, where the tablets of local worthies were revered (see Plate 1).[8] The Shrine of Local Worthies held tablets of those residents of the county who it was felt should be formally remembered for their bravery or exemplary lives.

Brief biographies of those magistrates considered worthy of being honoured in the Shrine of Illustrious Officials in the county Temple of Confucius are included in the "Men: Illustrious Officials" (人物志: 名宦) section of the 1688 gazetteer. The biographies in this section are grouped into two subsections, "Those Worshipped in the Shrine of Illustrious Officials" (崇祀名宦), and "List of Worthy Officials" (宦績列傳).[9] In the 1819 gazetteer, those magistrates, and other officials given a biography are in the "Record of the Biographies of Officials" (宦迹略) section: this section is divided into two subsections exactly as in the 1688 gazetteer, but the two subsections are not given separate subheadings.[10] The equivalent biographies in the provincial gazetteer are all included under the single heading, "Illustrious Officials" (名宦).[11]

This careful separation into two groups, but always under the overall heading of "Illustrious Officials", strongly suggests that there were two groups honoured in the shrine: "Illustrious Officials" and "Worthy Officials". The county magistrate in person was required to worship the enshrined illustrious officials in the spring and autumn of each year. There is no mention in the gazetteer of any formal requirement to worship the worthy officials, but, given that the worthy officials are entered alongside the illustrious officials in the 1688 gazetteer under the main heading "Illustrious Officials" (名宦), and, in the 1819 gazetteer under the same heading as the illustrious officials, and that both are subsumed under the single heading of "Illustrious Officials" in the provincial gazetteer, it would seem that both groups were, in fact, revered in much the same way. It seems probable, therefore, that the worthy officials were honoured in the same shrine as the illustrious officials, but on a side altar, with the worthy officials receiving a less formal annual worship.

By 1688 nine officials had biographies in the "Those Worshipped in the Shrine of Illustrious Officials" (崇祀名宦) section. They were all officials of the Ming dynasty: three provincial or prefectural officials (including Liu Wen, who was responsible for getting the new county of San On set up in 1573), three county magistrates, two county directors of education, and one county deputy director of education.[12] By 1819 nine further officials had been added to this group, two viceroys, four provincial governors, and three more county magistrates.[13]

These illustrious officials were represented in the shrine by a spirit tablet, presumably with the official's name carved on the front and with a short biography, doubtless written on the back of the tablet. The biographies of the enshrined illustrious officials as given in the gazetteer were, it would seem, drawn from those on the tablets enshrined in the temple, although the editor most likely reworked them for the gazetteer.[14] The biographies mostly stress the official's integrity, dedication, diligence, politeness, frugality, virtue, benevolence, compassion, sense of justice, and so forth: in other words they stress how close the official in question came to the standards expected of a Confucian superior man (君子). Only occasionally do they speak of particular achievements by the official in question. Many of the biographies included in the county gazetteer and the provincial gazetteer are, therefore, rather formal and somewhat uninformative.[15]

Since these tablets were spirit tablets, they seem from time to time to have been entered into the Shrine of Illustrious Officials after the death of the official in question had been announced to the county authorities, and perhaps on occasion some considerable time after the death. The tablet of Wu Daxun, who was the first county magistrate after the county was established in 1573 (1573–1576) was thus entered into the shrine as an illustrious official only in 1615, which was also when those of Qiu Tiqian (1586–1590), and Yu Zhu (1594–1599) were entered, presumably as the result of an initiative of the then county magistrate, Wang Tingyue (1614–1619; Wang Tingyue was not himself honoured with a tablet in the temple). However, in other instances the tablets were entered into the shrine well before the death of the official in question.

In total, 29 officials were honoured at the worthy officials level by the date of the 1688 gazetteer, including 13 county magistrates (both Zhou Xiyao and Li Kecheng were among these 13):[16] 38 more, including 19 further county magistrates, had been added by 1819. Some of the other worthy officials were county military officers, or county directors of education.[17] They seem to have been represented by tablets, much as the illustrious officials were, bearing biographies, which were later reworked and transcribed to the gazetteer. The biographies of the worthy officials are very similar in tone and content to those of the illustrious officials.

The local worthies were also, it would seem, divided into illustrious and worthy classes. The 1688 gazetteer divides the biographies of local worthies into a class of "those worshipped in the Shrine of Local Worthies" (崇祀鄉賢), and then another, headed "list of worthy residents" (名賢列傳), followed by two further groups, "those who showed proper behaviour" (行誼), and "righteous bravery" (忠勇) who were probably also worthy residents.[18] Ng Tso, the man who had petitioned that the county of San On be set up in 1573, was one of these local worthies "who showed proper behaviour", and Ho Chan, who so dominated the area in the early Ming, was also one of the worthy residents.[19] As with the illustrious and worthy officials, the biographies of both classes of local worthies were doubtless reworked and transcribed into the gazetteer from their tablets in the shrine.

As Table 1 shows, only a relatively small percentage of county magistrates were honoured as illustrious or worthy officials.[20] Of the 26 magistrates in post in the years 1573–1647 (the Ming magistrates), 3 were enshrined as illustrious officials (12%), and 6 as worthy officials (23%). Of the 14 early Qing magistrates (1647–1713), 2 were enshrined as illustrious officials (14%), and 7 as worthy officials (50%). Of the late Ming and early Qing magistrates taken together (1573–1713), only 45% were thus honoured. Of the 34 in post between 1713 and 1788, in the middle Qing, only 2 were enshrined as illustrious officials (6%)

and six as worthy officials (17%).[21] None of the 22 magistrates
in post between 1788 and 1819 had been honoured by the date
of the 1819 gazetteer: this may well be because none of the
magistrates who might have been designated as such were known
to have died by 1819. Taking the whole period 1573–1788
together, 6 of the 75 magistrates were honoured as illustrious
officials (8%), and 19 as worthy officials (25%) while the
remaining 63% were not honoured.

There was thus genuine discrimination between those
magistrates who were singled out as being worthy of honour, and
the rest.

Table 1
Illustrious and Worthy County Magistrates, San On, 1573–1788[22]

Name	Name in English	Dates	Illustrious Official	Worthy Official
明				
吳大訓	Wu Daxun (Ng Tai-fan)	1573–1576	✓	
曾孔志	Zeng Kongzhi (Tsang Hung-tsz)	1576–1579		✓
范經	Fan Jing (Fan King)	1579–1583		
鄒守約	Zou Shouyue (Chau Shau-yeuk)	1583–1584		
梁大皡	Liang Dahao (Leung Tai-ko)	1584–1586		
邱體乾	Qiu Tiqian (Yau Tai-kin)	1586–1590	✓	
宋臣熙	Song Chenxi (Sung Shan-hei)	1590–1594		
喻燭	Yu Zhu (Yue Tsuk)	1594–1599	✓	
葉宗舜	Ye Zungshun (Yip Tsung-shun)	1599–1601		

Name	Name in English	Dates	Illustrious Official	Worthy Official
李汝祥	Li Ruxiang (Lei Yue-cheung)	1601–1602		
李時偕	Li Shixie (Lei Sze-kai)	1602–1605		
林一圭	Lin Yigui (Lam Yat-kwai)	1605–1608		
俞堯衢	Yu Yaoqu (Yue Yiu-kui)	1608–1611		
鄧文照	Deng Wenzhao (Tang Man-chiu)	1611–1614		
王廷鉞	Wang Tingyue (Wong Ting-yuet)	1614-1619		
陶學修	Tao Xuexiu (To Hok-sau)	1619–1622		
陳良言	Chen Liangyan (Chan Leung-yin)	1622–1624		✓
黃繩卿	Huang Shengqing (Wong Shing-hing)	1624–1626		
喻承芳	Yu Shengfang (Yue Shing-fong)	1626–1628		
陳轂	Chen Gu (Chan Kuk)	1628–1631		✓
烏文明	Wu Wenming (Wu Man-ming)	1631–1635		
李鉉	Li Xuan (Lei Yin)	1635–1637		✓
彭允年	Peng Yunnian (Pang Wan-nin)	1637–1640		✓
周希曜	Zhou Xiyao (Chau Hei-yiu)	1640–1644		✓
孫文奎	Sun Wenkui (Suen Man-fui)	1644–1645		
楊昌	Yang Chang (Yeung Cheung)	1645–1647		

Name	Name in English	Dates	Illustrious Official	Worthy Official
清				
張文煋	Zhang Wenxing (Cheung Man-sing)	1647–1648		✓
楊美開	Yang Meikai (Yeung Mei-hoi)	1648–1650		
李君柱	Li Jungzhu (Lei Kwan-chue)	1650–1654		✓
何中賢	He Zhongxian (Ho Tsung-yin)	1654–1656		
馬以懋	Ma Yimao (Ma Yi-mau)	1656–1661		✓
張鵬彩	Zhang Pengcai (Cheung Pang-tsoi)	1661–1663		
張璞	Zhang Pu (Cheung Pok)	1663		
	County in Abeyance	1663–1670		
李可成	Li Kecheng (Lei Ho-shing)	1670–1675		✓
羅鳴珂	Luo Mingke (Law Ming-o)	1675–1678		
張明達	Zhang Mingda (Cheung Ming-tat)	1678–1684		✓
安宇枚	An Yumei (On Yue-mui)	1684–1687		✓
靳文謨	Jin Wenmo (Kan Man-mo)	1687–1694		✓
丁棠發	Ding Tangfa (Ting Tong-fat)	1694–1700	✓	
金啟貞	Jin Qizhen (Kam Kai-ching)	1700–1713	✓	
趙大焆	Zhao Damei (Chiu Tai-mei)	1713–1722		

Name	Name in English	Dates	Illustrious Official	Worthy Official
黃廷賢	Huang Tingxian (Wong Ting-yin)	1722–1724		
徐雲祥	Xu Yunxiang (Chui Wan-cheung)	1724		
段巘生	Duan Yansheng (Tuen Yin-sang)	1724–1725		✓
王師日	Wang Shiri (Wong Sze-yat)	1725–1730		
何夢篆	He Mengzhuan (Ho Mung-suen)	1730–1741		✓
湯登鼇	Tang Dengao (Tong Tang-ngo)	1741–1744		
唐若時	Tang Ruoshi (Tong Yeuk-sze)	1744–1745	✓	
鄧均	Dang Jun (Tang Kwan)	1745–1746		
汪鼎金	Wang Dingjin (Wong Ting-kam)	1746–1751		✓
趙長民	Chao Changmin (Chiu Cheung-man)	1751–1752		
胡	Hu (Wu)	1752–1753		
沈永寧	Shen Yongning (Sham Wing-ning)	1753–		
王文徽	Wang Wenwei (Wong Man-fai)			
書	Shu (Shue)			
嚴源	Yan Yuan (Yim Yuen)	1758–1762		
那嶼	Na Yu (Na Yue)	1762–1764		
楊士機	Yang Shiji (Yeung Sze-kei)	1764–1767		

Name	Name in English	Dates	Illustrious Official	Worthy Official
譚見龍	Tan Jianlong (Tam Kin-lung)	1767–1768		
鄭尚桂	Zheng Shanggui (Tseng Sheung-kwai)	1768–1771		
李文藻	Li Wenzao (Lei Man-tso)	1771		✓
楊士機	Yang Shiji (Yeung Sze-kei) (again)	1771		
富森布	Fu Senbu (Fu Sam-po)			
張之凌	Zhang Zhiling (Cheung Tsz-ling)			
曾璞	Zeng Pu (Tsang Pok)	1774–1775		
繆一經	Mou Yijing (Mau Yat-king)	1775		
高暎	Gao Ying (Ko Ying)	1775–1776		
楊任	Yang Ren (Yeung Yam)	1776		
舒明阿	Shu Minga (Shue Ming-a)	1776–1777		
蘇燦	Su Can (So Chan)	1777		
夏家瑜	Xia Jiayu (Ha Ka-yue)	1777–1778		
洪肇楷	Hong Zhaokai (Hung Shiu-kai)	1778–1779		
高質敬	Gao Zhijing (Ko Chat-king)	1779–1780		
吳沂	Wu Yi (Ng Yi)	1780–1784		✓
李大根	Li Dagen (Lei Tai-kan)	1784–1788		✓

The seven magistrates in post in the 43 years after the rescission of the Coastal Evacuation Decree (1670–1713, that is, during the early and middle period of the Kang Xi, 康熙, reign) would seem to have been of a particularly high quality (two were enshrined as illustrious officials and four as worthy officials — 86%). The only magistrate not honoured in this period was Luo Mingke (1675–1678), during whose tenure the county city was lost to a bandit attack. The percentage of magistrates enshrined from this period was very much higher than at any other.

* * *

The gazetteers are usually completely silent as to how magistrates appointed to San On were chosen, and surviving archival records of the board of civil appointments in the capital are mostly similarly unhelpful. How the choice was made usually has to be inferred. Unfortunately, this is not always possible. The normal practice for routine appointment of magistrates to ordinary counties, that is, counties which were not seen as sensitive and so which did not require special treatment and special hand-picked appointments, was for the board of civil appointments in Peking (北京, Beijing) to summon a group of men who were ready to be posted, who would then cast lots before the board officials for the positions then available, or soon to become available, thus avoiding any suggestion of favouritism.[23]

However, in Kwangtung and the south generally, the board of civil appointments would usually send batches of expectant officials, both men looking for a posting as magistrate and others looking for postings as official assistants, down to the viceroy, who would use them in his office as he needed for whatever duties he had in hand, or as acting officials in some county where a temporary vacancy had arisen, until a full vacancy came up in some non-sensitive county, and then he would slot one of his expectant officials in.[24] The viceroy would then inform the board as to where the expectant official had been posted. It is probable that the viceroy always had some expectant officials in his entourage.[25] It is likely that those chosen to be sent to the viceroy as expectant officials were sent in this way because that was how the lots fell for them. Furthermore, particularly from the middle Qing, the viceroy felt he had the right to move his magistrates around from county to county at his own discretion.

This procedure of sending expectant officials to the viceroy was essential to ensure that prompt action could be taken where a vacancy arose suddenly, and without warning. It obviated the otherwise inevitably very long interval before news of a vacancy could be sent to Peking and someone could be found to make the long journey south to take over in a county like San On, should the previous incumbent have died, resigned, or had to take urgent leave (especially, that is, if one of his parents had died, when leave of absence was automatic). This interval would normally be at least a full year.

This accelerated process can be seen clearly in the case of Zhou Xiyao. He resigned his post at Chinese New Year, 1644, and his successor, Sun Wenkui, arrived in San On within a few weeks, long before the authorities in Peking could even have been informed that the post was vacant. Much the same happened in 1751, when magistrate Wang Dingjin (1746–1751) died in office ("of overwork" according to his biography: 惜以勞瘁, 卒于官):[26] there was no delay before his successor, Chao Changmin (1751–1752), arrived to take over. In the case of Chao Changmin, he was moved to San On from his previous post as magistrate of Chiu Yeung (朝陽, Chaoyang), probably by the viceroy exercising his power of moving magistrates from one county to another; presumably, the viceroy moved one of his expectant officials into Chiu Yeung.[27]

However, the board of civil appointments would hand-pick magistrates for counties seen as being sensitive for some reason. Some counties were always sensitive because of their heavy workload or other special factors, and their magistrates would be appointed from carefully chosen candidates who were felt to have the youth, strength, vigour, intelligence, and high standards such a sensitive posting would require. Usually they would also be men with experience in other testing counties. In such circumstances, lots would probably not be used, although, if two or three such sensitive counties came up at one time, a small hand-picked group of candidates might cast lots as to which each would get. The counties which were seen as always in need of carefully hand-picked magistrates were especially those which were highly urbanized, major centres of trade, and which had very large populations, and consequently many crimes to be dealt with, and difficult commercial disputes to handle. The two counties which divided Canton city and its suburbs (Nam Hoi, 南海, Nanhai, and Pun Yue, 番禺, Panyu) were cases in point.[28]

Other counties, normally seen as ordinary, might, however, at times become sensitive because of political developments, serious outbreaks of violence, and so forth. This was so for San On, which was usually seen as just a quiet, rural county, but which became sensitive during the period 1630–1713, because of its exposure to serious attacks by bandits and others, attacks requiring vigorous and especially competent magistrates to deal with.

* * *

Throughout the first part of this period of disturbance, 1630–1647, the period of the late Ming collapse and the consequential explosion of brigandage, San On seems to have suffered more than most other Kwangtung counties. Nam Tau, the San On County city, was besieged by bandits (or rebel armies) no less than three times in this period (1630, 1634, 1635), and the county was attacked, in 1633 and 1641, by yet other large pirate gangs, although these gangs did not try to take the county city.[29]

The county was further ravaged, in the very early Qing (1647–1661), by large bandit gangs operating out of the fortress city of Tai Pang, in the east of the county (Tai Pang city stands just inland from the shores of Mirs Bay), under the leadership at first of Chan Yiu (陳耀, Chen Yao), and then of Lei Man-wing (李萬榮, Li Wanrong) between 1647 and 1657. In 1647, the year the San On magistracy was to acknowledge the Qing, the bandit Chan Yiu captured Tai Pang: he managed to break through the city walls. It was probably also Chan Yiu who besieged the county city of Nam Tau for three months later in 1647, trapping the magistrate, Zhang Wenxing, inside.

Chan Yiu did not stay in Tai Pang for long — he was probably killed when a Qing military force arrived suddenly and unexpectedly, to relieve the siege of Nam Tau, when a good number of the bandits were captured and killed.[30] However, when he left the scene, the bandit chief Lei Man-wing took over Tai Pang as his base. Lei Man-wing also probably besieged Nam Tau (at some point in the period 1656–1657). He was to rule in Tai Pang for nine years, and was only ejected after a three-month siege in 1657.[31] These bandits claimed to be a rebel army, supporting the southern Ming imperial claimant. To add to the chaos of these years, 1648 was a year when a terrible famine struck San On, and, in the same year, plague (probably an outbreak of the bubonic plague which spread out round the world at this precise period). The gazetteer says that "more than half the people died" (民之死亡過半) in this plague, and that the price of food rose so high that cases of cannibalism occurred. While these comments may be exaggerations, 1648 was clearly a disastrously bad year.[32]

In the last part of this period, after the Coastal Evacuation, from 1669 onwards until 1713, Nam Tau was attacked yet again by bandit gangs, in 1672, 1676, and 1680. The 1676 attack led to yet another siege of Nam Tau: on this occasion, the city actually fell to the bandits, and was held by them for several months.[33] Furthermore, the county was, after 1669, in a very weak state following the devastation of the Coastal Evacuation (the population may have dropped by 1670 to a quarter or third of what it had been in 1640, as is discussed later), and was thus in grave need of careful rehabilitation, which again demanded better than average county magistrates.

In total, San On thus suffered 11 major pirate or bandit attacks in the 50 years 1630–1680, and Nam Tau was put under siege no less than 6 times during this same period (see Table 2, in Chapter 7 below).

San On was vital to the defence of the Pearl River, and the approaches to Canton. It was, as both Zhou Xiyao and Li Kecheng pointed out, "the outer defence of Canton".[34] Any attack on San On, if not repulsed, would be likely to spill over into the rest of the Pearl River area, and cause significant problems for Canton, and the province as a whole.

Throughout this 1630–1713 period, therefore, unless gifted, vigorous, and trustworthy men were posted to San On as magistrate, then the attacks by the bandits and pirates might not be repulsed, the defence of the whole Pearl River would be called into question, Canton's security would be at risk, and the rehabilitation of the county would be unnecessarily delayed. Throughout this period it is likely that hand-picked men were appointed as magistrates to San On, either routinely or at least frequently.

* * *

The evidence in the gazetteer does not allow us to know exactly how the late Ming San On magistrates, in the early part of this 1630–1713 period of disturbance were appointed: it is likely that some, at least, were hand-picked for the post (this is particularly so for Li Xuan, 1635–1637).

In the second part of this period of disturbance, 1647–1661, when southern Ming forces were still active in Kwangtung, and Koxinga and his supporters were active along the Kwangtung coast, the Qing government clearly felt that it would be too risky to appoint any Ming graduates to the coastal counties of Kwangtung, especially to so sensitive a post as county magistrate of San On, since the county controlled the entrance to the Pearl River and the sea route to Canton: only men known to be loyal to the Qing would do. Apart from Ma Yimao (1656–1661), a Kui Yan from Shaanxi (陝西, Shensi) Province, who was probably a graduate of one of the very first Qing examinations, all the San On magistrates in the period 1647–1662 were "candidates" (貢生, 歲貢, or 撥貢, gongsheng); at these dates there were still very few Qing graduates. It is probable that all the early Qing San On magistrates in the period before Shang Kexi came to power (1647–1655) were hand-picked for the position as effective, dependable, and trustworthy: this was certainly true at least of Zhang Wenxing (1647–1648).

The first Qing magistrate of San On, Zhang Wenxing, was appointed "in the third year of Shunzhi, when Tong, the commander-in-chief, entered Canton" (順治三年隨佟軍門入粵).[35] The third year of Shunzhi ended at Chinese New Year, 5 February 1647, and Tong Yangjia entered Canton on 20 January 1647. Zhang Wenxing, therefore, must have been appointed to San On within a very few days of General Tong's entry into Canton. He was a "candidate", but must have been travelling in the entourage of General Tong as an expectant official, and one earmarked as able to take over a sensitive county without delay. He was an ethnic Chinese from Manchuria, from Fengtien (奉天) Province,[36] and can be assumed to have been a man trusted by the Qing authorities. Zhang Wenxing and his successors, Yang Meikai (1648–1650), Li Jungzhu (1650–1654), and He Zhongxia (1654–1656), were appointed before Shang Kexi rose to power in Kwangtung as Pingnan Wang.

It is not known exactly how the system for appointments to counties in Kwangtung worked during the period 1655–1661, the first part of the period during which Shang Kexi ruled the province as Pingnan Wang. Jonathan Spence states that the central Qing authorities sent viceroys and provincial governors to Kwangtung during this period, but that they had only nominal power, since Shang Kexi kept all real power in his own hands.[37] It seems probable that county magistrates and other local officials sent to Kwangtung were also chosen by the board of civil appointments in Peking, but presumably Shang Kexi would have had some sort of veto over them. Probably all appointments were made by sending batches of expectant officials to Shang Kexi, who would have used them until satisfied with their services, and then slotted them into whatever vacancies had arisen. All the San

On magistrates appointed in the Shunzhi reign part of Shang Kexi's period of rule (that is, between 1655 and 1661: Ma Yimao, 1656–1661; Zhang Pengcai, 1661–1663; and also Zhang Pok, 1663) came from the north of China, but not from Shang Kexi's home region, Manchuria, and do not seem likely to have been close to Shang Kexi before they were sent into Kwangtung.

Shang Kexi clearly had little spare time to interest himself in local problems, as the lack of action against Lei Man-wing between 1647 and 1657 shows, and his magistrates were expected to fend for themselves, being left to a large degree to their own devices. At the same time, it has to be said that several of them certainly acted as magistrates should, especially Ma Yimao, whose conduct when besieged in Nam Tau in 1656–1657 was well regarded by the county community.

Between 1663 and 1670 the county of San On was in abeyance since all the residents had been driven away because of the Coastal Evacuation.

***

In the third part of this period of disturbance, 1670–1713, in the early Kang Xi period, the San On magistrates seem to have been hand-picked and sent directly to the county by the board of civil appointments in the capital. This was probably also the case for some of the other counties in the Pearl River area at this time. Most of the magistrates appointed to San On were ethnically Chinese men with close ties to the Qing, dating back to before 1644. For instance, Li Kecheng (1670–1675), was a man born in Liaodong (遼東) Province, in Manchuria. He was a guansheng (官生, also called yinsheng, 蔭生), a man awarded a Kui Yan degree without examination by the imperial Qing authorities because of the services to the Qing of his father, who had been a high civil official of the Qing as kings of Manchuria, before they went on to conquer the rest of China in 1644. His successor, Luo Mingke (1675–1678) was also born in Liaodong, in Manchuria, just as Li Kecheng had been, but the gazetteer says nothing further about his background.

Both Li Kecheng and Luo Mingke were appointed during the latter part of the period of Shang Kexi's rule in Kwangtung: both must have been acceptable to him. Li Kecheng was the son of a high civil officer of the kings of Manchuria before 1644, and Shang Kexi himself had been a high military officer (a general) of the Qing in that same pre–1644 period. There is every possibility, therefore, that Shang Kexi would have known Li Kecheng's father personally, and very possibly Li Kecheng also. Li Kecheng's native place was about a hundred miles to the south of Shang Kexi's birthplace (it is not known whereabouts in Liaodong Luo Mingke was born), but the Li and Shang families may well have been living near each other in the Manchurian capital of Mukden (沈 陽, Shenyang) before 1644. At the same time, Li Kecheng must have been appointed by the central Qing authorities, and then submitted to Shang Kexi for approval, since only those central authorities could have awarded him a guansheng degree. While this is not stated expressly in the gazetteer, there can be little doubt that Luo Mingke was, like Li Kecheng, also the son of a man who had supported the kings of Manchuria before the conquest of the rest of China: he must have been born well before the conquest.

Luo Mingke's successor, Zhang Mingda (1678–1684), appointed to San On after the fall of Shang Zhimin, was born in Fengtien Province, in Manchuria: he was, in addition, an ethnically Chinese bannerman (the son of an officer in the Qing

Army before 1644). Zhang Mingda's successor, An Yumei (1684–
1687) was, like Li Kecheng and Luo Mingke, born in Liaodong, in
Manchuria: he, too, was an ethnically Chinese bannerman. Both
Zhang Mingda and An Yumei must have been born in Manchuria
before the Qing conquered the rest of China in 1644: they were
doubtless the sons of trusted officers who were involved in the
conquest. These bannermen can be assumed to have had a good
deal of military knowledge, and may thus have been seen as
particularly suitable for posting to a county in danger of attacks
by bandits.[38]

John Watt has shown that the Kang Xi government awarded
substantial numbers of jiansheng (監生) degrees to ethnically
Chinese bannermen, sons of trusted army officers in this period
(especially after 1677, and the end of the Rebellion of the
Three Feudatories). Watt assumes these jiansheng degrees were
purchased (as was usual for jiansheng degrees later), and that
cash shortages were the reason for this surge of jiansheng degree
holder appointments, but this seems unlikely.[39] If cash shortages
were behind this, then it would seem unlikely that only ethnically
Chinese Manchuria-born bannermen would have bought these
degrees. It is much more likely that these jiansheng degrees were
awarded to ethnically Chinese men close to the Qing, and deemed
completely trustworthy, with those men then posted to sensitive
counties where the central Qing authorities wanted men they
trusted in post. Zhang Mingda and An Yumei are both examples:
both held jiansheng degrees, which can be assumed were awarded,
rather than purchased (it is not known what sort of qualification
Luo Mingke held).

Jin Qizhen (1700–1713) was another bannerman posted to
San On with a jiansheng degree, and, again, it can similarly be

assumed that this was awarded, not purchased. He may have been born after the conquest of the rest of China in 1644, but was certainly a man trusted by the emperor. Given his surname (金: "Golden"), it is possible that Jin Qizhen was a member of the imperial clan, since the imperial clan took Jin, (the translation of their Manchu surname, Aisin-Goryo) as their Chinese surname. If so, he was the only ethnically Manchu man appointed to San On in this period. Jin Qizhen was certainly born in Manchuria, although the gazetteer gives no details.

Most of these magistrates stayed in San On for longer than the usual two to three years (Li Kecheng, five years; Zhang Mingda, six years; Jin Qizhen thirteen years), again suggesting that they were trusted by the central Qing authorities.

In the whole period 1670–1713, therefore, only two magistrates cannot be seen to have had a close connection with the Qing as kings of Manchuria: Jin Wenmo (1687–1694) and Ding Tangfa (1694–1700). Jin Wenmo came from the southernmost tip of today's Hebei (河北) Province, and Ding Tangfa came from Jiashan County (嘉善, Ka Shin) in Zhejiang Province, just west of Shanghai. Both were Tsun Sz, graduates of the highest, national, level of the imperial examinations, from one of the examinations held in the early Kang Xi period. Except for Ma Yimao, these were the first graduates appointed as San On magistrates in the Qing. There was probably some reason which does not come out in the details given in the gazetteer why the Kang Xi administration trusted Jin Wenmo and Ding Tangfa; certainly, like most of the other Kang Xi appointees, Jin Wenmo and Ding Tangfa stayed in San On for longer than usual: seven and six years respectively.

These early Kang Xi magistrates were thus men close to and presumably seen as trustworthy by the central government (and, between 1655 and 1676, by Shang Kexi as well) but they were also gifted and effective. Most were in due course to be honoured with a tablet in the Shrine of Illustrious Officials in the San On Temple of Confucius: Zhang Wenxing, Li Jungzhu, Ma Yimao, Li Kecheng, Zhang Mingda, An Yumei, and Jin Wenmo as worthy officials, and Ding Tangfa and Jin Qizhen as illustrious officials.

* * *

The need for rehabilitation after the Coastal Evacuation is still mentioned in the gazetteer as a priority for magistrate Jin Qizhen (1700–1713), but this need does not appear thereafter.[40] The threat from pirates and bandits was also, by then, much less than it had been (no pirate or bandit attack on San On is mentioned in the gazetteer between 1680 and 1804). After 1713, therefore, the conditions in the county had, once again, become normal, and the county was viewed again as ordinary and not sensitive. Therefore, there no longer seems to have been any special care given to choice of magistrates for San On. No ethnically Chinese men born in Manchuria, for instance, seem to have been posted to San On as magistrate in the middle Qing period, between 1713 and 1819, and no ethnically Chinese bannermen seem to have been appointed, as opposed to four or five in the period 1670–1713.[41] If, in the early Qing, before 1713, most of the magistrates were hand-picked for the magistracy of San On — as seems likely from the breakdown of their backgrounds — after 1713, with the county no longer sensitive, and its problems behind it, it seems that most were appointed after drawing lots in the usual manner for routine appointments, or else, more likely, were chosen by the viceroy from the expectant officials in his entourage, or were posted by the viceroy using his powers to transfer magistrates from county to county within his jurisdiction. The San On magistrates He Mengzhuan (1730–1741), Tang Ruoshi (1744–1745), Chao Changmin (1751–1752), Yan Yuen (1758–1762), Zheng Shanggui (1768–1771), Li Wenzao (1771), and Li Dagen (1784–1788) were all appointed magistrates, as their first appointment, to counties in Kwangtung other than San On. Probably all these magistrates were transferred to San On by the viceroy, although the surviving records do not specifically state that such a transfer utilizing the viceroy's powers took place, except in the case of He Mengzhuan.[42]

As well as Jin Qizhen, who may have been ethnically Manchu, ethnically Manchu or Mongol bannermen were occasionally appointed as San On magistrates in the later eighteenth century. Magistrates Wang Wenwei (dates unknown, in period 1753–1758), and Shu (dates unknown, in period 1753–1758), may have been ethnically Manchu. Magistrates Na Yu (1762–1764), Fu Senbu (dates unknown, in period 1771–1774), and Shu Minga (1776–1777) were certainly ethnically Manchu or Mongol, and Zhang Zhiling (dates unknown, in period 1771–1774), and Mou Yijing (1775) probably were.[43] It will be noted that most of these magistrates were posted to San On only for brief periods, and most were appointed in the two periods when the administration of San On was endangered by strings of ephemeral magistrates (1752–1758 and 1771–1777).

Magistrate Shen Yongning (1753) purchased a jiansheng degree. He was initially (at age 29) appointed as a deputy county magistrate (縣丞), but later paid a further sum to the central government to allow himself to be appointed magistrate. He was eventually transferred to San On from another Kwangtung county, presumably by the viceroy. Magistrate Gao Zhijing (1779–1780) was a Kui Yan by examination, but paid a "donation" so that he could be considered for appointment as magistrate (at this period it was usually only Tsun Sz who were appointed as magistrates): he was also eventually transferred to San On from another Kwangtung county, presumably by the viceroy.[44]

The imperial government normally, as noted above, appointed as county magistrates men who had graduated from the imperial examinations at a sufficiently high level. Sometimes, however, men graduated at the required level, but at a relatively advanced age, or else, in many cases, they had to wait for a decade or more after graduation before a post could be found for them, since the number of graduates was always greater than the number of posts available for them to be appointed to. Such men would eventually be appointed county magistrates, but would usually only serve for one term, or perhaps two, and then retire. John R. Watt has shown that the problem of what to do with men who were elderly when they came up for appointment was a long-standing concern for the Qing government, but it was equally a problem in the Ming.[45]

*　*　*

Men appointed as San On County magistrates were, typically in the late Ming, Kui Yan, graduates of the second, provincial, level of the imperial examinations, with only one Tsun Sz, a graduate of the third, national level of the examinations being appointed in the Ming.[46] The early Qing appointees from the period 1647–1662, and the Kang Xi appointees between 1670 and 1713 were special cases, but, after 1713 until 1745 most Qing appointees were Tsun Sz. As noted above, some men who had purchased degrees were appointed as San On magistrates, later in the imperial period, but all the Ming and early Qing magistrates discussed here either graduated or were, it would seem, awarded degrees.[47]

Men appointed to San On in the Ming were normally men in their thirties or forties when they graduated as Kui Yan, and typically were about 55 or even older when they were first given an official appointment as county magistrate. In the middle Qing period we have the ages on appointment of several San On magistrates: most were relatively elderly. Duan Yansheng (1724–1725) was 74, He Mengzhuan (1730–1741) was 50, Chao Changmin (1751–1752) was 44, and Li Dagen (1784–1788) was 60.[48] Given their age when they were installed in San On, it is not surprising that relatively few San On magistrates went on to take a second post in the bureaucracy: it would seem that almost all of them retired after their single term as magistrate, and most of those who did take a second posting did not move on to highly prestigious posts. This was, it would seem, true of many ordinary counties in this period.

Of the Ming magistrates about whom it has been possible to find details, Qiu Tiqian (1586–1590) graduated as Kui Yan in 1579, and thus waited for seven years before he got his first post in the bureaucracy, in San On. His native place gazetteer does not record him taking any second post: he may have graduated rather later than the average age of between 30 and 35.[49] Yu Zhu (1594–1599) graduated as Kui Yan in 1576, but was only posted to San On 18 years later, by when he must have been at least 50 years old; he did not take a second post after quitting San On.[50] Li Shixie (1602–1605) graduated in 1585, and must also have been at least 50 when he arrived in San On; nor did he take a second post after he left.[51] Peng Yunnian (1637–1640) graduated as Kui Yan in 1624, but was only posted to San On in 1637, 13 years later; his native place gazetteer does not record any second posting, and he was probably well into his fifties by the time he concluded his appointment as San On magistrate.[52]

In fact, of all the 40 late Ming or early Qing magistrates of San On (that is, those recorded in the 1688 gazetteer, plus Jin Qizhen), only eight or nine are recorded in the gazetteer, or in the gazetteer of their native place (where it has been possible to consult it), or the provincial gazetteer, as being offered a second posting on their departure from San On. Zeng Kongzhi (1576–1579) was promoted from San On to assistant sub-prefect (通判) of Ko Chau (高州, Kaozhou) in the far west of Kwangtung. Tao Xuexiu (1619–1622) was promoted to be prefect of Kunyang (昆明, another name for Kunming), in Guizhou (貴州昆陽府).[53] Chen Liangyan (1622–1624) graduated as Kui Yan in 1594, but was only given the post of San On magistrate 28 years later, in 1622, by when he must have been well over 50. His native place gazetteer does not say what he did during these 28 years, but does record that he was moved on from San On to another county, and was then promoted to magistrate of two successive Zhou counties: he must have been well over 60 when he retired from the last of these posts.[54]

Chen Gu (1628–1631), who graduated in 1600, did not get posted to San On until 1628, by when he must have been well into his middle or late fifties. He had been given a post as director of education in Wuxi (無錫), in Jiangsu (江蘇) Province, and had been promoted from that post to the magistracy of San On. By the time he left San On for the magistracy of Lanshan (藍山) he must have been close to sixty, if not even older than that.[55] Lanshan is a remote border county in Hunan, high in the mountains between

Kwangtung and Hunan, in the late Ming mostly inhabited by Yao people. Lanshan was in a state of unrest and disturbance when Chen Gu was posted there (probably this unrest was connected with the earliest stages of the Yao rebellion, which broke out in full force a few years later, in 1643, when the Kwangtung army was deployed against the Yao people in Kwangtung), and he was forced to "exert all his strength in pacifying the people" (勤于撫綏). This posting to Lanshan may well have been a punishment posting, as he was forced to leave San On because he had offended a "rich and powerful man" (以忤權貴去). He stayed in Lanshan for some years, and was "successful in quieting the area, so that he was praised for his efforts" (民有寧一之頌), and then retired to his native place, where he died at the age of 69.[56]

Wu Wenming (1631–1635) was promoted to assistant sub-prefect of Canton.[57] Zhou Xiyao (1640–1644) graduated as Kui Yan in 1624, and thus waited 16 years for a posting: he must have been about 50 when he came to San On; he declined the offer of a promotion to prefect of Jinning in Guizhou (貴州晉寧) in 1644.[58] Magistrate An Yumei (1684–1687) left San On when his mother became ill; he was given a second posting, to the county of Po Ning (普寧, Puning, in Kwangtung), in 1691, presumably after the period of mourning for his mother was over. An Yumei does not seem to have taken any further post after his time in Po Ning.[59]

In the case of Ding Tangfa, the San On Gazetteer states that he was "promoted" (on this occasion the graduates and elders of the county put up an inscription to him at the south gate of Nam Tau; it no longer survives), but gives no details. According to the gazetteer of his native place, Jiashin County, in Zhejiang Province (浙江嘉善縣), he graduated as Kui Yan in 1677, and then as Tsun Sz 11 years later, in 1688 (this was at the fourth examination after

the one at which he graduated as Kui Yan). He was not posted
to San On until 1694: it is not known what he did between 1688
and 1694. By 1694, he must have been at least 50 years old.
According to the gazetteer of his native place, in 1700 when he
left San On, he was posted as censor, (監察御史), at Jingjidao (京畿
道, King Kei To, probably the area around Xi'an, 西安, in Shaanxi,
陝西, Shensi, Province).[60] By the time he had completed his task
there, he must have been over 60 years old: he seems not to have
taken another post but to have retired.

Of the Ming and early Qing San On magistrates, only Li
Xuan (1635–1637) and Jin Wenmo (1687–1694) seem to have
been offered the opportunity of a genuine bureaucratic career. Li
Xuan was much younger than the average San On magistrate. He
graduated as Kui Yan in 1633, and then as Tsun Sz at the very
next examination, in 1634, and was immediately posted to San
On, arriving there in 1635. He cannot have been much older than
about 35. He was in due course transferred from San On to Hoi
Fung (海豐, Haifeng) in Kwangtung, as county magistrate (he was
in Hoi Fung as county magistrate from 1637 to 1639). Officials
were eligible for substantive promotion after serving two terms
as county magistrate.[61] Li Xuan was accordingly promoted into a
senior provincial post (as intendant) after his service in Hoi Fung.
According to his native place gazetteer, his post as intendant was
titled "intendant of the coastal region of Kwangtung" (粵海巡
憲): this is probably the same post as Liu Wen had held in 1573,
although in the case of Liu Wen the title of the post is given in the
San On County Gazetteer as 巡視海道.[62]

He held this post from 1639 until he retired in 1646, at the
coming of the Qing. He was probably forced to retire because
of Qing security concerns: given the continuing presence of

Ming claimants to the throne in the Kwangtung area, and pro-
Ming forces from Taiwan threatening the Kwangtung coast,
it is probable that Ming graduates were seen as politically
unacceptable in such important positions along the coast. The
coming of the Qing thus brought an abrupt end to what might
otherwise have been a promising career. Li Xuan, however,
was very atypical as a San On magistrate, as he was a Tsun Sz,
rather than a Kui Yan, the first and only Tsun Sz appointed to
the magistracy of San On in the Ming, and was also very much
younger than most: he was probably still only about 45 when he
retired in 1646. He must have been hand-picked for his posting to
San On.

Jin Wenmo was also very atypical as a San On magistrate. He
graduated as Kui Yan in 1669, and as Tsun Sz at the next but one
examination, in 1673. He was probably only about 30 or 35 years
old, or thereabouts, then. He was only, however, posted to San
On, his first position in the bureaucracy, in 1687, 14 years later:
it is not known what he did during the intervening period. His
biography in the gazetteer of Kaizhou (開州, in Hebei Province),
his native place,[63] states that, after labouring with all his strength
in San On to relieve the distress of the people following the
Coastal Evacuation, he was named censor, and sent to conduct
an enquiry into the operation of the county jails in the south and
east of Shandong (山東) Province. While he was there a famine
struck, and he used his powers to petition the emperor directly to
provide relief. After the successful conclusion of this task, he was
appointed intendant in Henan (河南) Province. He was then sent
to Fujian (福建) Province, to head the salt monopoly there (巡視
福建鹽政). He died while he was in that post, at about 55 years
of age. Like Li Xuan, therefore, Jin Wenmo started a promising

career which was brought to an abrupt end, in this case by his early death.

Connected with the posting of relatively elderly men to San On is the tendency, in the late Ming and early Qing, to post men to San On as their first posting. Only Chen Gu (1628–1631) of all the late Ming or early Qing magistrates is known to have had a post in the bureaucracy before his posting to San On: he had previously been director of education in Wuxi (無錫).

In the middle Qing period, however, it was common for the posting to San On to be the second or subsequent posting. Duan Yansheng (1724–1725) had been posted as county magistrate in Shanghang (上杭) and Tingzhou (汀州) both in Fujian Province, before his posting to San On, but he was under a cloud and had been dismissed by the central authorities for poor behaviour towards his junior staff in Fukien after only a very brief time in post there: his posting to San On was specifically said to be a "last chance".[64] As noted above, many of the other middle Qing San On magistrates were transferred to San On by the viceroy from some other Kwangtung county: this is specifically said of He Mengzhuan (1730–1741), transferred by the viceroy from the county of Fung Chuen (封川, Fengchuan), but is implied for several others.

This posting of relatively elderly men to San On, or other small and rural counties, as their first or second posting, must have been a definite policy of the imperial government, especially in those periods when San On was not seen as being sensitive. Men likely to be too old to undertake more than one or two postings, or three at the outside, were appointed to the more remote and rural counties, while younger men with the vigour of youth, or men with higher-level degrees and so more likely to be able to sustain a career of several decades, were usually posted to the bigger, more urban, "busy and difficult" counties, or to counties seen as being in special need of a younger magistrate with a good Tsun Sz degree. This does not imply that San On was less than a normal county: most of the counties of China were small, remote, and rural, and San On was, in fact, rather typical. It was the large, busy, urban counties which were atypical.[65]

Li Xuan, Jin Wenmo, and Ding Tangfa, young men with Tsun Sz degrees, and Li Kecheng and the bannermen posted to San On in the period 1670–1713, were doubtless given this appointment because San On had suddenly become, in the late Ming, and then again in the early Qing, a dangerous and difficult posting, as noted, and so demanded a man better qualified than the average San On magistrate. As mentioned, the county city had suffered almost continuous bandit attacks in the late Ming and early Qing: thus it required a skilled magistrate. Similarly, in the Kang Xi period, the government needed especially competent and trustworthy magistrates in this pirate and bandit-wracked county still reeling from the Coastal Evacuation.

* * *

While the biographies of magistrates as given in the gazetteer are, in many ways, rather formal and uninformative, in one respect they give a good deal of information. In most, the views of the leaders of the county community as to the life and worthiness of the magistrates, and as to how they were remembered by the county community, are stressed. This is particularly so in the biographies of magistrates from the late Ming and early Qing. It was the county magistrate who was responsible for entering the tablets of illustrious officials into the shrine, like magistrate Wang Ting-yue in 1615, but it seems very likely that the magistrate took careful note of the views of the leading men of the county (who would, unlike the magistrate, have had actual memories of how the magistrate in question had behaved) before making any decision as to which magistrates (and other senior officials) were to be thus honoured, and which not.

Thus, in the case of Zeng Kongzhi (1576–1579, a worthy official) his biography in the gazetteer states: "The people were at peace" (民甚安之),[66] and, in his biography in the provincial gazetteer it states:

> During his years in post, everything was relaxed and at peace, when the day came for him to leave, the people wept, and tried to stop him leaving...they erected an inscription to him (在任數年 閒左乂安, 去之日民籲, 大吏留之...立留賢碑).[67]

Of Qiu Tiqian (1586–1590, an illustrious official), his biography states: "His reforms were all sensible, and the people thought what he did was good" (所因革皆宜民善俗),[68] and of Chen Liangyan (1622–1624, a worthy official) it states:

> The scholars liked him for his frugality and simple manners: the ordinary people sang in pleasure: when he was transferred elsewhere, everyone remembered him for his good governance (士 欣樸械, 民樂弦歌, 惜任未幾別調, 闔邑士民, 有甘棠之思).[69]

Of Chen Gu (1628–1632, a worthy official), the gazetteer states: "[When he left office], the elders wailed, and blocked his way, so that his carriage could not move" (父老攀號者遮道,車不得前); the gazetteer of his native place, Tong'an (同安), in Fujian Province, adds to his biography as given there, "The people loved him" (民 思其德)[70] — both gazetteers also record that the people of the county erected temples to him at both Nam Tau and Sai Heung (西鄉, Xixiang). He was forced out of office because he had offended some "rich and powerful man" (以忤權貴去), presumably in Canton, but the biographies in both the San On and Tong'an gazetteers make it very clear that the San On County community did not support the views of this man. Of Li Xuan (1635–1637, a worthy official), the gazetteer states: "The people loved him: 民多德之";[71] and of Peng Yunnian (1637–1640, a worthy official), it states: "The people of the County missed him so much that they built a shrine to him, and today they sacrifice to him" (邑人思慕, 今附祀, 議建祠), and, in his biography in his native place gazetteer it states: "The people loved him" (邑人甚德之), a comment repeated in his biography in the provincial gazetteer (邑人思之).[72] Of Zhang Wenxing (1647–1648, a worthy official), his biography in the provincial gazetteer states: "The people all said to one another how good he was" (口碑磧磧焉).[73] Of Ma Yimao (1656–1661, a worthy official), his biography in the provincial gazetteer states "the County was not disturbed" (邑無擾).[74] Of Li Kecheng (1670–1675, a worthy official) it states: "He was not only praised within the county, but was widely admired within all the neighbouring counties" (其惠澤不獨蒸被一邑鄰封皆嚮慕之; Appendix 3). Of Zhang Mingda (1678–1684, a worthy official) it states: "Contemporary opinion held him in high esteem" (時論韙之); his biography in the provincial gazetteer suggests that his efforts to ensure that no trouble was caused to the people by the census in 1681 brought him a great deal of public admiration.[75] Of An Yumei (1684–1687, a worthy official) the gazetteer states that when he announced his resignation because of his mother's ill health: "The people felt as if they had lost their parents", and, when he left: "The people all gathered around, young and old, all weeping, they were so unwilling that he leave" (士民聞者, 如失怙恃, 去之日, 闔邑童叟悉會集遠送, 垂別號泣, 依依不舍云). The biography in the provincial gazetteer notes that he went from San

On to Po Ning County, and that the people in Po Ning so loved him that they built a shrine to him, and put up an inscription to him.[76] Of Jin Wenmo (1687–1694, a worthy official) the gazetteer states: "He touched the hearts of the people" (悉得其情), and his biography in the provincial gazetteer states: "the officials and the people felt his administration was good, like in ancient times" (士民倡有古良吏風).[77] Of Ding Tangfa (1694–1700, an illustrious official), it states: "When he was promoted, all the Graduates and Elders of the County erected a memorial inscription, which still stands inside the South Gate" (及行取升任之日, 闔邑紳耆為立去思碑, 至今存南門內).[78] Of Tang Ruoshi (1744–1745, an illustrious official) it states: "He benefitted the people, who considered him a fine administrator" (撫民以惠, 邑由是大治). Of Duan Yansheng (1724–1725, a worthy official), it states: "The people thought what he did was good" (咸藉首倡); and of He Mengzhuan (1730–1741, a worthy official), it states: "The people still miss him" (至今民猶慕之).[79]

It is not known what formal requirements had to be met, if any, before the tablet of an official was placed in the Shrine of Illustrious Officials, but it would seem that popular feeling in their favour was a major factor: at the least these comments show what a good reputation these magistrates left behind them. The comments, therefore, are a valuable source for the magistrates. Of course, all these biographies were written by scholars, mostly scholars from the elite of the county community, and, by "popular feeling" the implication must be the feeling of the elite of the county community. There is, therefore, likely to be bias in the comments. However, while the reputation of Jin Qizhen doubtless rested in part on the feelings of the county elite after he relieved them of the obligation to pay any taxes in arrears from ancestral trust funds, at the same time, the remarks on many of the other magistrates stress their care for the poor and low-ranking, as with Yu Zhu, Li Xuan, and Zhou Zhiyao, with their care for the salt workers, always the very bottom of local society, or Li Kecheng's care for the poor farmers dying of want. The bias in the biographies, therefore, while it cannot be entirely ignored, does not seem to be overwhelming.

What can be said, however, is that the views of the high provincial authorities in Canton seem to have played relatively little part in the decision as to which magistrates were to be honoured. Chen Gu was forced out of post by the high provincial authorities because of the ill will of some "rich and powerful man", probably in Canton, and Duan Yansheng was actually dismissed twice by the high provincial authorities, firstly in Fujian, then in Kwangtung, because he had a short temper and abused his subordinates when they did something wrong (in other words, he failed to act as a Confucian superior man ought). Both of these magistrates must, therefore, be assumed to have been unacceptable to the high provincial authorities, but both were, nonetheless, honoured with a tablet in the county shrine. This is made very clear in what the biography of Duan Yansheng says, with its statement that the county community "thought what he did was good", even if the high provincial authorities thought that his actions warranted dismissal.

Some writings left by some of the San On magistrates can be found in the "Fine Writings" (藝文志) section of the gazetteer:[80] these writings occasionally allow us to see what the magistrate was trying to achieve — this is an important source for both Zhou Xiyao and Li Kecheng.

Unfortunately, passages were chosen for inclusion in this section of the gazetteer solely on account of the beauty and elegance of the language, not the historical significance of the writing. Fourteen edicts (條議) of Zhou Xiyao are included in this section[81] (at least two others are excerpted),[82] together with six of his "occasional writings" (reports sent to his senior officers in Canton, prefaces for the county gazetteer, and inscriptions placed in the county school or various temples to mark their restoration),[83] as well as eight poems (see Plate 2).[84] Eight of Li Kecheng's edicts are included (see Plate 3),[85] together with two occasional writings,[86] and twelve poems.[87] Clearly, the editor of the 1688 gazetteer, Tang Man-wai, had a high opinion of the quality of the writing displayed by these two magistrates.

However, of the remaining 37 magistrates of the period 1573–1700, only seven had writings which Tang Man-wai considered elegant enough for this section: among them two edicts by magistrate Yu Zhu (1594–1599),[88] and two edicts and an occasional writing by magistrate Li Xuan (1635–1637; another important occasional writing, probably by Li Xuan, an impassioned plea for action to be taken to reform the way sales of excess salt were being handled, is excerpted in the text).[89] In most cases, however, it is only from the edicts that anything very detailed can be gleaned about the magistrates and their aims; furthermore, the edicts often clarify comments in the biographies, enabling those biographies to be understood more fully. It is possible, therefore, to form some idea of the aims and achievements of these four magistrates from their surviving writings, in particular of Zhou Xiyao and Li Kecheng, but more difficult to do so for other magistrates.

In addition to the writings of these magistrates, Tang Man-wai included single occasional writings of magistrates Deng Wenzhao (1611–1614),[90] Jin Wenmo (1687–1694),[91] and Ding Tangfa (1694–1700; a further occasional paper by one of the late seventeenth-century magistrates, an impassioned appeal for the salt taxes to be reduced, is excerpted in the text),[92] two occasional writings by magistrate Zhang Mingda (1678–1684),[93] and two occasional writings and a poem by magistrate Qiu Tiqian (1586–1590).[94] All of these magistrates were in due course to be honoured in the Temple of Confucius as worthy officials, except Qiu Tiqian, who was enshrined as an illustrious official, and Deng Wenzhao, who, alone of all these magistrates, did not have a tablet of honour in the temple.

The editor of the 1819 gazetteer was even less impressed by the quality of the writings of the late Ming and early Qing magistrates: he dropped from the new gazetteer a good number of those chosen by Tang Man-wai for the 1688 gazetteer, and he included only one further piece written by any of the magistrates of the period 1700–1819 in the "Fine Writings" section: a single occasional writing by magistrate Duan Yansheng (1724–1725).[95] It is a particular regret that he did not feel it desirable to include any writings by Jin Qizhen (1700–1713).

It is, therefore, the case that, of the 26 magistrates honoured as illustrious or worthy officials in the Temple of Confucius between 1573 and 1788, and who thus can be assumed to have contributed significantly to the county, only ten (38%) have any of their writings included in the gazetteer, and only four or five have any of their edicts included (11%). Because the editors of the two gazetteers included so few writings by magistrates other than Zhou Xiyao and Li Kecheng — and, to some extent, Yu Zhu and Li Xuan — and given the rather formal and uninformative character of many of the biographies included, the gazetteer is unfortunately of less value than would be ideal in giving any detail of the work of these other magistrates, although whatever can be gathered has been utilized in the following chapters.

3

The Work of the County Magistrates
and Their Magistracies

For 2,000 years the county magistrates (知縣), as the administrative heads of the counties, were the lowest level of the imperial bureaucracy. They were the local representatives of the imperial government and the essential centre of district life and development, not just in the Hong Kong area, but everywhere in China.

The Chinese imperial government ran a very strict examination system, based entirely on the Confucian classics. This examination system was designed to ensure that the graduates were entirely familiar with the classics, and so had a deep understanding of the Confucian way: all magistrates were expected to administer their counties in accordance with these principles. From the ninth and tenth centuries onwards, officials of the imperial government were normally chosen from those who passed these examinations.[1] Almost all men were eligible to sit these.[2] The primary level of the examinations was taken at the local prefectural city (for San On, this was Canton) after preliminary tests at the county level; the second was taken at the provincial city (for San On, at most dates, this was also Canton), and the third at the national capital. A pass was a precondition of taking any of the higher-level examinations. Appointment as an official normally required a suitable pass in the examinations: either a pass at the third, national, level, or at least a good pass at the second, provincial, level, although provincial graduates often had to wait some years or decades before they could take up a post. Barely one in a hundred candidates who passed the prefectural examination eventually passed the national examination. In many cases, graduates who were expectant officials and were awaiting a vacancy to be posted to would, in the meantime, become unofficial advisors to the magistrate of their home county (as with Tang Man-wai in San On), or would at least observe the magistrates of their home county in action and form views as to how they felt magistrates ought to behave. Usually, a graduate would be appointed to a post as county magistrate as his first posting.

County magistrates were supervised by several ranks of senior provincial officials (assistant prefects, prefects, intendants (taotai), provincial governors, and viceroys, together with the provincial treasurer and provincial judge), to whom the county magistrate had to send regular returns. The magistrate's superiors regularly came to the county to check on their work.[3]

County magistrates had a number of official assistants who would usually also be graduates, but with lower grades, below the level at which they could look for appointment as magistrates. However, promotion from an official assistant post to a post of county magistrate was possible, as with Chen Gu (1628–1631) Zheng Sanggui (1768–1771), and Wu Yi (1780–1784) in San On. Chen Gu was promoted to the magistracy of San On from the post of county director of education at Wuxi, Zheng Sanggui from a junior post in the salt monopoly in Fukien, and Wu Yi from a post as director of education, like Chen Gu.[4] However, such promotions were rare. All the junior staff of the magistracies, below the level of the official assistants, were appointed by the magistrate from residents of the county, and could be dismissed by the magistrate.

After two successful postings as county magistrate, an official could hope for promotion to a higher level post, either within the provincial bureaucracy, or in the capital. In the whole of China there were only a few thousand officials.

Occasionally, the imperial authorities would award degrees to men of proven loyalty and intelligence, but who had not graduated, and then post them as county magistrates to sensitive counties: this, as discussed previously, affected San On in the period 1647–1713. Later, again as already discussed, from the later eighteenth century, some men who had purchased degrees were posted as county magistrates, but this development does not seem to have affected San On in the late Ming and early Qing period.

In order to reduce the risk of corruption, no official of the rank of county magistrate or above was permitted to serve in his home province, nor in the home province of his wife or concubine, nor in a province where his father, or any other close relative, was serving. For the same reason, a magistrate was forbidden to marry, or to take as a concubine, a girl from a family of the province to which he was posted.

Since the magistrate was thus required by law to be a native of a province other than Kwangtung, very few, if any, of the San On magistrates could understand the Cantonese or Hakka (客家, Kejia) speech of the ordinary people of San On, and a vital duty of the clerks of the San On magistracy was to act as interpreters to the magistrate: as the gazetteer points out,

> The country people cannot speak the language of the officials, and, if the magistracy issues summonses, or has any judicial proceeding, then the magistracy underlings must handle the questioning (山人不通官話, 官府召訊必令衙役答話).[5]

The whole system was managed and controlled by the board of civil appointments in the capital. The army was organized similarly: military examinations were held, and the successful graduates given a post, with the management of the system being run by the board of war in the capital.

* * *

The county magistrates had a number of routine duties. They were responsible for the collection of the taxes, especially the major revenue-producing tax, the land tax, and for remitting it properly to the provincial authorities: this required them to manage the county granaries, where tax-grain was stored, or where the grain bought with silver paid in as tax was held, and to ensure that disbursements from the granaries were handled properly. From the late Ming, the great majority of the land tax in San On was paid in silver at a fixed and immutable rate of commutation; this may well have been made obligatory in San On by Zhou Xiyao in the late Ming (see below). Silver paid in as tax had to be refined to a standard fineness, cast into standard weight ingots, and stored in the county treasury strongroom under careful guard, until it could be sent under guard to the provincial treasurer (for San On, in Canton). The local operations of the salt monopoly, the other major revenue producing arm of the government, were, in San On, under the supervision of the magistrate, but the San On magistrate was not himself responsible for the collection of the tax. Huang Liu-hung notes that in most upcountry counties in the late Ming–early Qing the magistrate had to handle the collection of salt tax himself by ensuring that the county's quota of taxed salt was sold. But this was not so in San On, where the magistrate had merely to keep in view the operations of the salt monopoly, and to alert the provincial authorities when things were going wrong, although this was no small matter (see Chapter 6).[6]

During the Ming dynasty, the magistrates had to meet all central government expenditure in their county, especially the salaries and subsistence rations of the military posted there, from the tax revenue received by the county authorities, and to account for such expenditure.

In ordinary rural counties like San On, tax collection, and the concomitant careful control of the granaries and treasury, were the major routine duties of the county magistrates in the late Ming and early Qing — as Djang Chu remarks: "Tax collection was undoubtedly the most important duty of the magistrate".[7] This was certainly the view of Huang Liu-hung also, who consistently puts the collection of taxes in the first place in his discussions of a magistrate's duties.[8] However, in addition to these duties, they were also the local judges and police authorities, with responsibility for ensuring that crime was kept in check and that criminals were appropriately punished to maintain civil peace: as such they also presided over the county jail and execution ground. They managed the county land tax registry, so that disputes about the ownership of arable land — the essential factor underpinning the subsistence of the people — could be, if necessary, properly adjudicated. They also arbitrated any other inter-personal lawsuits which arose in the county, and which could not be settled by arbitration by the local elders.

Furthermore, the local, preliminary, level of the imperial examination system was run by them. They also had to conduct the prescribed rituals, season by season, especially those performed at the County Altar of Land and Grain (社稷壇) outside the south gate of the county city, at the City God Temple (城隍廟) within the walls of the city, and at the Temple of Confucius (文廟). These rituals ensured that the people of the county remained in a good relationship with the deities. Finally, they oversaw the imperial courier services, which carried official letters from place to place.

As well as these routine duties, however, the county magistrates also had other, less regular, but possibly even more important responsibilities. They were, in the first place, required to keep in close contact with the leaders of the people — scholars, clan elders, graduates of the imperial examinations, guild masters, salt merchants, and so forth — to ensure that they knew what the problems of the county were. Where intractable social problems arose, the magistrate had to adjudicate them, and arrive at a suitable compromise between the parties. Proposals to deal with serious problems had to be formulated and implemented by the county magistrates (in some circumstances, they had to seek approval from the provincial authorities before implementation). Above all they had to ensure that the county remained at peace, and that there were no social problems or heterodox religious ideas brewing which might cause the peace to be disturbed. It was

these duties which led to the county magistrate's Chinese title —
"He who knows everything about the County" (知縣).

When a natural disaster afflicted their county they had to take
appropriate action to mitigate the effects. In San On, magistrates
Chen Gu (1628–1631) and Zhou Xiyao thus had to face major
outbreaks of an epidemic disease, probably bubonic plague.
Chen Gu ordered that all the houses should be scrubbed clean to
eradicate ticks and fleas (in 1628), while Zhou Xiyao (probably
in 1643) organized a major ritual to the city god, beseeching the
God to rid the county of this disease. Li Kecheng had to deal with
widespread starvation in the county, arising from the aftermath
of the Coastal Evacuation. He dealt with this by directly and
personally encouraging the farmers to work hard, and supporting
them with donations of seeds and cattle from his private income.

Direct action was also taken by magistrate Li Dagen (1784–
1788). In 1786–1787 there was a terrible famine: the gazetteer
states in the "Disasters" (災異) section that locusts destroyed the
crop in 1786, and that both 1786 and 1787 were years of serious
drought, so that rice rose to a price of one silver dollar for ten
catties, and many people died of starvation.[9] The magistrate took
grain from the granaries, and "boiled it up into congee, which
preserved many people from starvation" (邑中饑, 糜粥賑濟, 民賴
以存活者甚多).[10] Magistrate Ma Yimao (1656–1661) also had to
deal with starvation when Nam Tau was besieged by the bandit
Lei Man-wing in 1656–1657: the gazetteer says that he found a
solution, but does not say what it was — probably, like Li Dagen
later, Ma Yimao used grain from the county granaries to make a
congee to feed the people.[11]

The magistrates had to liaise with the local military authorities
to stamp out any irruption of banditry or piracy (the local

military forces were not under the magistrate's direct control, but he was expected to maintain cordial and close relations with the local military officers), and to ensure that no rebellious elements arose among the local people. Where any serious bout of banditry did occur, the magistrate normally took temporary control of the county military forces, that is, of both the local militia and the soldiers posted to the county, until the crisis was ended — in San On both Zhou Xiyao and Li Kecheng did this (see below).[12]

The magistrates were also expected to encourage the people to live decent and virtuous lives. In the first place this required the magistrate to ensure that there were good schools in their counties, providing education of a high moral character, to encourage the common people to study.[13] Charitable activity among the people had to be encouraged. They were expected to foster righteous behaviour among the people generally, primarily by their own example, but also by honouring local men and women who were seen to have shown exemplary behaviour: they were, for instance, required to invite representatives of the elderly who had lived unblemished lives to dinner on an annual basis. In the Qing, they also had to arrange for regular public readings of the sacred edict, an imperial rescript which reminded people of their duty to live virtuously and decently.[14] In 1736 an inscription urging people not to fall into the "four evils" (drunkenness, banditry, prostitution, and gambling) was engraved onto stone and displayed in a central location within the city of Nam Tau (within one of the gatehouses leading to the yamen, 衙門), where it still stands. It is unclear who was responsible for the erection of this inscription, but the then magistrate, He Mengzhuang, probably at the least inspired the placement (see Plate 4). It was as part of these duties that the Shrine of Local Worthies was maintained in the county Temple of Confucius, where the magistrate worshipped every year the tablets of local residents who had lived exemplary lives.

Above all, they had to provide benevolent moral leadership, and dedicated, efficient, intelligent, and public-spirited service to the people. In addition, they had to present a grave, austere, frugal, and scrupulously polite demeanour, and to live a life marked with integrity and love of the people,[15] in other words a life in accordance with the Confucian way, as Confucian superior men (君子), so that the people would admire them and try to emulate their selfless hard work and dedication to good order, peace, and security.

* * *

Philip C.C. Huang has, however, stated that county magistrates were, in the Qing, heavily engaged in hearing interpersonal civil cases (戶婚田房案) in their courts, even in the smallest and most rural of counties. He states that the local people were rather litigious, so that large numbers of interpersonal lawsuits were always being started. Hearing cases arising from disputes over land, and other interpersonal civil disputes, was, he believes, the single most time-consuming task, and the heaviest burden facing the magistrates. He states that 50 interpersonal civil cases a year was a minimum figure for even a small rural county; John R. Watt, Bradly Reed, and Linxia Liang take much the same line.[16] Huang goes on to suggest that magistrates were, or quickly became, experts in the law, with many of them becoming notable jurisprudential scholars. The evidence used by Huang, Liang, Watt and Reed is taken, however, from the very late Qing, from relatively few counties, mostly from north China, and almost all from large, densely populated, urban counties with large volumes of trade, and, as such, it is questionable as to how much this evidence illuminates the position in small, quiet, rural counties, such as San On, in the late Ming and early Qing.

Civil lawsuits in traditional China were initiated by a complainant submitting a plaint (呈) to the magistrate: these were written documents in the form of a petition, which could not exceed a certain length, which detailed the grievance, and begged for justice. They could only be submitted on specified days, and had to be received by the magistrate in person.[17] The magistrate then added a short comment giving his prima facie views on the case. In many cases the magistrate noted that the plaint did not give enough evidence, or was of dubious veracity,[18] and thus required further information before the case could be proceeded with. In some instances he rejected the plaint outright. In others he accepted the case as worthy of action. The complainant might then submit a further plaint, giving more details.

Actual judicial action beyond this prima facie stage usually began when the defendant submitted a counter-plaint in rebuttal, rejecting the original plaint, and giving his version of events. The magistrate would then usually start an investigation. Further plaints from both parties would be submitted as points which they felt the magistrate would need to be aware of. Philip C.C. Huang suggests that only a minority of plaints received were initiatory plaints: the majority were counter-plaints, rebuttals, and subsequent procedural plaints of various kinds. Eventually, once all the evidence had been presented, reports had been submitted from magistracy underlings with the conclusions of any investigations they had undertaken or any interrogations they had carried out at the magistrate's command, and the parties and witnesses had been gathered together, the magistrate would proceed to a formal judgement.

It seems that the majority of civil cases where an initiating plaint was submitted to the magistracy proceeded no further than this.[19] It cost about a tael[20] of silver to submit a plaint — much more than that if the complainant lived far from the county city and would need to travel and stay one or more nights there (some areas of San On were four days or more travel away from the county city) — and this would have been a very high price for most villagers. To proceed to a formal judgement would usually cost the parties several tens of taels, on occasion even more than that. It seems probable that, in most cases, the initiating plaint was not designed primarily to start litigation, but to use the threat of an expensive case to force an unwilling opponent to go to arbitration.[21]

Criminal cases were also often initiated by submission of a plaint by the aggrieved party, especially relatively minor cases. However, plaints in these cases could be submitted on any day, and, in the magistrate's absence, whoever was in charge of the yamen could receive them and initiate action. Other avenues for initiating a criminal case existed, which were used in particular for serious crimes. In some yamen a gong or drum was placed at the main gate of the yamen: anyone beating it would be taken immediately to the magistrate, or to whoever was in charge of the yamen at the time, and the aggrieved party could then initiate action verbally (although anyone who undertook this course of action for frivolous purposes was punished). This method was considered by Huang Liu-hung as the normal way of initiating a serious criminal case. In other yamen the magistrate could be interrupted in his business in the court hall by someone "raising a clamour" (喊稟, or 大聲呼冤, or 大堂聞有喊冤): this was the method used in Kwong Ning. It is not known which method was used in San On. In all cases, any delay in initiating the case was seen as suspicious and likely to indicate perjury or exaggeration.[22]

Of those civil cases where a counter-plaint was submitted, and the formal judicial process started, again, the majority did not proceed to a formal judgement but were ended by arbitration.

Every county was required to maintain a case register, into which all legal cases formally handled by the magistracy (i.e. all serious criminal cases, and civil cases where a counter-plaint was filed, and formal investigation started) were entered. This register was the most important single archive which would be checked by the magistrate's superiors when they visited the county. The case register for Baodi County survives for the years 1833–1835 and 1861–1881.[23] The Baodi case register shows that, for the years 1833–1835, 1864, 1868–1870, and 1879–1881, the numbers of interpersonal "civil" cases registered in Baodi County varied from 10 to 19, and averaged 12.8 a year. For the years 1861–1863, 1865–1868, and 1871–1878, however, the cases registered varied from 1 to 8, and averaged 4.6 a year.

Philip C.C. Huang assumes that the number of civil cases entered onto the Baodi case register throughout this half-century was deliberately under registered by a long succession of Baodi magistrates to reduce the chance of negative findings being made on inspection by senior officials, and that the actual number of civil cases formally heard was in fact much higher, "50 or so cases a year". However, no evidence is given by Huang to support this assumption that only 5% or 10% of Baodi civil cases were registered. If supervising officers were to find out that the Baodi cases had been deliberately and seriously under registered for a long period, then the negative results of any such finding would, in all likelihood, have been more serious than the ill handling of any individual case. It seems at least tentatively worth accepting the Baodi figures for civil cases heard as they stand, particularly as these figures are similar to those disclosed by the diary of Du Fengzhi for Kwong Ning in 1866–1867.

However, it could also be possible that the ten years of higher than average registrations of civil cases in the Baodi case register represent Baodi magistrates who registered all cases where investigation was begun after receipt of a counter-plaint, and the years of lower registrations magistrates who registered only cases which proceeded to formal judicial rulings. In either case, the number of cases heard would have been moderate, and cannot be seen as implying a heavy caseload. It would imply that formal investigations began in 10 to 20 interpersonal civil cases there each year in the late Qing, with about a half or a quarter of these proceeding to a formal judicial ruling. It is unlikely that cases which did not proceed beyond the magistrate's prima facie note were registered at any date, since these cases did not proceed to a formal investigation.

This tentative finding is supported by the figures for interpersonal civil cases heard in Kwong Ning County during this same late Qing period by magistrate Du Fengzhi. He took over his post there in the tenth moon of 1866. During the first month of his incumbency, he received probably about 180 plaints; these plaints represent a backlog which had built up before his arrival in Kwong Ning.[24] During the fifth moon of 1867 he received 145 plaints. In the eighth moon he received about 100 plaints.

However, during the ninth and tenth moons of 1867 he was absent from the yamen, either working for a time in Canton, or out suppressing bandits: it is likely that no civil plaints were received in Kwong Ning during these two months. Based on these figures it seems that the total number of plaints received over a full year would have been about a thousand. These plaints covered both civil and criminal cases, and both initiating and subsequent plaints.[25]

Cheung Yin suggests that Du Fengzhi heard rather less than 50 judicial cases a year in the period 1866–1867, including both criminal and civil cases: all the cases Du Fengzhi heard are discussed in his diary.[26] He notes that Du Fengzhi heard 11 murder cases, 14 robbery cases (ranging from major episodes of banditry to mere pilfering and minor theft), and 20 cases he classifies as "civil" (戶婚田房案), plus one other civil case which is not included in his table of civil cases: he also notes five or six cases where the yamen helped a landlord by chasing unpaid rents.[27] However, only a very small minority of these civil cases proceeded to a formal judicial ruling. Furthermore, many of the cases classified as "civil" by Cheung Yin are only doubtfully really to be seen as being truly interpersonal civil cases.

Two of the civil cases as classified by Cheung Yin are more realistically to be seen as criminal cases. One refers to the abduction and rape of two married women. The other is a case where a very poor man who had a young son, and saw no need to continue to support a wife, sold her to a relatively well-off merchant. However, the merchant did not pay over the sum agreed, and the poor man therefore brought a case for abduction of the wife (Du Fengzhi considered the case "shameless", and required the poor man to take the wife back, and his younger brother, a soldier, to guarantee that the elder brother would not thereafter try to sell her again).

Most of the other civil cases heard were disputes arising between gentry clans or families about the boundaries of their areas of influence. Very few were cases resulting from quarrels between ordinary villagers. Thus, eleven cases were "mountain cases" (爭山案, or 爭山木案), all of which were cases of this kind.[28] Kwong Ning was famous in this period as an exporter of bamboo and wood. In the late Qing the trade in fuel became extremely lucrative, as most areas near the bigger cities had by that date become completely bare of trees and bamboo. The cities (Canton in the case of Kwong Ning) nonetheless had an insatiable demand for both bamboo and firewood, which could thus only be met by imports from further afield. The subsoil landlords[29] in areas which still had stands of trees or bamboo, such as Kwong Ning, wanted to deny access to these hillside woodlands to commercial woodcutters, or, indeed, to their topsoil tenants unless the landlords were paid a rent for the privilege. Usually each tenant village would have had a small area where they could cut wood for their own fires, but it was the areas which could be exploited commercially which the subsoil landlords wanted to restrict access to.

They similarly wanted to ensure that no one could enter the hills to reclaim land without the reclaimer accepting a tenancy status from the subsoil landlord. They also wanted to ensure that graves could only be made with their consent on their hillsides: a further two of the civil cases were disputes as to which gentry group could control burials on specific hillsides. All these 13 cases were thus disputes between gentry clans, or by rival groups within one gentry clan, as to the boundaries of their areas of influence, or as to which group actually had the right to control these hills. These cases, therefore, are more about the limits of the powers of subsoil landlords, and the boundaries of the areas they each controlled, than genuine interpersonal civil cases. They should be seen as "political" cases, quarrels about local power and domination, and attempts to clarify the respective rights of subsoil landlords and topsoil tenants.[30]

Only about six Kwong Ning cases, therefore, are likely to have been genuine interpersonal civil cases arising between ordinary villagers. One of these cases was a quarrel between close relatives over the exact boundaries of a house lot, another included a claim that a nephew was cheating a widow out of an inheritance, while a third was a dispute between villages about the division of expenditure for a Ta Tsiu celebration.[31] The rest were mostly about land. At least some of these cases were probably also disputes between gentry figures: this is especially so for the case about Ta Tsiu expenses.

The number of genuine interpersonal cases in Kwong Ning, therefore, leaving aside the "mountain cases" and other political cases of the gentry, is thus rather fewer than perhaps might be expected considering the evidence from the Baodi case register, if the figures surviving for the Baodi register are taken at face value. Kwong Ning, however, was substantially more rural than Baodi, and this finding is not entirely unexpected. The Kwong Ning figures suggest that the numbers of cases registered in the case register of Baodi County as it has survived are likely to be at least not wildly under registered, and calls into question Huang's belief that "50 civil cases a year" was a minimum figure for civil cases proceeding to judgement in any county in the late Qing, no matter how small and rural.

That criminal judicial activity was more significant than civil is also suggested by Huang Liu-hung's comments on the judicial work of magistrates in the early Qing. He gives nine volumes (卷) of discussion on criminal cases (201 pages in translation), and only part of one volume on civil cases (8 pages in translation): he clearly felt that criminal cases were by far the most significant part of a magistrate's judicial duties.[32]

Of course, the late Ming and early Qing San On magistrates must have heard interpersonal cases in their Court. San On, in these years, however, was less urbanized than late-Qing Baodi, or even Kwong Ning, and had a far lower population. It is very unlikely that more interpersonal civil cases arose in San On in this period than in late Qing Kwong Ning, very probably fewer.

The imperial Chinese legal code did not clearly distinguish between criminal and civil cases. However, there was a sharp difference in administrative practice in the magistracies between the two. The magistrate thus had to inform his superiors of every serious crime occurring in his county (that is, crimes punishable by penal servitude or exile, or which might involve the culprit being executed — murder, wounding, rape, robbery, kidnapping, brigandage, etc) and the magistrate might be fined, or even dismissed, if he did not solve these cases within a given time.[33] For less serious crimes — brawling, cursing, insulting others, pilfering, immoral behaviour, and the like — the magistrate had to send a return listing the number and type of such cases and how the magistrate had solved them, and the penalty imposed. All such cases had to be entered into the county case register. When the magistrate's superiors came to the county to check on the work, it was an essential part of this review that the superior officer look over the papers to satisfy himself that these cases had been handled properly, and that the punishments imposed were appropriate. The magistrate, would, therefore, treat any criminal case reported to him as an urgent matter, and would himself initiate action and pursue it to a solution; as Djang Chu notes, "Criminal cases had to be reported to the magistrate immediately, and received priority attention".[34]

Interpersonal cases, however, such as debt cases, breaches of contract, commercial disputes, land disputes such as tenancy disputes, boundary disputes, or succession disputes, marriage or other family disputes, minor misdemeanours and the like, would only be taken up by the magistrate if the elders involved could not achieve an amicable consensus, or if their arbitration failed. Any initiatory plaint in such a case which did not mention that the complainant had tried to get the matter arbitrated would be unlikely to be accepted by the magistrate at the prima facie stage. The magistrate would certainly give time for arbitration in such cases, and would only take the matter up if local arbitration had clearly failed. He might then send the case to the gentry of the county for arbitration at a higher level. He would normally only proceed formally to judgement if all arbitration opportunities had failed, and if the parties were willing to pay all the fees involved.[35] This was certainly the line taken by Du Fengzhi, who consistently demanded that the Kwong Ning gentry adjudicate all such disputes; thus leaving for his own judgement mostly only those cases which were disputes between gentry groups, and which thus could not realistically be arbitrated by the gentry.[36]

The great majority of legal cases which are referred to in the San On Gazetteer were criminal cases, mostly serious, initiated by the magistrate, and not interpersonal cases initiated by one party to a dispute. In addition, both Zhou Xiyao and Li Kecheng, but particularly the former, found it difficult to get criminal cases decided, as the people would go to great lengths to avoid attending Court, even as witnesses, absconding, giving false names or addresses, and so forth, so that it seems most unlikely that any substantial numbers were coming voluntarily to the court to lay charges against their neighbours.

This presumption is borne out by the oral evidence from the New Territories. Village elders born there in the later nineteenth or early twentieth century all stated to scholars who asked them about their lives that the idea of approaching the yamen filled them, and their fathers and forefathers, with horror. As a Hong Kong government official observed in 1906: "The people never went to a Chinese yamen unless obliged",[37] or, as Stewart Lockhart noted in 1900: "The inhabitants [are] distrustful of officials", and show a "want of faith in the justice of government".[38] Stewart Lockhart also noted that, when civil disputes arose, they were always handled by the council of elders of the village or clan in question, from whence they might be taken by appeal to the council of elders of that division ("Tung" 洞) of the county, and then to the Tung Ping Kuk (東平局), the council of elders for the eastern roads half of the county, and only then, if the complainant was still unsatisfied, would the matter go to the magistrate.[39] This suggests that interpersonal cases that were sent to the magistrate for a hearing in late Qing San On were few, except, presumably, for disputes breaking out between gentry groups.

In fact, hardly anything written about any late Ming or early Qing San On magistrate, in any entry in the gazetteer, mentions any interpersonal civil cases coming before them: almost every comment on the legal work of these magistrates mentions only criminal cases. Thus Zeng Kongzhi (1576–1579) is mentioned as being concerned about legal cases, but what is said of his actions is that he dealt with cases quickly, so that people were not kept for any length of time in jail, thus suggesting that his actions were concerned primarily with criminal cases.[40] The same sort of comment, that he dealt with criminal cases expeditiously, is made of magistrates Chen Liangyen (1622–1624), Li Kecheng (1670–1675), An Yumei (1684–1687), Jin Wenmo (1687–1694), and Li Wenzao (1771).

A story is included in the biography in the provincial gazetteer of magistrate Qiu Tiqian (1586–1590) that credits him with subtlety in criminal investigation worthy of magistrate Dee, or other famous judges. A Nam Tau silversmith lusted after the wife of one of his neighbours, and he had this man murdered so that his path to the lady would be clear. However, she rebuffed all his advances, and threatened to commit suicide if he did not let her be. The silversmith gathered some friends, enemies of the murdered man, and made a formal complaint to the magistrate that the lady was a woman of loose morals, and had committed adultery, entertaining men in her husband's house and bed. She was arrested for adultery and thrown into the county jail.

However, the magistrate held court immediately, and listened very carefully to everything that was said, especially the words of the lady, and the underlying implications of what was said. He was convinced that she was quite innocent of the complaint of adultery and loose morals, and had her released. However, his suspicions were aroused, and he had her secretly watched. The silversmith immediately sent a matchmaker to her, to make a proposal that she become his concubine, as he felt that the lady would now be too frightened of being called back to the jail to refuse him. The magistrate, on being informed of this, immediately arrested the silversmith, arguing that no man would accuse a lady of having loose morals, and then offer to wed her a day or two later. In court, the magistrate's subtle questioning soon exposed the whole affair, and the silversmith paid the price for the murder. Magistrate Qiu was widely praised for his handling of this case, which was seen as exemplary.[41] Magistrate Qiu is particularly praised, not only for listening carefully to whatever people said in court, but also for ensuring that he understood exactly what they were saying and the implications. Chen Liangyen (1622–1624) is also credited with taking great care to ensure he understood the inferences of everything that was said in his court.[42]

There are other specific comments made about the attitude towards criminal cases of some of the magistrates. An Yumei is said to have refused to extend punishments to the relatives of convicted criminals. Duan Yansheng (1724–1725) is said to have kept punishments (i.e. for convicted criminals) to a low number. Wu Yi (1780–1784) is praised for his astuteness in finding the culprit in a murder case which had been left unsolved for over a year by his predecessor, Gao Zhijing (1779–1780).[43]

* * *

Given all this, it is very difficult to believe that there were large numbers of interpersonal or land disputes coming before the San On magistrates. In fact, the only comment in the San On Gazetteer on any of the magistrates which refers to interpersonal cases refers to Li Kecheng (1670–1675). His biography in the provincial gazetteer states that "he always tried to achieve conciliation in any dispute arising among the people" (民有訟者必力勸息之),[44] and this comment does not suggest large numbers were coming into his court for a judicial ruling, and specifically implies that, where any did, he would seek arbitration from the elders of the county before any formal hearing.

Furthermore, were the magistrate to decide any interpersonal land case, then the decision of the magistrate would become the very best possible land deed, being an indefeasible statement of right, and would doubtless have been carefully preserved. However not even one such decision by any San On magistrate is believed to survive, at least within the three hundred or so Qing period land deeds surviving in today's New Territories. Those land dispute decisions by the magistrate which have survived seem all to have been cases where two communities (two rival villages, or a village and the gentry communal trust which was the subsoil landlord of the village), rather than two persons, were involved: in every case these disputes were as much political as economic, and centred on which village community was the dominant player in the local area involved, on the limits of the powers of the subsoil landlords, and the rights of their topsoil tenants. In these cases, the magistrate's decision was carefully preserved — in two cases being inscribed onto stone. However, no more than about four or five such cases are known, dating from the 150 years prior to the takeover of the Hong Kong area by the British, and, certainly, there is no evidence to suggest that such cases were at all numerous.[45]

There can be little doubt, therefore, that the local villagers of the San On area were at all dates, and particularly in the late Ming and early Qing, in fact rather non-litigious, and did everything they could to avoid being brought before the magistrate, and that there was no heavy burden on the magistrate to hear interpersonal civil lawsuits. It is at least possible that, in this regard, San On was at one with the majority of rural counties, certainly those in south China, as the great majority of the south China counties were just as rural and unsophisticated as San On. The bulk of the legal work of these rural magistrates was undoubtedly criminal.

This certainly seems to be true, not only of late Ming and early Qing San On, but also of Kwong Ning during Du Fengzhi's tenure there. He heard about 25 serious criminal cases during this time, plus several minor criminal cases, as against only about 6 genuinely interpersonal civil cases, as noted above, suggesting that in Kwong Ning criminal cases took up a good deal more of the magistrate's time than civil interpersonal cases. Much the same seems to be true of Baodi, where the case register shows nearly twice as many serious criminal cases as civil cases registered, plus, in addition, more cases of brawls, fights, and assaults than all the civil cases.[46]

It would seem, therefore, that, in the late Qing, small rural counties did not see very large numbers of interpersonal civil cases, that they were substantially outnumbered by criminal cases, and that hearing civil cases did not create an excessive workload for the magistrates of such counties. The suggestion that interpersonal civil cases were extremely numerous, and a heavy burden on the magistrates in the late Qing should, therefore, be seen as applying only to highly urban counties with large populations and a substantial commercial life, or else to other counties which were special in some regard. In the late Ming and early Qing, in counties like San On with low levels of urbanization and low levels of population, this divergence is likely to have been even more pronounced.

* * *

To help administer the range of his duties, the county magistrates had, in all counties, a small staff. In San On County the magistrate had, in the late Ming and early Qing, five official assistants, including the county director of education and his deputy, and a formal establishment of something like a hundred junior staff, although it is probable that there were perhaps about twice this number actually employed.[47] In 1723 the establishment of the county was increased, and a sixth official assistant (a deputy magistrate, 縣丞) was added.[48] This establishment of official assistants was rather above the national average. Every county had a director and deputy director of education, but otherwise most counties only had about one or two other official assistants on average; the larger number in San On was probably due to the county's large area and difficult terrain.[49]

The director and deputy director of education, while they were regarded as staff of the magistracy, were also supervised by the provincial director of education, and there were severe limits on what the magistrate could ask of these officials.

In all counties, the official assistants, like the magistrate himself, were posted to the county by the central government. Their careers were supervised by the board of civil appointments, which kept records of appointment, leave, and retirement (or dismissal). The magistrates could therefore not dismiss these official assistants. Because the official assistants were thus officers of the state, the county also kept details of their postings, and these are recorded in the gazetteer after the record of the appointments of the magistrates.

It is often stated that the official assistant posts were "sinecures", without any real duties, but this seems to be rather doubtful. Other than the director and deputy director of education, who had certain specific duties, they had no duties which were specifically theirs, and they were not allowed to make any judicial rulings, but they were available to assist in whatever way the magistrate saw fit. Some magistrates gave them very little, others more, but, in general, each of them had enough work to keep a clerk busy.

* * *

Throughout the empire, the magistrate and his official assistants, each had their own offices, or yamen: these were laid out in similar ways in every county, but there were relatively minor differences between yamen in large counties, and those in smaller counties, where the administration was simpler. These latter yamen consisted of a number of buildings arranged around a series of courtyards. In the case of the San On magistrate's yamen, in the centre of the county city of Nam Tau (see Plate 5), there was firstly a small court opening off a side street, entered through two small gateways, left and right (this courtyard was there for feng shui, 風水, reasons, to ensure good luck for the magistracy, and was left empty of buildings).[50] The yamen was separated from the main east-west street of the city by a row of shops owned and operated by merchant families; the three alleyways between the main east-west street and the side street to which the yamen opened were provided with gatehouses (門樓, see Plates 6 and 7).[51] The yamen faced south, also for feng shui reasons.

Behind this feng shui court was the front court, reached through the imposing main gate (see Plate 8). On top of the main gate was the Drum Tower (譙樓, also called 鼓樓), where the great drum was placed which was used to warn residents of outbreaks of fire, attack by bandits, or other serious matters.[52] In this front court, to the left and right, were the entrances to the main county granaries, and the earth-god shrine of the magistracy. Opposite the main gate was the ceremonial gate (儀門), this was set in the centre of an elegant ceremonial hall, which was where the magistrate would greet important visitors. Across the front of this hall was a high balustrade of polished wood, with four gates in it: the middle two were opened only on ceremonial occasions, and usually only the easternmost gate was used.

Behind the ceremonial gate was the main court. On either side of this were the offices of the magistracy clerks with the general archives of the magistracy (see Plate 9),[53] and the buildings housing the magistrate's treasury guards, and "runners" (差役, see Plates 5 and 8). At the back, to one side, were the stables and the building housing the courier soldiers.

On the west side of the main court in the Nam Tau yamen was the gateway which led to the access corridor to the jail (the jail was located in the middle of the granary area on the west side of the court, for greater security). Also accessed from this corridor was a small enclosed courtyard behind the western clerks' office. This had a small building standing in its centre. Since this courtyard was very secure, it is possible that this building was the county treasury, where refined silver awaiting shipment to the provincial treasurer was stored, and where the treasury clerk's office was to be found. Opposite this courtyard, behind the eastern clerks' office, was another enclosed courtyard, identical with the western one, accessed through a corridor opening to the front court. In the centre of this courtyard was a building, shown as identical to the building in the western courtyard. This eastern courtyard was also very secure, and the ground floor of the building in this courtyard was possibly used as the granary office (the granary office functioned as the land tax office), housing the land tax register and archive, with the office of the clerk of the land tax register, and a strongroom holding the unrefined sycee silver handed in as tax.[54] Somewhere in this area would have been the magistracy shroff office where payments to the magistracy would be made, and the quality of the silver paid in tested.

At the back of this main court, opposite the main gate and the ceremonial gate, up a flight of steps, was the court hall (大堂, see Plate 10). In front of the court hall, at the top of the steps, was a platform, fronted by a high balustrade (the risk of flooding led to the buildings of the San On yamen being built on platforms raised several feet above the courtyard, so that balustrades were needed to obviate the risk of falling down). Access to the court hall of the magistracy required passing between the buildings housing the treasury guards and runners. The court hall was where the magistrate would hear most of his judicial cases, and conduct all his formal, public duties.

Behind the court hall, in the private part of the yamen, were the second hall (二堂), a library, and the private office of the magistrate. In the second hall the magistrate would hear cases which were thought to be too sensitive to be heard in public. Behind this again were a series of courtyards which separated the various buildings of the magistrate's residence, with gardens on either side. The whole complex was surrounded by a stout wall.[55]

The yamen of the official assistants were smaller, but followed the same basic pattern. One of these official assistants had the title in San On of "supervisor of documents", more usually translated as "chief of police" where San On is concerned (典史): he was the administrative head of the magistracy, and his job was to assist the magistrate and ensure that the junior staff, especially the runners, did their work properly. In Nam Tau, his yamen lay within the magistrate's yamen complex, immediately to the east of the magistrate's private office (see Plate 2): it consisted of a main gate, a front court with some subsidiary buildings, a main hall, and a rear court with residential buildings. To the far side of this yamen of the chief of police was, it is believed, the back entrance to the yamen, which would be used by people with private business with the magistrate or his household, and which gave access from the yamen to the Kwan Tai Temple just outside.

The San On County director and deputy director of education had their yamen within the walls of Nam Tau, but not within the magistrate's yamen complex. They were similar to the yamen of the chief of police, but rather larger, especially that of the director.

The other two official assistants of the San On magistracy in the late Ming and early Qing were the two assistant magistrates, whose yamen were outside Nam Tau. These yamen were earlier in date than the magistrate's yamen, since these two assistant magistracies had been, before 1573, two of the assistant magistracies of the county of Tung Kwun, and had been transferred to San On when the areas they supervised were passed to the new county when it was established. Each of these assistant magistrates aided the magistrate by supervising the countryside areas. One had his yamen in the small market town of Fuk Wing (福永, Fuyong), some 12 miles outside Nam Tau: he was responsible for assisting the magistrate in matters arising in the area north-west of Nam Tau, that is, the "western roads" (西路) part of the county. This area was called the "western roads" area since it was accessed by the road which left Nam Tau by the west gate of the city.

The other assistant magistrate was known as the Kwun Fu assistant magistrate (官富巡檢): this name reflected the fact that, in the Yuan dynasty, the yamen of this officer had been at Kowloon City, then usually known as Kwun Fu. In the late Ming and early Qing he was responsible for the vast area to the north, east and south-east of Nam Tau, comprising about three-quarters of the county (this was the "eastern roads", 東路, part of the county: that is, the area accessed by the roads which left Nam Tau by the east gate). The yamen of the Kwun Fu assistant magistrate was, in the late Ming and early Qing, at the village of Chek Mei, about a mile west of the market town of Sham Chun (深圳, Shenzhen), and was housed in buildings rented from the villagers. The yamen of this official was moved back to Kowloon City in 1847, when the central government wanted an official on the spot to keep an eye on the British in their new city of Hong Kong, just across the harbour. After 1723, the easternmost part of this huge eastern roads area was put under the supervision of the new deputy magistrate, stationed at Tai Pang. The yamen of the two assistant magistrates were similar in size to that of the director of education.

Nothing whatsoever survives today of the San On yamen, nor of any of the yamen of the official assistants, except for the main hall of the nineteenth-century assistant magistrate's yamen in Kowloon City. A building survives in Nam Tau which was probably the gunpowder store of the military yamen there (see Plate 11).

* * *

In San On the magistrate himself, along with the chief of police, directly supervised the area within the walls of Nam Tau City, together with its suburbs, including the mercantile community of the city, the Nam Tau Tsan (南頭鎮). This lay to the south (the walled city of Nam Tau was essentially a government cantonment, with few shops and little commercial life). The magistrate and the chief of police also directly supervised the small area accessed by the roads which left Nam Tau by the south gate and the bridge over the river. There was also a north gate to Nam Tau, but this gate was blocked up for feng shui reasons; the northern roads had, shortly after the county was established, been diverted around the city to the east gate, and the area accessed by these northern roads thus formed part of the "eastern roads" area (the north gate of Tai Pang was similarly closed for feng shui reasons; see Plate 28). These roads from the south gate led through the mercantile area. There were two roads, initially running almost parallel to each other, approximately north-south. The one to the east ran to the important ferry pier at She Hau (蛇口, Shekou), which took traffic across the mouth of Deep Bay (後海灣) and so on to Lantau, Cheung Chau (長洲, Zhangzhou), Yuen Long, Kowloon City, and Tai Po. The road to the west ran to the important Tin Hau Temple (天后廟) at Chek Wan (赤灣, Chiwan); this was the main temple of the Nam Tau area (see Maps 3 and 4).

Below the magistrate and his official assistants every county had a number of minor staff.[56] The most important of these were the clerks (吏). There was a formal establishment of seven document clerks (典吏) in the magistrate's yamen in San On in 1688, handling the land tax registry and the general archives of the magistracy, with, in addition, a receipt and dispatch clerk (承發), a granary clerk (倉吏), and a treasury clerk (庫吏): a total establishment of ten clerks. There was also one general clerk (司吏: this title means "office clerk") in each of the yamen of the chief of police and the two assistant magistrates.[57] These are all listed in the 1688 gazetteer, since their salaries and essential expenses were a charge on the tax income.[58] The 1819 San On Gazetteer mentions yet one more clerk, a general clerk (司吏) serving the director of education: it is probable that the post of this clerk, who is not mentioned in the 1688 gazetteer, was omitted from that earlier gazetteer as the result of an editorial oversight (there was an equivalent clerk in the establishment in Tung Kwun in 1464).[59]

The establishment of clerks in San On had only been raised by one by 1819, with one further general clerk (司吏) established to service the new deputy magistrate post, in 1723.[60] In the time of Zhou Xiyao, there were, in addition, a senior clerk (大吏) and a disbursement clerk (攢典) in each of the Wing Yung and Yue Pei granaries in Nam Tau (永盈倉, 預備倉). These posts were included in the "old gazetteer" (the gazetteer issued in 1643, in Zhou Xiyao's time, which no longer survives),[61] but the posts had been abolished, along with the granaries they served, by the time the 1688 gazetteer was issued, a reform put in place by Zhou Xiyao.[62]

Documents generated in the yamen were divided into six subject areas (房) in most magistracies:[63] the seven document clerks in the establishment in San On represented one clerk to each of these six subject areas, plus a clerk to care for the land tax registry.

The Tung Kwun Gazetteer of 1464 states that a similar situation was in place in Tung Kwun at that date. Tung Kwun had six "office clerks" (司吏) in the establishment there (吏...六房每房司吏一名). The six subject areas, both in Tung Kwun in 1464, and in San On in 1688, were: clerks (吏), dealing with personnel matters of the clerks and officials within the yamen; households (戶), dealing with the small taxes, especially the salt tax, and the corvée (徭役), and matters arising from the bao-jia (保甲);[64] rituals (禮), looking after the rituals conducted by the magistrate; soldiers (兵), overseeing relations with the military, and with personnel and other matters for the courier soldiers and runners; legal (刑), with responsibility over all documents arising from court cases; and works (工), with responsibility for documents arising from public works matters.[65]

In addition to the six office clerks in Tung Kwun in 1464, there were also a receipt and dispatch clerk (承發典吏), as in San On later, and two "document clerks" (典吏), who presumably cared for the land tax registry (these would probably have worked under the granary clerk), whose duties were conducted in San On by a single clerk. Tung Kwun also had a clerk who checked documents for errors (勘合科司吏) and one other, whose title and duties cannot be read in the gazetteer as it has survived. There was no clerk in San On in 1688 whose duties corresponded with these latter two clerks. There were also a chief clerk and a disbursement clerk in the "tax office" (税科局大使: 攢典) in Tung Kwun in 1464: these would have been the granary clerks working in the granary within the Tung Kwun yamen. The granary clerk would have dealt with the land tax, and would have kept the land tax archive, presumably with the assistance of the two document clerks. The duties of these two clerks were undertaken in San On by the single granary clerk there.[66] There were, in addition, other officials in Tung Kwun: a "keeper of the records" (主薄) and a "private secretary and supervisor of the records" (幕官典史). The private secretary was a public officer, paid from the taxes, not a private employee of the magistrate, and was presumably the Tung Kwun equivalent of the San On chief of police. The keeper of the records was probably in charge of the yamen's accounts.[67]

The San On Gazetteer states that there were nine "fong" (in essence "room") in the yamen in San On. Compared with Tung Kwun, San On had fewer clerks on the establishment from 1573, but the responsibilities of the clerks were very similar to those of the clerks in Tung Kwun a century earlier. Of the clerks of the nine fong in San On, six were identical with the six office clerks in Tung Kwun a century earlier, and the other three were the granary clerk, the treasury clerk, and the receipt and despatch clerk (the clerk of the land tax registry probably worked under the granary clerk, rather than forming a separate fong).[68]

The six clerks occupied two small buildings in the main court in the San On yamen (see Plates 8 and 9). The clerks' buildings in the main court were called 各吏房, meaning "rooms of the clerks of the subject areas". The clerks' building on the eastern side of the main court housed the clerks of the clerks, households, and rituals fong, and the building on the west those of the soldiers, legal and works fong. The clerks of each fong occupied a room or cubicle of the building, accessed from an open verandah along the front face of the building, protected by a high balustrade. A fourth room in the eastern building housed the receipt and despatch clerk; the fourth room in the western building was probably the general archive of the yamen. The eastern building had a further room, housing another clerk, the "supervisor of the eastern building" (東司) and the western building similarly had a room for the "supervisor of the western building" (西司). These were probably alternative titles for the granary clerk and the treasury clerk.[69] The granary clerk (in charge of the land tax registry) and the treasury clerk were the general managers of those vital parts of the yamen in addition, it would seem, to supervising the other clerks.

There is no clear reference to a chief clerk in San On in either the 1688 gazetteer or the 1819 gazetteer. It is unlikely that San On did not have such a position, however. The chief clerk (usually called the 大寫) was a figure of great importance and authority in all yamen, and his advice was vital to the magistrate. The 1688 gazetteer does, however, say that the duties of the clerks in San On were "distributed in accordance with expenditure by the Supervisor of Documents" (戶分典司), and this "Supervisor of Documents" may well be the San On chief clerk: presumably either the supervisor of the eastern building or the supervisor of the western building, whichever was the more senior at the time, would have acted as chief clerk in San On.[70]

The clerks of the magistracy had to be well educated, and had to be able to write a fluid, graceful, and easily readable hand. They also had to be able to speak Mandarin fluently, so as to be able to converse with the magistrate, and to translate for him. Documents written by the magistrate would be passed in draft to the clerks, who would then write out a fair copy for dispatch (or several copies: some of the annual returns sent to the provincial authorities had to be sent in sextuplicate), and another fair copy for entry into the archive. Routine documents, including warrants, would be drafted by the clerks, and issued after the magistrate had approved them and marked them as suitable for dispatch. The clerks prepared the annual and quarterly returns required to be sent to the provincial authorities.

The granary clerk was in charge of the land tax office, and was responsible for keeping the books recording tax payments and arrears, and for informing the magistrate when arrears were such that enforcement action to collect the taxes was needed. He also kept the granary books, recording the entries and disbursements of grain. The land tax registry clerk would have worked for the granary clerk.

Procurement was handled by the clerks: everything needed by the magistracy, from food, firewood, and stationery to horses for the courier soldiers (see below) and armour and arms for the treasury guards, was purchased by them. The rituals clerk was responsible for making all the arrangements for the prescribed rituals which the magistrate was required to undertake (this would have included ensuring that the county graduates were notified to attend). The filing system was operated by them (presumably this work was supervised by the receipt and despatch clerk), with every incoming or outgoing document being properly docketed, and entered onto the shelves of the archive room, to ensure that the magistrate could retrieve it as needed.

If disputes among the people arose which could not be settled by the elders, especially over land, it was the clerks who would normally handle the matter first, hearing the parties, advising them and urging restraint where appropriate, in an effort to bring about an agreement. A plaint from a complainant in a civil dispute would only be accepted, and a formal hearing in the court hall, or the involvement of one of the official assistants initiated, when the clerks had failed to bring about an agreement. This, as noted previously, seems to have been relatively rare in San On (presumably this sort of arbitration work, where it involved disputes over landholding, would normally have been handled, or supervised, by the granary clerk). If a criminal case arose, it would presumably have been the legal clerk who would deal with the essential preliminaries, before the matter was put before the magistrate for authority to issue summonses and arrest warrants. Similarly, if social or political disputes broke out, then it would usually be the clerks who would hear the parties first, and seek to reach an amicable compromise, to avoid, if possible, the magistrate or one of his official assistants becoming involved. Sometimes this would involve a clerk going out to the place where the dispute had arisen, and holding meetings there, before preparing a report, if necessary, for the magistrate. In all these matters, the clerks would work alongside the official assistants.

In addition to the clerks, there were courier soldiers (舖 兵), treasury guards (卒), and runners employed by the San On magistracy.[71] In some counties there were more categories of such junior staff, but it seems likely that a simpler tripartite classification was used in San On.[72]

The courier soldiers manned the imperial postal services (see Plate 12) which carried official letters. There were two postal routes which ran from Nam Tau in the late Ming and early Qing. One ran north, to Tung Kwun City, where it connected with a route from Tung Kwun to Canton: this route carried official letters to and from San On and the provincial authorities, and from San On to and from the other magistracies in the broader area. The other route linked Nam Tau with the important fortress city of Tai Pang in the east of San On. The courier soldiers carried letters on horseback: the routes used by the courier soldiers were perhaps the only roads in the county capable of being ridden on. There was an establishment of 27 courier soldiers, 14 to man the Tung Kwun route, and 13 to man the Tai Pang route. They required 25 new horses every year.[73] This would have allowed two, perhaps even three, couriers to leave on each route each day if necessary. The horses of the courier soldiers could be commandeered by any senior officials passing through the county, or imperial messengers carrying urgent messages; this was probably a less serious problem in relatively remote San On than in more centrally located counties.[74] In most yamen the courier soldiers had their local headquarters outside the yamen complex, but the courier soldiers probably had their Nam Tau headquarters and stables at the back of the main court within the yamen: they would usually have lived with their families in houses within the walls. The San On military establishment also included a small group of 20 mounted soldiers (馬兵), with 25 "war horses" (戰 馬): these were probably mostly used to carry messages from the county military headquarters to the various military posts in the county.[75]

Neither the 1688 nor the 1819 county gazetteers state what the formal establishment of treasury guards and runners was in San On, but the provincial gazetteer states that the joint establishment for these two groups was 83 in total. There were about 60 runners employed in the county at the end of the nineteenth century.[76] The treasury guards were men who had had some military training, such that they could act as guards for the magistracy, and especially for the treasury, the granary and its associated land tax office, and the county jail. Their essential duties were defending the magistracy against riot or banditry; guarding the county jail, the county treasury, and the land tax office (in both places silver paid in as tax was stored, on the one hand the standard fineness ingots awaiting convoy to the provincial treasurer, and, on the other, the loose sycee as paid in to the magistracy, awaiting refining to standard weight ingots); acting as guards to carry silver back to the magistracy from the place where it was paid in (in San On most tax silver was paid in at the place where the taxpayer resided, not at the magistracy);[77] and to guard convoys of silver from San On to the provincial treasury in Canton as needed. Since the magistracy had to be under guard at all hours, the treasury guards would have worked shifts: only a percentage would have been on duty at any time, probably no more than about 10 or 15. However, if the magistracy faced a major attack, then the general military forces would be deployed: there was a general military yamen (遊府署) in Nam Tau, headed by a major, a couple of hundred yards from the magistrate's yamen, with a significant garrison of troops.[78] When the magistrate left the magistracy on formal business, he would be accompanied by a couple of treasury guards as a bodyguard. Each of the assistant magistrates also had an establishment of two treasury guards to provide security for their yamen. As with the courier soldiers, the treasury guards, when not on duty, would live with their families in small houses within the walls (see Plates 13 to 15: these Plates are of surviving residences for junior military officers in Tai Pang — none survive in Nam Tau).

The runners were the general low-level support staff of the magistracy. They were required to be literate: they had to be able to read summonses and warrants, and to produce written reports on their return to the yamen after undertaking any work outside. The magistrates would frequently order runners to go out to investigate problems where plaints had been submitted, or even to interrogate witnesses, and their reports on these would have been an essential feature of many cases heard in the magistracy.[79] They also had to be able to speak basic Mandarin. They get their English name because one of their most important duties was, literally, to run messages for the magistrate within the county. They managed the county jail, under the supervision of the chief of police.[80] Because of their duties in managing the county jail, and in providing the watch at the watchtower, both of which had to be manned at all times, the runners also had to work shifts. It is probable that no more than about 20 were on duty at any one time. In San On, they were sent out, (in the Qing, together with a clerk and a treasury guard), to collect the taxes, sub-district by sub-district, twice each year, at the appropriate seasons. A vital duty of the runners was to act as policemen: they would be sent out to execute warrants for the arrest of suspects, to summons witnesses to attend court cases, or to gather evidence about criminal or other cases in hand. Apart from these duties, the runners were available to the magistrate to act as general support staff for anything the magistrate needed to have done.

The clerks, courier soldiers, treasury guards, and runners were paid their salaries and some essential operational expenses from the taxes: the establishment of these staff was thus official. However, the pay was minimal: pay for the runners and treasury guards was just 30 cash a day in the late Ming and early Qing, far less than the pay of an unskilled labourer or coolie, while pay for the clerks was stopped altogether, in a nationwide cost-cutting exercise, in 1662. Most of their income came instead from customary fees. These junior staff were, however, all recruited from the residents of the county. As such, the magistrate undoubtedly used them as intermediaries between the magistracy and the village areas from whence they had been recruited, and as advisors as to feeling in those village areas.[81] Equally the villages used their co-villagers working within the yamen as sources of information, and expected them to give advance warning of action in hand that might affect them.[82]

It should be noted that there was no establishment for servants in the yamen. There was thus no official arrangement for people to clean, cook, care for, or repair the buildings, and no one hired to do these jobs could be paid from the tax income of the county, neither were there any official funds available to meet the costs of any such work. The magistrate had to pay for all these jobs from his own pocket,[83] or from excess tax income; Zhou Xiyao, at least, found the lack of a quota for servants a problem.[84] The lack of funds for repair and maintenance of the yamen meant that yamen buildings were usually not regularly repaired or maintained, and were normally dilapidated, every magistrate hoping that the inevitable collapse would occur after he had left the county. The lack of regular repair and maintenance left the yamen buildings at severe risk of collapse when typhoons or floods hit them.[85]

* * *

In some counties, there were substantial numbers of staff employed extra to the formal establishment despite the prohibition in the Ming code for any supernumeraries other than simple copyists.[86] T'ung-tsu Chü gives figures suggesting that at least 100–200 supernumerary clerks and copyists would be employed, in even a small county (up to 2,000 in a large one), and up to 7,000 supernumerary runners and treasury guards, and he suggests that, even in small counties, there would be four or five times as many supernumeraries as there were runners and treasury guards in the establishment.[87] In addition, he states, magistrates felt that they needed to insert private servants of their own into their yamen, people they trusted, to stand over the formal clerks and check everything they did, to try to ensure that corruption was eradicated. He suggests that at least four or five such private servants of the magistrate were normally to be found within any yamen.[88]

It would seem, however, doubtful if anything like these numbers of supernumeraries were employed in San On in the late Ming and early Qing. Huang Liu-hung mentions additional clerks and runners, but does not suggest that they were at all numerous.[89] None of the documents that survive from San On from the late Ming and early Qing in fact make mention of any supernumeraries, although there were probably some employed there. This is particularly marked in the edicts of Zhou Xiyao and Li Kecheng on the reforms they were hoping to institute to improve control over their runners: in these edicts it would have been natural for mention of supernumerary runners to have been made if there had been any significant number of them in the county at the time.[90] Furthermore, the plan of the San On yamen in the 1819 gazetteer (Plate 8) marks the clerks' buildings, and shows the buildings housing the runners and treasury guards: these are far too small to have housed more than perhaps 20 clerks (the buildings are each shown as little bigger than the court hall of the magistrate), or more than a moderate number of runners or treasury guards. This seems to be true of all the yamen which have survived from the Qing: none of the clerks' rooms could have housed more than perhaps three men, four at the most, even in the larger yamen, and the same is true of the rooms used by the runners and treasury guards in those yamen: the rooms of the supervising clerks almost certainly housed only the one man (see Plate 9).[91]

Bradly Reed discusses the rules governing the appointment of clerks and runners in Ba County (巴縣) in Sichuan in the late nineteenth century: they required a certain number of established clerks or senior runners to endorse any applicant seeking employment as suitable and properly competent, and for one of the most senior to guarantee the applicant. The appointee would then take a post as trainee clerk, or assistant runner, and only later would he be promoted to an established post, when a vacancy arose.[92] It is likely that a similar procedure was in place in San On in the late Ming and early Qing, although probably operating under simpler rules than in Reed's highly urbanized and very busy late Qing Ba County.[93] It was the rule that clerks should be employed for only five years, but in San On the general tone of comments suggests that this rule was not followed, and that the clerks worked on a permanent basis.

In the late Ming and early Qing, San On County probably, therefore, employed a few copyists and supernumerary trainee clerks, (especially copyists),[94] and a number of assistant runners: perhaps a dozen supernumerary clerks and copyists, and perhaps about the same number of supernumerary runners. As noted above, the formal establishment of treasury guards and runners together was 83 in San On. However, Stewart Lockhart, after discussions with the then county magistrate in the context of the upcoming takeover of the New Territories, stated that there were about 60 runners employed in San On in 1899, implying that there could not have been more than a relatively few supernumerary runners in the county then.[95] Since there had to be treasury guards and runners on duty 24 hours a day, only at best about a third, ten to twenty or so of both treasury guards and runners, would have been on duty at any time.

Reed notes that, in Ba County, in the very late Qing, clerks were divided into three groups, and only one group was on duty at any time (each group served for three months at a time). The same was true of Neixiang County, in Henan Province.[96] It is, however, unlikely that this was a standard feature routinely found in the late Ming and early Qing. There is no mention of this as a standard requirement in the Ming code, and Huang Liu-hung makes no mention of any such practice, so it seems most unlikely

that it was in place in the counties he was appointed to. Where
three month stints were in place, the clerks were required to
reside within the yamen, in rooms provided for them, and could
only leave the yamen when under instructions from the magistrate
to do so. However, in San On, the residences of the clerks were
all converted to additional granary space in the early Qing, in
the late seventeenth and early eighteenth centuries, strongly
suggesting that this practice was not followed in San On. There
does not seem to have been any such three month stints among
the Kwong Ning underlings in 1866. Perhaps this practice was
not followed in Kwangtung generally in the Qing. There is also
no hint in any of the documents which survive suggesting that
private servants of the magistrates had been employed to stand
over and double-check the work of the clerks in San On: Huang
Liu-hung was aware that some magistrates used such employees,
but his view of them was that there was "really no need for these
private servants".[97] It is probable that use of private servants of
this character was not a feature of San On in the late Ming and
Early Qing.[98]

T'ung-tsu Chü's figures are taken from prohibitions in the
Qing law, and from minatory handbooks issued by famous
administrators. In both cases these sources would be describing
extreme cases, and may well have been exaggerating (Reed's far
more exact figures for Ba County imply only about a quarter
as many supernumeraries as Chü suggests, even for that very
urbanized and busy county). They should be taken as applying at
best only to the late Qing, and to very large and busy urban and
suburban counties. Neixiang had 292 clerks, or about 97 in each
stint: most of these clerks must have been supernumeraries.[99] It
is, however, very difficult to conceive of where these clerks could

have been housed in Neixiang, where the surviving clerks' rooms could not possibly have housed more than about 30 at most; perhaps the yamen rented premises outside the yamen for the excess clerks. In fact, it is difficult to conceive of how so large a number of clerks could have been fully employed, given the quiet and rural character of Neixiang County. Clearly, though, when the Neixiang yamen was built, in the Ming, and renovated, in the early Qing, it was designed and built for a far smaller number than 292 or 97 clerks. The surviving Nanyang prefectural yamen (Neixiang County lay within the Nanyang prefecture) usually housed about 30 clerks, which is more in line with the size of the rooms available for them, and would seem to be about the number the Neixiang yamen was designed for.[100]

Small, remote, and rural counties like San On should be regarded as quite modest in their employment of supernumeraries, especially in the late Ming and early Qing. San On was just too poor to have supported anything like the army of supernumeraries T'ung-tsu Chü suggests was normal. It is unlikely that San On had more than perhaps 20–25 clerks in total in that period, established and supernumerary.

The same arguments apply to the runners and treasury guards. Again, the rooms available to house them in San On (and in the other surviving Qing yamen) could not possibly have housed more than a small number — perhaps 10 or 20, at most perhaps 30, at any time; given the shifts they would have worked, this would imply about 30 to 90 employed overall. Space for more than this number simply could not have been found in the San On yamen, nor yet in any other of the surviving Qing yamen. The 60 runners employed in San On at the very end of the nineteenth century (perhaps 20 in any shift) are more likely to be the norm.

Many magistrates, especially in the large, urban counties, in the late Qing, where pressure of public duties was immense, had personal advisors, or private secretaries (幕友, usually called 師爺), to advise them, so that they could cope with the demands made of them. These normally included scholars expert in the law, and in the taxation and administrative systems.[101] They were paid for by the magistrate from his personal income. However, there is no hint in any of the surviving documents that any of the late Ming or early Qing San On magistrates employed such private secretaries; probably, again, the poverty of the county would have made employment of private secretaries at that period financially difficult. Huang Liu-hung was one exception, but they were clearly regarded by him as less than essential to the work of most magistrates: he states that they were only necessary in very busy counties, such as the two he was appointed to.[102] Employment of private secretaries in fact only became a widespread practice from the mid-eighteenth century.[103] While it remains quite possible that a few late Ming or early Qing San On magistrates might have employed such private secretaries, there is no evidence for this. By 1899, however, there were three private secretaries in the county.[104] The relative lack of complex legal cases in late Ming and early Qing San On would also have made such private secretaries less necessary.

* * *

Since it was a major duty of the magistrate to keep in close touch with the views and feelings of the leaders of the county community, it is to be expected that institutions arose to ensure that the magistrate could contact those leaders easily. The register of the San On graduates of the imperial examinations was kept by the county director of education. Graduates were expected to attend the ceremonies honouring Confucius at the Temple of Confucius along with those at the County Altar of Land and Grain and at the City God Temple each year. Late nineteenth-century documents suggest that, by the end of the Qing, the graduates had established a trust among themselves to gather funds for a dinner to be held by the graduates at the time of the annual rituals, and possibly at other times as well. It may have been that the graduates used premises in the Temple of Confucius complex (possibly in the Ming Lun Hall, 明倫堂, see Plate 1), for this dinner.[105] It is entirely unknown when this arrangement arose, but if there was such a trust, with an elected manager to run it, this would certainly have made it easy for the San On magistrate to contact the local graduates. At all events, the graduates would have attended the rituals in the Temple of Confucius and the ceremonies at the County Altar of Land and Grain from the Ming, when the magistrates would have met them. They would have had at least an informal set of leaders to represent them then.

In the 1670s the leader of the San On graduates seems to have been Tang Man-wai. He graduated as Kui Yan in 1657. He was one of only ten San On natives who graduated as Kui Yan between 1651 and 1675, and seems to have been the only one who was active in public life within San On in the 1670s. Two other San On natives who became Kui Yan in 1651 and 1663 respectively went on to become Tsun Sz in 1660 and 1676, that is, graduates of the third, national, level of the imperial examinations, and left the province to become county magistrates away from Kwangtung. Tang Man-wai himself also went on to become a Tsun Sz in 1685, and became a magistrate immediately on graduating, in Zhejiang. All the other San On graduates in this period were Sau Tsoi (秀才, Xiucai, graduates of the first, prefectural, level of the examinations: there were about 20 Sau Tsoi in the county in the 1670s).[106] As a Kui Yan, Tang Man-wai was the social equal of the San On magistrates and would have been a natural, if unofficial, advisor to the magistrate, both in his own name, and as the leader and representative of the county graduates. In due course he became the editor of the 1688 San On Gazetteer, and it is clear from the gazetteer that he was close to Li Kecheng in particular, and, it must be assumed, was an important, if unofficial, advisor to him.

However, the county elite did not consist only of the graduates. Many of the dominant clans of the area had no graduates, but were far too important for the magistrate to ignore, or else were dominated by men who did not have degrees.[107] The result was the establishment of bodies which represented the county elite, including both graduates and non-graduates, and which the magistrate could seek advice from.

In the eastern roads part of the county, the most important of these bodies was the Tung Ping Kuk (東平局, Dongpingju; "council for peace in the east"). This comprised the eastern roads graduates, and the heads of the dominant clans of that area, whether they had degrees or not. It is unclear when this organisation was set up, but it was at the latest by the early Qing: in the later Qing it had a meeting hall in Sham Chun. The eastern roads area was divided into a number of sub-districts, or tung (洞); many, probably all, of these had similar bodies representing the leaders of those sub-district communities. These bodies similarly included both graduates and non-degree holding clan elders from the dominant clans of the area. Most is known of the body which was set up in the Sheung Yue Tung sub-district (雙魚洞, Shuangyudong), in the Sheung Shui (上水, Shangshui) area. This was the Po Tak Alliance (報德約, Baodeyue), which met in the Po Tak Temple (報德祠) at Sheung Shui.[108] It is believed that there were analogous bodies in the western roads part of the county.[109]

When magistrate Ding Tangfa (1694–1700) left the county on promotion, the inscription in his honour was erected by "all the graduates and elders of the County" (闔邑紳耆), that is, by all the county elite, whether they had degrees or not. It is likely that this inscription was put up jointly by the Tung Ping Kuk and the equivalent western roads body. When Li Xuan (1635–1637) informed the provincial authorities that he had received complaints from the "scholars and people" (士民) of the county as to the deplorable conditions of the salt workers, it is probable that this again implies an initiative from the Tung Ping Kuk and the equivalent western roads body. In both these cases it is clear that the magistrate considered the elite of the county to comprise both graduates and non-graduate elders.

However, if these bodies were originally designed to make it easier for the magistrate to contact the dominant clans of the county, in due course the magistrate found himself obliged to consult with them. If he failed to do so, then he would risk the dominant clans withdrawing their support, and the magistrate would find it far more difficult to administer the county, since much of his work depended on a continuing close co-operation with the leaders of the county community. This is particularly so because the magistrate needed to get donations from the leaders of the county community on a regular basis to pay for public works projects in the county (on this, see below). If the magistrate failed to consult them, they might decline to help with donations. This would have been disastrous for the magistrate's effective administration of the county.

This caused problems at the very beginning of the nineteenth century. Hakka-speaking settlers had moved into the eastern part of San On County from the very end of the seventeenth century. However, the Tung Ping Kuk and the councils of the eastern roads tung were all exclusively Punti (本地, Bendi, "Cantonese-speaking"). The San On Hakka were allowed to take the imperial examinations in San On from 1805 (before 1805, they could only take the examinations in the counties from which their ancestors had emigrated to San On). The Hakka graduates and the elders from the major Hakka clans in the Hakka speaking areas of the county became unhappy that they were excluded from the bodies which were the normal advisors of the magistrate. They therefore formed a body of their own, the Tung Wo Kuk (東和局, Dongheju, also meaning "council for peace in the east"); it met in the newly founded market of Sha Tau Kok (沙頭角), whose formal name was Tung Wo Hui (東和墟, "eastern peace market"). This was about 1800–1820, and they demanded that the magistrate consult with that body, as well as with the Tung Ping Kuk, and so with the Hakka elite as well as the Punti elite.[110]

4

The Ming Magistrates: Zhou Xiyao and His Predecessors

There are three Ming San On magistrates with edicts surviving in the 1688 gazetteer, Yu Zhu (1594–1599), Li Xuan (1635–1637), and Zhou Xiyao (1640–1644). Yu Zhu (his alternative name was Xiyu, 熙宇, Hei-yue) came from Xinjian (新建, San Kin) county in Jiangxi Province. Xinjian County is a suburban county of Nanchang (南昌, Nam Cheung), the provincial capital of Jiangxi, covering part of the city of Nanchang and the suburban area to the west and north of the city. This is a very rich area, flat and fertile, comprising the delta of the Kan River (贛江) as it reaches the Poyang Lake (鄱陽湖). There were a substantial number of Ming graduates from Xinjian County sharing the same, somewhat uncommon, surname as Yu Zhu (喻), and it is probable that he came from a scholarly family. He graduated as Kui Yan in 1576.[1] He therefore waited 18 years after graduation before his appointment as magistrate in San On.

He was probably about 50 years old, or a little more than that, on appointment, and probably approaching 60, or even more, when he left San On. He did not take a second post.

Li Xuan (his alternative name was Baiwei, 伯韡, Pak-wai), came from Zhangping (漳平, Tseung Ping) County in Fujian Province. This county lies about 80 miles inland from Amoy (廈門, Xiamen), up the Jiulong River (九龍江). This is an area of great natural beauty, where the river winds between the forested hills of the Boping Ling Range (博平嶺). The county is famous for tea. Li Xuan graduated as Kui Yan in 1633, and as Tsun Sz at the very next examination, in 1634. He was immediately posted to San On, arriving there a few months later, in 1635. He was, as noted previously, very much out of the normal run of San On magistrates. He was the only Tsun Sz posted there in the Ming, and was much younger than most San On magistrates: he cannot have been more than mid-thirties when he arrived there. A young Tsun Sz like Li Xuan was, presumably, hand-picked for San On because of the growing sensitivity of the county in this period, due to its heavy exposure to pirate and bandit attack.

He went on from San On to a second posting as county magistrate in Hoi Fung county, in Kwangtung (1637–1639; Hoi Fung was another county wracked by bandits and pirates in this period). And then went on to serve in a post called 粵海巡憲 in his biography in the Hoi Fung Gazetteer: this was probably the same post as Liu Wen held in 1573, that is, intendant of the Kwangtung coastal region (in Liu Wen's case this post is called 巡視海道). In all his postings he was well regarded: the people of San On "loved him" (民多德之); the people of Hoi Fung "so liked his good policies that they erected a temple to him" (多善政民立祠), and he was twice promoted in rank while working as intendant. However, with the coming of the Qing he retired (1646), or was required to retire (as a Ming graduate in a highly sensitive coastal post he would have been unacceptable to the new Qing authorities), and returned to Zhangping, by when he was probably still only in his mid-forties.[2]

Zhou Xiyao (his alternative name was Daosheng, 道升, To-shing) was born in Zhaofang (招坊), in Jingde County (旌德縣) in today's Anhui Province (in the Ming, Jingde lay in Jiangnan Province, 江南). Anhui is a rich province, centred on the highly fertile lands along the Yangtze River. However, some 60 miles to the east of the Yangtze lies the mountain range of Huang Shan (黄山). This area is of great natural beauty, but is poorer than the lands nearer the great river. Jingde County lies in the heart of this mountain range. Despite its mountainous terrain and relative poverty, however, Jingde had a long and deep tradition of scholarship and learning.[3] Zhou Xiyao came from a family with an impressive record of scholarship. At least nine or ten members of the Zhou clan of Zhaofang secured imperial examination successes during the Ming. In the last generation of the Ming, as well as Zhou Xiyao, Zhou Xishun (周希舜, Chau Hei-shun), and Zhou Xiyuan (周希元, Chau Hei-yuen) of Zhaofang graduated; given their names, sharing the same first character, they were probably close relatives of Zhou Xiyao's. Despite Zhou Xiyao's family record of scholarship, however, he does not seem to have been very wealthy: his writings as county magistrate of San On suggest that he had little private income, and was essentially dependent on his salary for his subsistence.

Zhou Xiyao was probably born about 1590. He graduated as Kui Yan in 1624.[4] He thus waited 16 years after graduating before getting his first official position, in 1640, in San On. This was very similar to the delay Yu Zhu experienced before he was posted to San On: such delays were not unusual in this period. He must thus have been about 50 or so years old when he took up the position.

He left San On in the spring of 1644 after being offered a promotion to the post of prefect in Jinning Zhou (晉寧州知州), in Yunnan Province.[5] He declined the promotion on the grounds that his father was in poor health and needed to be looked after, and resigned his position in San On.[6] However, the increasing chaos of this period (the last Ming emperor committed suicide and the first Qing emperor assumed the throne only a few weeks later) was also a factor in his decision.

At the Chinese New Year, 1644, Zhou Xiyao traveled to Shiu Hing (肇慶, Zhaoqing). Shiu Hing was, at this date, the seat of the governor of Kwangtung. Zhou Xiyao presumably went to Shiu Hing to hand in his resignation in person, and to decline the offered promotion. Chinese New Year's Day in 1644 was 8 February, although Zhou Xiyao probably arrived at Shiu Hing somewhat after the day itself. He would have presented himself to the governor on, or shortly after, the thirtieth day of the first moon, 10 March, when the governor's office would have reopened after the closure for the new year holiday. While in Shiu Hing he visited the famous site, the Seven Stars Crag (七星岩). There he came across a three-stanza poem which had been written by Guo Daoxian, the governor of Jiangxi (郭道賢; his alternative name was Guo Tianmen, 郭天門). This had been inscribed on a rock a year before (in the first moon of 1643). Guo Daoxian had presumably taken advantage of the New Year holiday, and come to Shiu Hing to consult with his colleague, the governor of Kwangtung, probably on the problems posed by the imminent collapse of the Ming state. His poem, while ostensibly on the beauties of the Seven Stars Crag, also, in veiled words, expresses his foreboding and despair at the position things were in:

> The pole stars are obscured, the truth is blacked out, everywhere is entangled with weeds, and you cannot fail to think about the past...Canton is again full of errors, how can it be that the stars are hanging upside-down?" (北斗名疑幻, 南官墨逼真, 一鉤蘿影外, 緱嶺憶前身...錯落仍珠海, 於為星倒懸?)

Guo Daoxian was to refuse to surrender to the incoming Qing, and ended his life as a rather embittered wandering Buddhist monk.[7]

Zhou Xiyao composed another three-stanza poem to Guo Daoxian's, which was eventually inscribed below and to one side of the earlier inscription (see Plates 16 and 17). This poem, which is also superficially on the beauties of the Seven Stars Crag, similarly conveys in veiled words, his despair at the state things were in: "Now I have resigned, I shall wander in the clouds. This situation will swallow up the whole of Kwangtung, the Heavens will take back the light [and night will fall]" (折腰事甫竣, 蕩滌在雲中, 气勢吞全粵, 光鋩接太空).[8] These remarks, and his evident agreement with the views expressed by Guo Daoxian, make it very likely that the desperate state of things in the country was behind his resignation.

After his resignation Zhou Xiyao retired to the quiet and serenity of his home and its garden in Jingde, where he occupied himself writing a book, *A Collection of Miscellaneous Jottings from South China* (南華草等集).[9] He never took another official post. It is not known when he died. He was not the only author among the San On magistrates: He Mengzhuan (1730–1741) wrote two books, a collection of poems and, a collection of essays,[10] and Li Wenzhao (1771) also wrote a book, but the gazetteer gives no details.[11]

**

Zhou Xiyao took up his post in San On in a very difficult period. The Ming dynasty was hastening to its final collapse. Brigandage was rife. The central government was riven with cliques and corruption. Tax income was collapsing. The basic services of government were in meltdown. Everything we can see of Zhou Xiyao's time in San On suggests he struggled to try and stem the drift to final collapse, but nothing he did could postpone the inevitable end. Nonetheless, his writings show a man of probity and selflessness, shocked at the laxity and corruption he found, and trying to do something about it.

After he had been in post for some months, Zhou Xiyao wrote a paper, "All the Problems of this Place" (地方諸難), identifying the problems he had to face as county magistrate in San On.[12] This paper was, presumably, a report sent to the prefect of Canton, the immediate superior of the county magistrate of San On. He said in this paper that, "to be a county magistrate anywhere was difficult, but it was particularly so in San On, because of the major problems the county faced" (為今日之吏難, 為新安今日之吏更難). He identified four systemic problems: piracy, a population with too many bad elements, inadequate resources, and problems involved in enforcing the criminal law.

Zhou Xiyao regarded piracy as the "highest level of difficulty" (誠與上難例合), in the problems he had to face. He noted that San On was the "outer defence of Canton" (為會省門戶邇). It was San On which guarded the entrance to the Pearl River: if the county magistracy could not control piracy in the waters off San On, problems would inevitably arise in Canton (see Map 5).

Piracy was, indeed, a serious problem. As previously stated, the county gazetteer mentions, in the "Bandits" (寇盜) section, five major attacks by pirate fleets on San On between 1623 and 1635, that is, during the 18 years before Zhou Xiyao took up the post of county magistrate. The county city, Nam Tau, was actually besieged by pirates in 1630 and 1635, and a siege was at least threatened in 1634 (a typhoon eventually drove the pirates off in that year, when the siege had just begun).[13]

These pirate attacks were serious events: the 1630 attack required "over a hundred" government ships to drive it off, with the suburbs of the city (including most of the city's shops and merchant houses) being burnt by the pirates. The 1634 attack was by a pirate fleet of "more than two hundred ships"; and the 1635 siege lasted over a month, with the suburbs of the city being once again burnt to the ground.[14] The gazetteer notes another pirate attack, which is not mentioned in the "Bandits" section, in 1633, in the biography of Lau Kwan-pui (劉君培, Liu Junpei), who was killed during the attack, in circumstances of some bravery.[15]

The Portuguese were another threat: they had occupied "Tamaõ Island" (屯門島, probably Lantau) between 1514 and 1521, and had threatened the critically important passage through today's Victoria Harbour in 1623.[16] Zhou Xiyao notes in his "All the Problems" paper that:

foreign ships regularly moored off Nam Tau, causing great anxiety. The foreigners attacked: the city, behind its strong walls, was safe, but almost all the coastal villages were sacked (紅彝艎寇, 數逼縣城, 固雉堞守禦無虞, 而鄉村殘落殆).

Clearly, a major disaster was indeed a real possibility.

Zhou Xiyao's first response to this problem was to "make strenuous efforts to reassure the people" (迄今安撫大費心力), but this was, clearly, not enough.[17]

Originally, Nam Tau city lay several hundred yards inland from the coast. Between the city and the coast was a shallow tidal river, and, on the other side of the river from the city, a strip of sandy land (called "the Nam Tau sandbank" 南頭沙). The shops and merchant houses of Nam Tau were built on the highest part of this sandbank, on either side of the roads which left the south gate of the city, to the south of the bridge over the river (see Maps 3 and 4). This mercantile part of Nam Tau was called Nam Tau Tsan (南頭鎮), and stretched along the coast to the south of the city. The northern part of this sandbank area formed a very low-lying, narrow peninsula, known as Kap Yat (甲一, Jiayi), between the river and the sea. This petered out to the west into muddy, shallow water. The shore to the north of the river mouth had, long before the Ming, been used to build salt fields. Hardly anything survives of the walled city of Qing Nam Tau except for two of the gates (see Plates 18 and 19), and very little either of the Qing mercantile settlement. Within the walls, the only significant surviving Qing buildings are the meeting house of the Tung Kwun natives (東莞會館, see Plate 20), and a memorial temple to the great Song patriot, Man Tin-cheung, (文天祥, Wen Tianxiang, the 信國公文氏祠, see Plate 21). Within the mercantile settlement all that survives from the Qing are a couple of heavily restored ancestral halls (see Plate 22), a small temple, and a couple of rundown shops (see Plate 23).

It is likely that boats originally came in on the high tide to the landing place on the Kap Yat shore, rested on the mud at low tide, and were unloaded by coolies crossing the mud to and from the shore on planks laid on the mud. This would not only have been awkward and inconvenient, but very dangerous if a storm suddenly rose up while ships were helpless on the mud. At some date, it would seem, a pier was constructed to provide a better landing place, where the ships need not ground on the mud. It is unclear when this was done, but a date in the later sixteenth century is possible. The pier was, in the 1630s and 1640s, under the control of the imperial salt monopoly, and it is probable that it had been constructed by the salt monopoly, primarily to make it easier to ship salt out from the salt fields near Nam Tau.

The new pier at Nam Tau would have made life much easier for traders, especially salt traders, but it also would have become a magnet for pirates. The attacks on Nam Tau in 1630, 1634, and 1635, perhaps also in 1633, may well have begun with the pirates seizing the pier, and then using it to unload troops to attack the city, although it is not specifically recorded in the gazetteer that the pirates took the pier before investing the city.

Zhou Xiyao took steps to deal with this problem. He first of all had the walls of Nam Tau raised by five feet to make the city stronger (1640).[18] He was not the first magistrate to try and take steps to strengthen the city: magistrate Chen Gu (1628–1631), a decade earlier, had built two strong lookout towers on the highest point of the walls of the city, on the northern section of the circuit, to improve the defences.[19] The main part of Zhou Xiyao's solution, however, was to build a strong fort in the middle of the Kap Yat area, on the seaward side of the city, close to the foot of the pier, so that it would be much more difficult for bandits or pirates to use the pier (1641).[20] Unfortunately, Zhou Xiyao could not access any government funds to permit the construction of this fort. He was able to convince the gentry of San On and the merchants of Nam Tau to pay from their private funds for the building of the fort and the purchase of its armaments, while he found soldiers to man it by transferring soldiers from other, inland, posts, so that no increase in government recurrent expenditure was required.

This fort is shown as "now in ruins" (今廢) on the map of
Nam Tau included in the 1688 gazetteer, and there is no trace of
it on the map in the 1819 gazetteer. It is probable that the pier
had been destroyed and the fort ruined, in the great storm of
1686, with the pier then replaced by new landing places a little
further away. Since the new landing places would no longer have
been close to Zhou Xiyao's fort, that fort would have become
superfluous, and hence would not have been rebuilt.

While new coastal defences, like the fort at Nam Tau, were
helpful in reducing the risk of attack by pirate fleets, at the end of
the day, when such an attack was launched it had to be opposed
by force. Where possible, the bandits or pirates were attacked
in the open, although sometimes all that could be done was
for the county magistrate to raise morale and stiffen resolve, as
magistrates Chen Gu (1628–1631), Wu Wenming (1631–1635),
Zhang Wenxing (1647–1648), and Ma Yimao (1656–1661)
did when besieged in Nam Tau in 1630, 1634, 1635, 1647, and
1656–1657.[21]

These battles with the bandits or pirates were very bloody
affairs (details are in the "Bandits", 寇盜, section of the
gazetteer).[22] The leaders of the imperial forces attacking bandits
or pirates in San On were killed in the fighting in 1533, 1551,
1570, and 1630. In 1633 the bandits killed all the defenders of the
forts at the Bogue. In 1680, when a walled village in San On tried
to withstand a bandit attack but eventually fell to the attackers,
the result was that everyone in the village, young and old, was
murdered by the bandits. When the imperial forces defeated the
bandits or pirates this was usually followed by the execution
of all those captured. In 1493 the bandits taken prisoner were
thus "executed" (討之), in 1551 they were "destroyed" (剿之),

in 1566 they were "executed" (討之), in 1570 they were "put to death" (死之), and in 1630 the crews of seven pirate vessels were "decapitated" (馘之).[23] It was regarded as evidence of a very unusually kind-hearted man that magistrate Zhang Wenxing (1647–1648), after being besieged in Nam Tau for three months in 1647, when he was relieved and the relieving force had captured the bandits and he found that most of them were "mere boys, and desperately poor", said he was "reluctant to execute them" (大師之後, 仍念弄兵皆赤子, 而不肯加誅, 愷悌之政, 剿靖之功, 嘖嘖口碑矣).[24]

In the Eleventh Moon, 1641, there was another attack by a large bandit force, which attacked Lung Yeuk Tau village (龍躍頭, Longyuetou). Zhou Xiyao took personal command of the county military forces, and produced a clever plan, which succeeded admirably. All the bandits were captured, and 300 of them, including 30 bandit captains, and the overall bandit chief, the "Cotton-Wool King", were beheaded. The matter was thus "cleared up" (擒其賊首棉花王等三十餘人, 斬首三百餘, 乃解). Zhou Xiyao thus fulfilled his duty of protecting the people and the peace of the county.[25]

* * *

Of course, as well as these major attacks by large bandit gangs or pirate fleets, there was also a significant problem of pirate attacks by single vessels attacking other ships at sea. There had long been a force of naval patrol ships (哨船) patrolling the seaways through San On waters, each patrol ship having its own patrol district, running from one coastal defence fort to the next, supported by smaller naval support vessels.

In the Tung Kwun Gazetteer of 1464 five "blockships" (站船) are mentioned, connected with three "marine guardposts"

(水驛). However, these are unlikely to have become the "patrol ships" (哨船) of the later Ming, since the guardposts all seem to be located within the East River Delta, and these "blockships" must have guarded only the inner waters, above the Bogue.[26] The establishment of ships in the Ming for the waters below the Bogue is given in the 1688 gazetteer: the numbers of warships and support vessels changed at various dates in the Ming, but there were usually eight to ten large patrol ships (eight war junks, 戰 船, and five "medium patrol ships", 中哨船, in the early Ming; ten patrol ships from 1592). From 1621 the largest vessels, however, seem to have been six-oared skulls. At most dates there were also several dozen small support vessels, sampans, and small skiffs.[27] None of these however, were still in existence by the date of the gazetteer in the late seventeenth century. In the eighteenth century, there were at first only a few six-oared skulls, but, in 1749 six "anti-smuggling" (查緝走私) ships were added, and in 1795 a force of six much larger vessels was built for the Pearl River, and a further five for the Tai Pang area. In 1817 this fleet was increased to 12, several of which were designed to go out into the open sea.[28] It was this fleet which the British defeated at the Battle of Kowloon Bay in 1839 and totally destroyed at the Battle of Tung Chung in 1859.

In the chaos of the late Ming, however, this system of patrol ships existed only on paper. It had become too expensive for the authorities to maintain any ships, or to pay for their crews on a full-time basis. Instead, only a few naval officers were kept on. Whenever there was a need for a patrol, the naval officer in charge of that patrol zone would hire a private vessel and its crew, and the vessel would become a part-time naval vessel, and its crew part-time naval personnel. This was a much cheaper option than keeping patrol ships on permanent standby. So that such a part-time naval vessel and crew could easily be distinguished from ships on private business, the vessel would fly a government flag, and each of the crew would have a government badge, and there would be a certificate held by the captain (the system assumed that the captain would usually be a full-time naval officer) detailing exactly who was part of the crew and hence was to be regarded as a part-time naval sailor. Zhou Xiyao found, to his absolute shock and horror, that the naval officers were renting out the government flags and even some of the waist badges to pirates. The pirates would then force ships to stop and be searched (which was what the government ships routinely did), and loot the ships of everything that could be carried off.[29]

It was the law that all ships had to stop when they passed a coastal defence fort, and be searched to check their bona fides. Only vessels flying a government flag were exempt from this requirement. False patrol ships, or pirates with government flags, could thus entirely escape detection by the coastal defence fort garrisons. Zhou Xiyao was outraged: "They are far worse than brigands...how can this evil be brought to an end" (其慘猶甚于寇...長此, 兇惡將安窮乎)?[30] His solution was drastic: the coastal defence forts were to stop and search all vessels, whether flying a government flag or not. If a vessel flying a government flag was stopped and it was found that only one or two of the men had waist badges, then the vessel was to be treated as a pirate, and all those on board were to be executed immediately and summarily without any further trial (許汛兵擒解正法). This decision was published as a county edict.

Unfortunately for Zhou Xiyao, he was soon to discover that the garrisons of the coastal defence forts were partners in crime with the naval officers, completely complicit in the corruption, and therefore could not be relied on to give any assistance. "The cats are lying down with the rats!" (同於貓鼠欲求!) he exclaimed.[31] He had some of the culprits from the army brought into his court, and he made his anger clear saying that they lied brazenly, committed perjury freely, and tried by all sorts of equivocations to put the blame on others. The edict he issued states that the military arrested innocent ships, claiming they were pirates. The corrupt soldiers used "villains" (土宄), claiming that the goods seized from the ships arrested by the military belonged to the "villains", and had been previously stolen from them by the ships arrested. The military miscreants also claimed that innocent passengers on the boats thus arrested were "pirate gang members". The naval and military authorities refused to accept responsibility, passing the buck backwards and forwards between them. The edict goes on to say that these sorts of evil practices caused people's lives to become more and more precarious, and the "atmosphere of banditry to get worse and worse" (以致盜氛日 熾, 而民命日危).

Zhou Xiyao proposed to set up new rules: whenever a case arose of theft by a "false government patrol ship" (假哨), then he would send a warrant to the appropriate naval patrol district commander and the appropriate coastal defence fort commander, ordering them to meet together to find and arrest the culprits. Both would be held jointly liable. If, after a month, no arrests had been made, and no suspects delivered to the magistrate, then the rations of the two garrisons would be cut day by day until the two garrisons were starved into doing their duty. Any member of the navy or army found to have colluded with pirates was to be bound and handed over for summary execution under military law. This edict reads rather as if Zhou Xiyao was desperately fishing for some remedy; it is unlikely that it had any substantial effect. It was only with the coming of the new dynasty, the Qing, when the army and navy were put under much more effective discipline, that this problem subsided.

The Tanka, the fisher people, were also implicated in piracies. At this period, they fished in groups: several small vessels supported by a larger one, in an organisation called a Kwu Pang (罟朋). Zhou Xiyao's description of the local fishery practices is so detailed that it is probable that he had gone out to sea to observe the Tanka at work.[32] Zhou Xiyao considered these cooperative practices an "excellent arrangement", but he recognised that there was a risk, when a Kwu Pang came across an isolated vessel at sea, that they might stop fishing and overwhelm it, taking everything on board (a successful piracy might have brought in as much as a whole season's fishing). His solution was to try to force the fishermen into bao-jia (保甲) groups, the mutual responsibility organisation which underpinned most Chinese social structures. The Tanka had never been entered into bao-jia groupings, but, if they could be, this, he felt, would stop piracies of this sort. His proposal did not take effect: the Tanka continued to live outside the bao-jia system. He issued a second edict when it became clear that the first was being ignored, but this second edict also had no effect.[33]

* * *

A particular problem, which exacerbated every attempt to deal with piracy, was "outsider evildoers" (異域奸棍). The San On County magistrate had jurisdiction only over San On and its waters, and could usually initiate criminal prosecution only where he had jurisdiction. If a boat whose home anchorage lay outside

San On committed a piracy outside San On, and then brought the stolen goods into the county to dispose of them, the magistrate faced very serious problems in taking any action. Similarly, if a boat whose home anchorage lay outside San On committed a piracy within the county waters, but then sailed out of the district to dispose of the proceeds of the crime in some other county upcountry, the San On magistrate was similarly very much restricted in what he could do. Zhou Xiyao issued two edicts to try and grapple with this problem of jurisdiction and "outsider evildoers".

The first of these edicts covered outsiders dealing with the Yao people of San On.[34] The gazetteer notes that the mountains along the north shore of Mirs Bay were the home of Yao people (猺, Zhou Xiyao calls them "Yi", 彝, "barbarians").[35] As was the normal situation with Yao areas, the county administration usually left the Yao people alone. Zhou Xiyao notes that the Yao people had some coastal markets. Outsiders took advantage of the absence of any government presence and came there to dispose of stolen goods arising from piracy, to hide there from any attempt by the county authorities to arrest them, and to dispose of kidnapped children sold off as slaves. Also, Ming imperial law forbade certain goods (charcoal and tobacco especially) from being sold to the Yao, but these outsiders brought in these forbidden goods and sold them at a high price. The naval patrol vessels did not patrol inside Mirs Bay: they only patrolled the sea ways, outside the entrance to the bay. Zhou Xiyao proposed to order the naval patrol vessels to patrol deep into Mirs Bay, as well as outside. All outsider boats were to be forbidden to enter Mirs Bay under any pretext, so that only local vessels would be permitted to bring local products to and from the Yao markets.

The naval patrol vessels would search all boats found in the area, and if they were found to be outsider boats, or to be carrying forbidden goods, then the boats would be seized as being in breach of a county edict, and the crews brought to the magistracy for trial. By making it illegal for outsider boats to enter Mirs Bay at all, Zhou Xiyao thus could bring any such boat found there within his area of responsibility.

The second edict specifically addressed the problem of outsider boats, (料船: this strictly means "boats carrying goods", but was used to mean ships coming from outside San On to trade, and especially to boats crossing over to San On from the Pearl River Delta area).[36]

It is probable that these late Ming "boats carrying goods" were vessels specially designed for very fast sea passage. In later years there was a specialist smuggling vessel which was common in the area, especially in periods when smuggling was more profitable than usual. A description of this sort of vessel was given in 1941, when large numbers (more than 50) were then using Tai O (大澳, Da'ao), on Lantau Island, as their home anchorage, from where they were used to smuggle salt into Japanese-controlled China. This description states "they are built like dragon boats" (龍舟樣): these smuggling boats were clearly designed for speed, being built long and narrow, with shallow draft. They were heavily sparred and manned. The 1941 writer notes that boats of this sort had for many generations been a feature of Tai O, at some dates the town had great numbers, at others just two or three, but always some.[37] As well as smuggling, they committed acts of piracy, their great speed giving them an edge over honest trading and fishing vessels. It is at least possible that it was this sort of vessel which was becoming common in the Pearl River area in the middle seventeenth century, and that it was boats like this which were the ones causing Zhou Xiyao concern. The "outsider boats" he was anxious about came to San On ostensibly to buy salt fish for legal export to the Pearl Delta, but in practice to smuggle salt into areas which should have been using taxed salt.

Zhou Xiyao proposed to require all outsider boats coming to buy salt fish to register themselves at the magistracy, noting the name of the owner, details of the local agent, and the date of every trip. The ship would have to enter a bond at the magistracy. For every trip they would take out papers which would then be checked by the military authorities at various checkpoints. Ships without appropriate papers, or found to be carrying salt rather than salt fish, would be arrested, but ships which had the correct papers and correct cargo would be allowed to proceed. This would, once again, bring these outsider boats within the San On magistracy's remit, as they could, if necessary, be proceeded against for breach of this county edict. Military collusion with malefactors would lead to the military being punished to the same degree as the sailors. These rules, with regimes of registration, the need to take out papers for every trip, and bonds, were very much the same as the rules governing the salt trade along the Yangtze and elsewhere, throughout the period from the Ming (and even earlier) down to the end of the imperial period, and would thus have been well within the usual Chinese bureaucratic norms.[38]

Zhou Xiyao was not the first magistrate to try to take action against "outsider evildoers". Li Xuan, five years previously, had made "clearing out the outsider evildoers his first priority on his arrival (in 1635)" (甫下車, 清外地之寇): his biography in the provincial gazetteer specifies that these outsider evildoers were from Tieshan (鐵山, Tit Shan), but where this Tieshan was is unclear.[39] Magistrate Zhang Mingda (1678–1684) is also said to have eradicated bandits, presumably outsider bandits, from the county.[40]

* * *

The second problem identified in Zhou Xiyao's "All the Problems" paper was bad elements among the population. He says in this paper of San On,

> It has on all sides deep mountains and great marshes, where outsiders skulk off and live, coming out and going in again, for the county is not a centrally located one, and the areas under the plough are constantly shifting (且鄰近深山大澤, 異族竄居出沒, 邑既不在腹裡, 加以流, 土充斥).[41]

In other words, the county was, in the late Ming, to some degree a frontier society. There were large areas of uninhabited land, and a steady drift of men coming in from outside the county looking for land to reclaim. According to their descendants (similar tales are told by many of the clan elders of the area today), these incomers were mostly unmarried men in their late teens or early twenties, who would build themselves a flimsy bamboo-and-thatch hut to live in while they tried to cut fields out of the wilderness. If, after ten or so years, it was clear that the land they had opened was fertile and viable, they would look to marry and start a family, and to replace the bamboo hut with a brick-and-tile house. However, if the venture failed, the young man would abandon it, and either return back to the place he had come from, or start all over again at some other spot in San On.

Any society with so large a number of rootless, single young men will have social problems. In the society of San On at this period these problems were made worse by the absence of the usual Chinese systems of social control — the clan community, the village community, and the bao-jia (保甲). If one of these incomers prospered, married, and had children, he would later be revered as the founding ancestor of the clan formed of his descendants, and as the founder of the village in which they lived, but, in his lifetime, he was just one man, and had neither clan nor village. As for the bao-jia, temporary residents did not have to register for this, and, until the settler had married and clearly taken his new home as his place of settlement, he was not expected to enter a San On bao-jia group. Not surprisingly, given the rootless and unsettled nature of so many of the residents, petty brigandage and opportunistic crime were common. Some more serious criminal gangs also took the opportunity to hide in the fastnesses of the San On forests and marshes.

There were, of course, some longer settled and better managed places in San On in the late Ming, in the lowlands around Nam Tau, along the Pearl River shore, around Yuen Long (元朗, Yuanlang) and in the Sham Chun River valley, where some villages were already a hundred, or even several hundred, years old by the seventeenth century. However, rootless and unsettled populations were clearly the norm over a large part of the county.

Zhou Xiyao issued three edicts which loosely cover aspects of this problem.[42] He was not the first county magistrate to try to grapple with it. Li Xuan started his research on the problem by trying to find out how many men there were actually legally resident in the county. He proposed to do this by studying the "yellow books" (黃冊), the registers of all able-bodied adult males resident in the county and liable for the corvée. He was shocked to find the registers in complete disarray. They were not properly housed, two or three out of every ten volumes were missing, and there was no-one who was responsible for looking after them.

Doubtless, they were also incomplete, and full of errors and omissions. He ordered a thorough reform of their housing and control.[43] It would, however, be several decades before they could be expected to give good, usable information.

The first of Zhou Xiyao's edicts on this problem, "Stop false identities to punish crafty villains" (禁詭冒以懲奸徒), dealt with the problem that criminals wanted for serious crimes in San On would usually abscond, crossing the border into Tung Kwun, or Wai Chau (惠州, Huizhou), where they were outside the San On magistracy's jurisdiction, and so effectively safe from pursuit.[44] In other cases, criminals claimed to be resident outside the county when they made fraudulent complaints to the magistracy, or else changed the place they claimed to be resident at every time they were approached by magistracy staff, or gave false names, complicating all criminal action undertaken.

Zhou Xiyao ordered that, in every criminal case, and particularly where any party claimed to be resident outside the county, the question of residence and identity was to be investigated and ruled on before the substantive criminal case was begun. To back this up, he had a new fort built on the Lotus Path (蓮花逕), the main footpath from Nam Tau to the north-east — this was the major road which would have entered Nam Tau through the north gate before that gate was blocked up, and which was then diverted round the city to enter through the east gate. This was the main road from San On to Tung Kwun and Wai Chau, and the fort facilitated the stopping and checking of the bona fides of all persons crossing the border (1642). This fort was built a little later than the fort at the foot of the Nam Tau pier, and, like that fort, the Lotus Path fort had to be built at the expense of the gentry and merchants of the county.[45]

The second of Zhou Xiyao's edicts relating to the rootless population was "Stop squeeze and venerate human life" (禁擄詐以重人命). This was designed to deal with an outbreak of rather sordid extortion. Criminals would take the bodies of dead paupers, give them false identities, and carry them off to some wealthy family, and claim that the family had either driven the dead man to suicide, or else were responsible for his murder, and hence demand a heavy pay-off.[46] If the matter was taken to the magistracy, perjury and brazen lies would keep the matter clouded. Zhou Xiyao was outraged: "This is worse than theft and brigandage" (此其為害慘於盜寇), he said. His solution was to require any case of murder or violent death to be dealt with first of all by an investigation, not at the magistracy, but at the place where the dead man had been resident, involving the neighbours, who were to view the body, and thus clarify the dead person's real identity. Anyone found using death to extort money was to be punished without mercy.

The third of Zhou Xiyao's edicts on these matters, "Bring an end to violence to bring peace to the people" (戢囂爭以按民堵) was aimed at the richer, longer settled clans, who were using their position to bully the incomers. They would come in force to where these isolated, single men were trying to open up land, and bully them, to make them accept a subordinate status as semi-free tenants (佃) of the longer settled clans, and, if necessary, kill or wound the recalcitrant. Zhou Xiyao was quite certain that it was the incomers that had the right to full ownership of the land they had opened from the waste[47] and it was entirely wrong for the richer clans to use force to make them tenants, particularly where, as he was sure was the case, the richer clans were using bully boys from over the border of the county to get their way.

He exclaimed:

> Alas, alas! What have the people of San On done to deserve such
> bitter evil, the people who have come and settled here in San
> On?...Since I have been given the post of local official, seeing
> the people of San On suffering, if I did not feel for them, but
> tolerated these evils, truly there would be no hope for the people
> of San On (嗟! 嗟! 新民何辜, 而遭此荼毒也, 蓋以業落新邑…在職有
> 地方之任, 視民有痛癢之關, 隱忍長惡, 尤而效之, 新安之民, 無噍類
> 矣).

His solution was to crack down on some ringleaders of the
trouble and punish them severely. Unfortunately, the ringleaders
would have been precisely those men from the wealthier, longer
settled clans on whom he relied for the money to build his new
forts and new school, and it is unlikely that he was able to
prosecute the ringleaders with the vigour he would have liked.

In the same edict Zhou Xiyao also promised harsh action
against the ringleaders of the wealthier clans who were instituting
inter-village wars over the control of local markets — violence
which would have hurt the poor men trying to open up new land
particularly severely. The rich clans were, without doubt, using
these men, now their tenants, as the front-line in their military
forces: Zhou Xiyao said, in tones of disgust: "Those tenants being
killed and wounded in these fights, are they not also San On
people" (殺傷各佃亦新民也)? But, again, his need for support from
these wealthy clan elders would have limited what he could do.[48]

* * *

More directly connected with the problems of a rootless
society was Zhou Xiyao's rebuilding of the county Temple of
Confucius and county school.

At all dates, primary education in San On was conducted
in schools in the villages. The schools were held in ancestral

halls, temples, or separate buildings, and managed by the clan or village elders. However, it was also necessary for there to be some provision for higher education, to equip youngsters to take the imperial examinations. A few of these village schools were good enough that they could bring students up to the point where they could consider taking the imperial examinations, but the great majority fell short of these standards. Good students from these latter schools had to move to another school after their primary education. They either moved to another village where better education was available to allow the student to progress higher, or else they went to the county city to enter themselves into an intermediate school. These were called the "Community Schools" (社學). There were six of these in and near Nam Tau in the late Ming.[49] The oldest of them, the "Tong Tseung Shuk Tsui, Dangxiang Shuxu" (党庠塾序) was founded in 1375 within the walls of Nam Tau. It is probable that some at least of the other schools were founded in the 1570s: the gazetteer notes of magistrate Zeng Kongzhi (1576–1579) that he "established schools" (興學校), and it was most likely these community schools in the suburbs of Nam Tau which were being referred to.[50] In 1641 Zhou Xiyao revised the curriculum and operating practices of the intermediate schools, or more likely, of the senior of them, the Tong Tseung Shuk Tsui, insisting that the school should train students in all the aspects of educated life, that is, in ritual, music, archery, horsemanship, books, and mathematics, so that they could become perfect gentlemen.[51] The aim was to equip graduates to enter into higher education at the county school, the heart of the county's provision for higher education.

The county Temple of Confucius and county school had been established on a large and magnificent scale in 1573 by the first county magistrate, Wu Daxun (1573–1576), on a small hillock (Man Kong, 文崗, Wengang) outside the east gate of the city, as part of the work needed to get the new county functional (see Plate 1).[52] Magistrate Qiu Tiqian (1586–1590) was able to get a substantial endowment for the county school, which assisted in establishing it firmly.[53] The establishment of the county required a great deal of work: the founding of the county Temple of Confucius and school was one of the very earliest actions taken, since Wu Daxun, the first magistrate, is specifically credited with undertaking this. He is also credited with completing the building of the yamen, in 1573–1574.[54] It was, however, not until the time of his successor as magistrate, Zeng Kongzhi (1576–1579), that the final planning and construction of the city walls, the drainage system within the walls, and the wells[55] (essential for the city's feng shui;[56] geomancy: see Plates 24 and 25) was finalized. Zeng Kongzhi is also credited with the firm establishment of the new county's bao-jia system.

The gazetteer says: "When the school was first opened, in the Ming Wanli period (1573–1619), the sound of the teaching spread far and wide" (新庠, 建自明萬曆改元之初, 聲教弘邕): clearly, therefore, the county school was actually functioning as a teaching centre at that period.[57] The temple and school, however, only stayed on the Man Kong site for 22 years: in 1595, magistrate Yu Zhu (1594–1599) moved it inside the walls of Nam Tau, to a site just inside the south gate. The reason given was that the old site, at Man Kong, was too exposed to wind and rain, and was awkward to access, but it is probable that it was the site's exposure to bandits which was the decisive factor. Magistrate Peng Yunnian (1637–1640) found money to provide scholarships for needy students at the resited school.[58]

Zhou Xiyao, however, moved the temple and school back to the original site at Man Kong in 1641. He was concerned that the new site for the temple and school chosen by Yu Zhu had very poor feng shui, and that this had led to only a very few examination successes, so it seems likely that teaching was still then conducted in the temple and school at the location inside the south gate. Zhou Xiyao wanted to take advantage of the excellent feng shui of the Man Kong site (the Man Kong site faced directly across Deep Bay, 後海灣 to Castle Peak, 青山) on a very powerful feng shui line). In addition, he felt that the site inside the walls was too restricted and cramped: he believed that the county school had to be large and imposing, to encourage a rough and uncultured population to study.[59] He recognised the threat from bandits, but felt that, nonetheless, the school and temple had to be moved back to the original site and be rebuilt to the original size and magnificence. They remained on the site outside the east gate until the end of the imperial period, although Zhou Xiyao's buildings had to be restored in 1671–1682, and in 1782–1784 (see Plate 1: nothing now survives of these buildings).[60] As with his two new forts, there was no government money to pay for the rebuilding of the school and temple, and Zhou Xiyao was obliged to use donations from the wealthy leaders of San On society to achieve his aim of getting a county school of elegance and stature.

However, while it seems likely that, during Zhou Xiyao's time, the county school was still receiving students, at a later date no teaching took place there. It became a venue used solely for rituals. Suitable students were entered onto the register of the county school in a ceremony at the temple, which entitled them to become candidates for the first level of the imperial examinations, but they had to go elsewhere for the further education they needed to get them to that level.

It is unclear when this occurrence took place; but it may well have been in the years immediately after the Coastal Evacuation. It is at this approximate period when this development occurred widely in China, but, in San On, it seems likely that local problems of the post-evacuation period triggered the change.

It may be useful to discuss the history of the county Temple of Confucius and county school further here, even though this will take us well into the Qing. The buildings of the county school and Temple of Confucius, as they had been rebuilt by Zhou Xiyao in 1641, were not destroyed in the Coastal Evacuation, out of respect for Confucius, but were wrecked beyond repair in a terrible typhoon in September 1671 and hence had to be rebuilt. There were no government funds for this restoration, and private donations had to be sought. Magistrate Li Kecheng gathered funds and began the work, but this was utterly thrown down when bandits captured the city of Nam Tau (1676–1677). Restoration work began again in 1679, and was completed in 1682, under magistrate Zhang Mingda (1678–1684).[61] Clearly, the temple and school were not available for a whole decade at least (1671–1682): it is likely that, when the temple was eventually available for use again in 1682, it was decided to leave it as a solely ritual facility. Higher education must have been carried on in some temporary facility during the period when the temple and school were unavailable. However, the community schools could not have been used for this purpose, for all of them had been rendered unusable in the Coastal Evacuation, and none were yet in a fit state by the date of the gazetteer.[62] While this is not specifically recorded, it is possible that classes were held in the yamen of the county director of education and deputy director.

A more formal response to the pressing need for a place where classes could be taught to candidates for the imperial examinations was made by magistrate Ding Tangfa (1694–1700). He established a free school (義學) in 1694, which he called the Po On Academy (寶安書院, Baoan Shuyuan). This was built immediately next to the Temple of Confucius, and was clearly designed to provide the classroom space which had, in the Ming, been available within the temple. The name of the school immediately suggests that it was a county facility, and the direct descendant of the teaching facilities in the Ming Temple (Po On, Baoan, was an ancient alternative name for San On).[63]

By 1724 the Po On Academy had become inadequate. In 1724–1725 magistrate Duan Yansheng (1724–1725) built a new academy, inside the walls of Nam Tau, near the west gate, which was considerably larger than Ding Tangfa's original establishment, (it had 29 rooms).[64] He called it the Man Kong Academy (文崗書院, Wengang Shuyuan). He was able to get donations which provided a substantial endowment for the school — land providing 75 tam of grain a year in rent — which was used to furnish needy students with scholarships.[65] Given the name Duan Yansheng gave to his school, taken from the place where the San On Temple of Confucius stood, it is clear that he intended his school to take over from the Po On Academy as the school where education preparatory to the imperial examinations could take place: clearly, this school was also felt to be a county facility. A little later, magistrate He Mengzhuan (1730–1741) found money to invite a series of famous scholars to come and give lectures in the new academy.[66] In due course, however, this institution itself fell into disrepair.

In 1800 magistrate Sun Shuxin (1800–1803) closed both the Man Kong Academy and the Po On Academy, which had, presumably, survived in some way in the meantime, perhaps as an intermediate school. The latter was re-opened as a temple, the Shui Sin Temple (水仙廟, Shuixianmiao), while the Man Kong Academy was left as a ruin — the site was used in recent years for the construction of a new Nam Tau school: the school houses the original inscribed stone from the doorway of Duan Yansheng's school. The magistrate founded a new school, the Fung Kong Academy (鳳崗書院, Fenggang Shuyuan), which opened in 1801.[67] This was established on the site which had been used for the Temple of Confucius between 1595 and 1641, just inside the south gate (he presumably was not as worried about the site's feng shui as Zhou Xiyao had been). This site had been used, after 1641, for various government offices, latterly the yamen of the salt superintendent of the Tung Kwun salt fields. That office had, however, been abolished in 1801, so the site was available for reuse.[68]

The magistrates, as well as being concerned about the physical condition of the county school and the academies and their endowments, occasionally went further. Several Qing San On magistrates are recorded as teaching the senior students in the county school in person, attending the examinations in the county in person, and spending their spare time with other scholars of the county, writing poems with them, or discussing the classics. This is stated of magistrates Ma Yimao (1656–1661), Jin Wenmo (1687–1694), Tang Ruoshi (1744–1745), and Wang Dingjin

(1746–1751): this would certainly have made scholarship seem socially a very prestigious thing.[69]

* * *

The third of the problems which Zhou Xiyao identified in his "All the Problems" paper was inadequate resources. By the end of his time in San On, however, he might have given it a higher priority. The basic core of the problem was that the Ming demanded that a county magistrate meet all government expenses in his county from the tax income received, and account to the provincial authorities only for the surplus remaining on his tax quota[70] after all these expenses had been met and accounted for. Unfortunately, San On had low income from tax, but high expenses. Since it was the outer defence of Canton, controlling access into the Pearl River, it had far higher numbers of military posts and garrisons than most counties (there are over 60 forts mentioned in the 1688 county gazetteer),[71] and all the rations and salaries of the soldiers of these forts had to be met by the county magistrate.

As a result, the expenses were often higher than the income, and rather than remitting a surplus to Canton, there was a shortfall. However, there was no provision for meeting such a shortfall: the county magistrate had to find a way around it — even if he had to borrow money (Zhou Xiyao had had to do this more than once: "I have several times had to make up the money by borrowing", 尚不足數, 復貸補額, he said).[72] In his "All the Problems" paper he noted that, at Nam Tau, "Within the city, everyone is a soldier" (城中盡是軍丁). If their rations and salaries were interrupted, it was fatally easy for them to take their weapons and training and switch to banditry. In such circumstances, the magistrate and his staff would be very exposed. So payments due to the military had to be his first priority. Finding extra income was, therefore, an urgent priority, but sometimes abuses crept in which conscientious magistrates would seek to reform.

One such area was procurement. The county magistrate had to buy new horses every year for the courier soldiers who manned the government postal service, 25 horses each year. Zhou Xiyao's predecessor as county magistrate, Yu Zhu (1594–1599), discovered, to his "deep distress" (本縣實切痛心) that his procurement officers were demanding that the horses be supplied at a sharp discount under the official price, and that this was remitted down the line, so that the actual breeders of the horses were only getting half of the price due. He ordered that this practice stop immediately, and instituted new, and much tougher, accounting rules to ensure that it did. His biography in the gazetteer summarises his work by saying that he "forbade under-the-table deals for horses, and instituted tough rules" (定里甲差馬之額, 嚴借辦私宰之禁, 立比卯十限之法).[73] Magistrate Li Kecheng, however, found in the 1670s that procurement of horses was again a problem, and again instituted reforms "completely understanding the difficulties of the people" (成洞恤民難).[74] Magistrate An Yumei (1684–1687) also had to take action against improprieties in the procurement of horses.[75]

Zhou Xiyao discovered that almost all his daily necessities were being provided free of charge by people in the Nam Tau market, firewood by the poor families living on boats, fish by the fish stores, rice, vegetables and so forth. He was "very distressed to learn this" (卑縣深為軫念): these were being handed over, in accordance with "evil customs" (陋規) by people who were very poor and just could not bear the burden. He forbade the practice absolutely; any trader offering to give something free in the future was to be cut off the list of businesses with which the magistracy would deal.[76] This had long been a matter which conscientious magistrates had tried to end. Magistrate Zeng Kongzhi (1576–1579) had "eradicated taxes paid in kind" (警粟税驅), which probably refers to this practice, rather than the payment of the land tax in grain.[77] A generation before Zhou Xiyao, Yu Zhu had also forbidden this practice: "he was very scrupulous in paying the exact market price for all his daily necessities, buying all his daily necessities from the people at the exact market price" (日用一絲一粟悉以平價市于民),[78] but this ancient practice was to prove difficult to eradicate: Li Kecheng also had to forbid it a generation after Zhou Xiyao, as did magistrates An Yumei (1684–1687), and Jin Wenmo (1687–1694).[79]

Unfortunately, having made this reform, Zhou Xiyao found he did not have enough money to buy the daily necessities that he needed: he was "short of man-power and food" (手口拮据), he had "no servants" (縣無額設夫役), and so was obliged to run around delivering his own messages, and he could afford only the "coarsest food to alleviate hunger" (脫粟且支饑) (see Plate 2).[80] It is this problem of inadequate income, such that the magistracy just could not support itself on its legal sources of income, that underlies whatever corruption there was. Zhou Xiyao might have been willing to eat coarse food and brown, unpolished, rice, but not everyone was.

* * *

Part of the problem was that the San On magistracy was, in the late Ming, finding it difficult to collect the taxes that were due. The county was divided into districts (都), which in turn were divided into sub-districts (圖). The taxes were collected by officers (runners) in each sub-district. Zhou Xiyao found them to be uniformly corrupt, embezzling the taxes, and claiming that taxes were in arrear when they had, in fact, pocketed them. He sacked all the runners involved in tax collection, and cancelled the posts. Instead, he required the bao-jia headmen to collect the taxes, as part of their corvée obligations.[81] This had been required by the first Ming emperor, and was stipulated in the Ming code, but had been generally abandoned long since: Zhou Xiyao was, therefore, attempting to revert to the situation as would have been found in the early Ming.[82] This reversion he found more effective than the use of runners. Nonetheless, there remained substantial arrears. Men accumulated arrears, and then fled over the border of the county when demands for payment were made, and did not make any appearance when summonsed to appear at the magistracy.[83] The people were poor, and the fields infertile: it was not easy for the families to meet the taxes. Clearly, there was not in San On, in the late Ming, any legal requirement for a taxpayer to register a guarantor who would meet the taxes if the taxpayer defaulted.[84] Zhou Xiyao felt he was making some progress with meeting defaults, but he would, he said, need some further years of hard work to break the back of the problem.

The county granaries were intimately connected with tax collection. Tax rice, or rice bought with taxes paid in silver, was stored in the county granaries, and disbursed to pay the wages of, and to provide rations for, the soldiers, and to provide a resource against famine in the county. Unfortunately, the rice held in the granaries (by far the largest holding of grain in the county) could be used to manipulate the grain market, and unscrupulous granary clerks could illegally sell grain whenever the price rose, falsifying the records of grain held. Control of the

San On granaries had thus long been a problem for the San On magistrates.[85]

Magistrate Yu Zhu (1594–1599) thus took action to reform the granary administration as soon as he arrived in San On. "The old granaries had many long-standing malpractices which were completely rectified: the deceitful clerks were all punished" (舊邑倉糧場課多積弊, 盡為釐革, 懲其滑胥).[86] Li Xuan (1635–1637) similarly "abolished the evil of the brokers dealing in tax-grain" (申經紀雜餉以豁重戾)[87]

In 1819 there were five granaries in Nam Tau. These were the Sheung Ping granary (常平倉), comprising twelve sections, the garrison granary (屯倉), with six sections (built in 1723), the Tso Wan granary (漕還倉), built in 1743, with three sections, and the Kam Kuk granary (監穀倉), built in 1738, with six sections. The three granaries built between 1723 and 1743 were all built within the magistrate's yamen complex, on the west side of the front court on what had been, in the late Ming and early Qing, the site of residences for junior yamen staff.[88] The Sheung Ping granary, which had been built in the sixteenth century when the yamen was first built, was also built within the yamen, on the east side of the front court. In addition to these four, there was, in 1819, the Fu Yau granary (富有倉), with six sections, built in 1745 a little west of the magistrate's yamen, in front of the Kwun Yam Temple (觀音閣).[89]

Before 1642, there had been two further granaries, the Wing Yung granary (永盈倉), and the Yue Pei granary (預備倉); both of these had been established in 1436, but had been moved, when the new county was founded in 1573, to a site next to the City God Temple in Nam Tau. In 1642, Zhou Xiyao "investigated them in detail, and wiped them out" (詳汰).[90] In the same year he cancelled the posts of the supervisory clerks for these granaries, that is, a chief clerk (大吏) and a disbursement clerk (攢典) for each granary.[91] In 1642, therefore, Zhou Xiyao was left with just one single granary in Nam Tau, the Sheung Ping granary, which was inside the yamen, and under the supervision of a single granary clerk (倉吏).

There had also been a granary in Tai Pang (大鵬倉) since 1436. There were no civil posts, however, for the management of this granary: it was probably managed by the military and functioned as a holding store for grain delivered to the military from Nam Tau as rations for the troops stationed at Tai Pang.[92] A further granary in Tai Pang, the Tai Pang garrison granary (大鵬屯倉), was built in 1669 (two sections), and extended in 1723 (a further six sections), and later a further three sections were added. This granary was brought under the management of the deputy magistrate in 1723.[93]

The closure of the Wing Yung and Yue Pei granaries by Zhou Xiyao was clearly a radical reform and involved a root-and-branch restructuring of the Nam Tau granaries. Clearly, Zhou Xiyao's aim was to have all the granary space inside the yamen, and so under his immediate eye, and under one single clerk, who could be held to account for the slightest shortfall or errors. In doing so, Zhou Xiyao probably lost something over half of his formal granary capacity. In 1819, the 27 granary sections then in existence in Nam Tau had a total formal capacity of 20,617 tam (擔, usually called 石, "shek", "shi" in the gazetteer: a tam is about a hundredweight).[94] The capacity of the county granaries in 1640, including the two granaries closed by Zhou Xiyao in 1642, must also have been close to 20,000 tam. The 12 sections of the single granary left after Zhou Xiyao's closures are, however, unlikely to

have had a formal capacity of more than about 9,000 tam. This
was in accord with Zhou Xiyao's stated aim of having in store
only the minimum amount of grain consonant with needs. He
felt that there was not enough grain being paid in, or able to be
bought with tax silver, to justify larger stocks. If more was held
in store than the minimum safe figure, then, he felt, irregularities
were inevitable.[95]

Zhou Xiyao may well have taken a further step. Up until his
time, the land tax was paid in San On either in grain or in silver
at a fixed and immutable rate of commutation, although the taxes
were always denominated in grain. Additional grain was then
bought, as needed, with the silver paid in as tax.[96] Zhou Xiyao
stated, "I have already collected 1,750 tam and I have converted
the money paid as tax into grain, but it is still not enough to
pay the wages" (已積糧一千七百五十石, 搜贖諸鍰, 捐之俸薪, 尚不
足數).[97] In the Qing, in San On, however, we hear, at most dates,
only of payment of the standard land tax in silver, and not of
payments of grain. Li Kecheng mentions improprieties in the tax
collection, but they are all ways of squeezing more silver out of
taxpayers, none involved grain payments. In 1898, a statement
of the annual income of the San On magistracy notes that the
standard land tax was all paid in silver, but that some other small
taxes were paid in grain, especially the tax on tuen tin (屯田, "land
originally allotted to soldiers"), and this was probably true of
the late Ming and early Qing as well.[98] Li Kecheng's biography
(Appendix 3) mentions tax payments in grain as well as silver;
this probably reflects payments in grain for the tuen tin (屯田) and
other small taxes, as in 1898.[99] The change from tax payments
in grain to universal commuted tax payments in silver for the
standard land tax seems thus to have come at some date in the

late Ming or early Qing. It is entirely possible that it was Zhou Xiyao who ordered that payments of land tax should be in silver for tax payments in San On. This would have allowed him to buy grain in bulk, and disburse it in bulk, and would avoid the huge administrative problems of grain being handed in tael by tael and catty by catty[100] by taxpayers. If grain were to be shipped in in bulk, distributed in bulk, and stores kept low, then malfeasance in the granary would be much less likely to occur. If this silver-only reform was not implemented by Zhou Xiyao, it is likely to have been introduced by one of his immediate successors, in the early Qing.

It will be seen, therefore, that, from 1642 until 1723, there was only one single granary under the control of the magistrate, and that this was within the walls of the magistrate's yamen, and, although more granary space was built in and after 1723, it was not until 1745 that there was any built once again outside the yamen complex. For over a century the San On granaries were thus all very closely under the magistrate's eye. This must have improved control and reduced corruption for several generations after Zhou Xiyao's time.

However, at some point in Zhou Xiyao's time as magistrate, the provincial authorities demanded that San On send 1,500 tam of grain (about 90 tons) to the provincial authorities, to assist them in paying the wages of the provincial army, which was fighting the Yao people (presumably in the context of the Yao rebellion of 1643), since the provincial authorities did not have enough in hand to meet this urgent requirement. Zhou Xiyao sent a report to his superiors on the situation: he felt the demand was quite impossible to meet.[101] San On was very poor, its fields infertile, and every ounce of grain that the county authorities took in tax, or bought with silver paid in as tax, had to go to the salaries of the soldiers stationed in San On or else there was a real risk of mutiny. Zhou Xiyao asked the provincial authorities to think about what had happened in 1630, 1634, and 1635: if Nam Tau had fallen then, there would have been a pirate fleet at the gates of Canton, and it would be the same if the Nam Tau soldiers were pushed into mutiny. San On only had 1,200 tam of grain in store (this was probably one year's expected disbursements). This was the essential buffer stock to ensure the supplies to the soldiers did not fail if the grain ships coming from Tung Kwun stopped, for whatever reason.[102] Zhou Xiyao said he could manage to send 500 tam (about 30 tons), but that would drain his buffer stock below the safe level, and there was a real risk of a mutiny if it were to be a poor year. But there could not possibly be any more. He ended his report with a veiled threat: if the 500 tam sent triggered a mutiny, then this must be forgiven by the provincial authorities. Zhou Xiyao's action in reducing the grain held in the San On granaries to the minimum required for expected normal disbursements doubtless helped him control the granaries, but must have exposed him seriously to this sudden demand for a huge payment to the provincial authorities above the taxes.

Zhou Xiyao's protestations seem to have been ignored. He received a note from his superiors — we do not have the text, only Zhou Xiyao's reply to it: the reply from the provincial authorities must have said that they had received the 500 tam he had sent, but that he still owed a further thousand tam, which had to be received before the end of the year. Zhou Xiyao sent a further report. He reiterated his protests (there is a faint sense in this second report that he is trying to hint: "do you ever read the reports I send?") He pointed out that disbursements to the military and the essential needs of the yamen took the great majority of the tax rice received as tax, or bought with tax silver, in San On. As he had said previously, San On was poor, its fields infertile, it produced very little grain, and tax revenue was low. Another heavy disbursement was a long-standing requirement on San On to send 160 tam a year to support the expenses of the metropolitan counties which divided the city and suburbs of Canton between them, that is, Nam Hoi (南海, Nanhai) and Pun Yu (番禺, Panyu). The expenses which had to be met in San On were often, indeed, in poor years, higher than the total amount of grain paid in as tax, or bought with silver paid in: in such circumstances, as noted above, he had "no option but to borrow money to bridge the shortfall: the salaries had to be paid, and this he had had to do several times" (捏者贖錢捐之俸薪尚不足數, 復貸補額). He could not manage to put into store more than 150 tam above disbursements in any quarter, at best. He could not meet this demand for 1,000 tam and begged that the figure required of him be dropped back to a much lower figure. He might be able to send 400 tam, but this would leave him very exposed, and nothing more was at all possible. It is unknown what the response to this was: probably the collapse of the Ming caused the whole issue to fall apart.

Zhou Xiyao's strenuous attempts to keep control of the granaries, and to ensure that demands by the provincial authorities did not push the magistracy into having to squeeze huge amounts of grain extra to the proper tax income from the county were appreciated by the elders of the county. In his biography in the gazetteer, it is stated as one of his major achievements, that "he coordinated the granaries to stop abuses" (併倉儲以革陋規).[103]

* * *

The final problem identified by Zhou Xiyao in his "All the Problems" paper was crime. In his various writings he mentions piracy, brigandage, corruption in the county tax office and the county military forces, disposal of stolen goods in quiet coastal markets, kidnapping, forcibly reducing free men to the status of unfree tenants, fighting (involving deaths and woundings) over the ownership of markets, and so on. Clearly, San On was not a safe or quiet area in his time. Mostly these crimes stemmed from the rootless frontier society of the area. It was the absence of effective clan, village, and bao-jia communities which underlay the high crime levels.

Zhou Xiyao noted in his "All the Problems" paper that he had great problems in getting cases into his court. Many witnesses were too poor to think of giving up a day's work to attend the court. Many suspects, when approached, gave false names, and were often supported in this by those living nearby. Others would abscond across the border. Zhou Xiyao did not make any specific proposals to deal with this problem, but it was a serious one.

Salt, and the problems of the commercial fishing trade (intimately bound up with the question of access to salt) are not included in Zhou Xiyao's "All the Problems" paper, but they clearly caused him a great deal of concern (he issued at least two edicts on these subjects), as they had his predecessors. These problems were to continue to plague his successors, right down to the end of the eighteenth century. Since these interlinked problems were a major problem throughout the period, from the establishment of the county, right down to the end of the middle Qing, they are discussed in a separate chapter.

Zhou Xiyao also faced a serious epidemic, in which several thousand people died. This was, in every likelihood, an outbreak of bubonic plague which had already attacked the county a few years before, in 1628, and which was to return, with even greater impact, in 1648. Zhou Xiyao sacrificed to the city god (城隍), and prepared a text which was recited before the god.[104] He besought the god's help: the people were too poor to pay for medicines, and their cries rose up on every side. The wealthy said it was punishment for sin, which Zhou Xiyao felt was ridiculous. He besought the god to send rain to wash out the disease, or thunder and lightning to drive it away, "then there won't be any need for medicines, and the epidemic will disappear" (或施甘雨和風而灑潤, 或驅迅雷, 疾電而除魔, 不事刀圭,全消瘴癘).[105] In the 1629 outbreak, magistrate Chen Gu (1628–1631) had ordered that the yamen and all the houses be scrubbed clean to eradicate ticks and fleas.[106] Zhou Xiyao was not the first San On magistrate to appeal formally to the city god: magistrate Chen Gu (1628–1631) had done so to avert an evil omen which was inducing hysteria among women.[107]

* * *

From stray remarks in his writings we can gather a little further information about Zhou Xiyao. He did not like the summer heat.[108] He lived through a typhoon, which demonstrated that the roofs of the yamen leaked — and, of course, he had no money to repair them.[109] This was presumably the typhoon of 10 June 1643, which brought "torrential rain, uprooted many trees, demolished houses, and capsized many boats and caused many deaths".[110] He enjoyed the San On New Year festivities.[111] He wrote a number of poems, mostly on aspects of his duties. Only one is on a local spot: perhaps, given his childhood in the midst of the glories of Huang Shan, the San On scenery did not impress him.[112] He was responsible for the restoration of the City God Temple in 1642.[113] He built a rest pavilion (臥里輕) in the gardens of the yamen (possibly the Western Pavilion, 西花廳, shown in the garden of the magistrate's residence in the 1819 drawing of the yamen, see Plate 5).[114]

He did not stay in his yamen and wait for cases to be brought to him, but went out to where cases had arisen, to judge them on the spot, in order, as noted above, to make it easier to get to the bottom of problems of identity and residence. This occasionally caused problems: taking a boat to reach the outer parts of the county left the magistrate at the mercy of the winds; if they failed he might be "becalmed for a whole day, unable to move, anchored in the middle of the sea, something which he found annoying" (若泛海往來, 必須候風, 往不得東南, 來不得西北, 羈楻中流, 動經旬日, 則往返之難).[115]

Zhou Xiyao's biography, presumably taken from his tablet as a worthy official (see Appendix 1) extols him, in the first place, for his compassion towards the poor: "he was greatly concerned about the sufferings of the people...and well acquainted with the facts of the hardships which affected the people" (留心民瘼...詳陳民瘼等事). In addition, he was "methodical" (井井有條).[116] China has a long tradition of eulogy, and this biography, written by a scholar for other scholars, is entirely within this tradition, giving everything good that can be said, and entirely omitting anything which could be called critical. However, these eulogistic praises from the biography are all supported from the writings he left, almost all of which show his compassion for the poor and his care for them (even taking into account the inevitable bias arising from using his own writings to understand him). He was desperately short of revenue, but was never prepared to resort to corruption or squeeze to get what he needed. The biography specifically notes that he "forbade squeeze" (禁投獻以絕擄詐). It also notes his "revival of the fishing and salt industries" (復魚鹽 以蘇土), presumably a reflection of his establishment of well-run salt fau, and notes that he "stabilised prices out of compassion for the merchants" (著平物價以恤行戶), presumably a reflection of his refusal to allow the magistracy any longer to take goods without paying the full market price for them. It also mentions as praiseworthy his coordination of the work of the granaries to eradicate abuses. Finally, the biography stresses the importance of his work in re-establishing the county school and Confucian temple.

5

Li Kecheng
and the Early Qing Magistrates

As previously mentioned, Li Kecheng was one of five magistrates who were in post as San On magistrates between 1670 and 1713 who came from Manchurian backgrounds and had close connections to the Qing as kings of Manchuria. These were men who it seems likely the central Qing authorities felt they could trust implicitly, and, in the case of Li Kecheng and his immediate successor, Luo Mingke, men who were trusted also by Shang Kexi. These magistrates, and especially Li Kecheng, could, therefore, be trusted to rehabilitate the county from the devastation it had suffered between 1647 and 1669, to eradicate the threat of bandit attacks, and bring the county into a firmly loyal commitment to the Qing. During these years San On was clearly seen as a problem, (in the circumstances of what the county had suffered between 1630 and 1670, not surprisingly).

Li Kecheng (his alternative name was Jiyou, 集有, Tsap-yau) was born in Tieling county (鐵嶺), Liaodong Province, Manchuria.

Tieling is a rich county, lying in the flat and fertile lands of the Liao river valley, about ten miles from the Manchurian capital of Mukden (沈陽, Shenyang). He was a guansheng (官生), that is, he was awarded a Kui Yan degree without examination as a mark of respect for his father's services. The guansheng degrees were awarded to the sons of ethnically Chinese men who had been high officials of the kings of Manchuria before the Qing took over the rest of China in 1644.

If his father had achieved high rank and position in Manchuria before 1644, it is unlikely that the father was born much later than 1580–1585. Li Kecheng was probably, therefore, born about 1605–1615. Unfortunately, the Tieling County Gazetteer does not mention Li Kecheng. Since his Kui Yan degree was awarded, not examined, the gazetteer ignores it, and he does not appear in the "Notable Men" or "Fine Writings" sections of that gazetteer.[1] Tieling County had two families of the Li surname with high ranking ministers to the kings of Manchuria in the years shortly before 1644; presumably Li Kecheng was the son of one of these families, but there is no clue as to which. What is, however, clear from the San On County Gazetteer is that Li Kecheng came from a wealthy family. He had access to copious private funds, and spent lavishly from those private funds on large numbers of county projects.

Li Kecheng must have been in his late fifties, or sixties, when he was posted to San On in 1670. It is, therefore, hardly surprising that there is no record of him taking another official post after he left San On in 1675: he doubtless retired to his home in Tieling to spend his last years there.

* * *

Li Kecheng, like Zhou Xiyao, came to San On at a very difficult time. The collapse of the Ming left a huge vacuum at the local level. Zhou Xiyao's resignation would only have taken effect when his successor arrived at San On to take over the seals of office. The next magistrate, Sun Wenkui, arrived to take over in "the 17th Year of the Chongzhen emperor" (崇禎十七年任). The Chongzhen emperor is normally credited with only 16 years, and this reference to the 17th Year means the period between Chinese New Year (8 February) and the date of the emperor's death (25 April, 1644). The reference, presumably, therefore, implies that Sun Wenkui arrived just a few weeks after Zhou Xiyao had handed in his resignation at Shiu Hing, that is, within the period 10 March 10–25 April 1644.[2]

Sun Wenkui, however, lasted in post for only about a year. He was succeeded by Yang Chang. The gazetteer is rather coy about the date when Yang Chang took over, saying only that it occurred "in the 2nd Year". This must be 1645, which was the 2nd Year of the Qing Shunzhi emperor, but which was also the 2nd Year of the southern Ming claimant, the Hongguang emperor (弘光). The gazetteer states that Yang Chang was a Ming appointee, so he must have supported the Hongguang emperor's claims. The Hongguang emperor was captured by the Qing in June 1645, and was executed the following year, in December 1646, when he was succeeded as southern Ming claimant by the Yongli (永曆) emperor.[3]

Yang Chang also lasted for only a year. The Qing attacked and took Canton in a surprise advance in January 1647. The first Qing appointee as San On magistrate, Zhang Wenxing (1647–1648), was, as noted above, appointed "in the 3rd Year of the Shunzhi emperor [...] when Tong, the commander-in-chief, entered Canton" (隨佟軍門入粵), that is, immediately following the Qing capture of Canton, very early in 1647, between 20 January and 5 February, Chinese New Year's Day.[4] Zhang Wenxing was from Fengtien, in Manchuria, and can be assumed to have been a loyal and committed supporter of the Qing. His appointment, following immediately on the capture of Canton, strongly suggests that he arrived in the entourage of General Tong Yangjia as an expectant official. From then on, the San On magistracy acknowledged the Qing. However, the southern Ming re-took Canton a little over a year later, following the defection of General Tong's deputy, General Li Chengdung. The Qing were only able to retake Canton after a siege in November 1650; the city was then sacked with terrible slaughter. It was only after the fall of Canton in 1650 that the Qing were able to begin to consolidate their hold on central Kwangtung. Magistrates Zhang Wenxing and his successors Yang Meikai (1648–1650) and Li Jungzhu (1650–1654), therefore, had to hold San On for the Qing while much of the province was still holding out for the southern Ming.

These disruptions, with six magistrates in post in six years, and with the county supporting the Qing while much of the rest of the province was supporting the southern Ming claimant for much of the time, must have caused considerable political instability and social difficulties for the area. This political sensitivity only eased after the Yongli emperor was pushed into the far west of Kwangsi in February 1652, then into Yunnan (雲南), in March 1656, and then over the border into Burma (June 1659) where he was captured and executed in January 1662.

As soon as Tong Yangjia took Canton and Zhang Wenxing took over the magistracy of San On, however, the county suffered its worst ever bandit disturbance. The bandit chief Chan Yiu attacked and captured the city of Tai Pang, and then went on to put Nam Tau under siege for more than three months (1647). That siege was lifted when a Qing army came to Nam Tau unexpectedly and raised the siege, albeit with considerable difficulty (多方墨守, 不少懈, 卒以平定). Chan Yiu was probably killed at this point, but Lei Man-wing, presumably one of his lieutenants, escaped back to Tai Pang with most of Chan Yiu's forces. He was able to rule from Tai Pang, and to ravage the county for the next nine years, until he was destroyed by a Qing army after a three-month siege of Tai Pang in 1657. Although Lei Man-wing and Chan Yiu seem to have been, in truth, little better than simple bandits, Lei Man-wing, and probably Chan Yiu as well, claimed that they were supporters of the southern Ming imperial claimant, who was still, at that date, holding out in south-west China.

During his time in San On, Lei Man-wing ransacked the county. The gazetteer says that he "pillaged in all directions for several years, destroying more than half of all the houses in the county, and killing or kidnapping tens of thousands of people" (四出流刦數載, 通縣鄉村房屋, 焚毀過半, 殺擄男女數萬).[5] There is always a tendency for figures in Chinese authorities to be exaggerated, but there is some evidence which suggests that the devastation caused by Chan Yiu and Lei Man-wing was indeed massive.

A census of the salt workers was conducted intermittently by the salt monopoly (supposedly once every ten years) in the Tung Kwun salt field area (these were the salt fields around Nam Tau city). The census of 1622 found 3,391 workers there, and the 1632 census found 3,417 workers. These figures are very similar to those from the previous censuses, of 1542 (3,051 workers),

1582 (2,267 workers, probably a printing error for 3,267 workers), 1593 (3,487 workers), 1603 (3,487 workers), and 1613 (4,487 workers, undoubtedly a printing error for 3,487 workers), and represent the normal workforce employed at these salt fields.[6] There were no salt field censuses taken between 1632 and 1662.

However, in 1662, just before the Coastal Evacuation, in the context of the salt field census of that year, the gazetteer states that 2,166 workers from this salt field were "killed by bandits in these last years" (先年寇亂殺絕). Zhou Xiyao makes no mention of any heavy loss of life among the salt workers, which makes it likely that the deaths came after he left San On in 1644.[7] The salt monopoly was forced to cut the production quota of salt here by 18% in 1650, "because of the loss of life by bandits and flight from them in these last years" (除去先年寇亂殺絕逃亡),[8] so it is probable that the loss of life was predominantly in the years 1644–1650. Since no bandit attacks are noted in the gazetteer for the years between 1644 and 1647, the loss of life was, presumably, therefore, because of deaths at the hands of Chan Yiu and Lei Man-wing between 1647 and 1650, although deaths in the 1648 plague might well be included in this figure as well. The 1650 reference says that the workers were killed, or else had fled, but, clearly, none of those "missing" in 1650 had returned by 1662, and hence by then they were declared dead.

The conclusions to be drawn from the salt field censuses are supported by comments in the biography of Ma Yimao (magistrate, 1656–1661), which states that

He regarded the sufferings of the people as if they had been his own, in his time warfare was constant, the fields were abandoned, there was frequent confusion, and the people had no food, but he sorted it all, keeping up the spirits of the people (有如己饑己溺, 時兵燹多事, 田地荒蕪, 開多混淆, 民苦虛粮, 悉為清出, 以免賠纍).[9]

Clearly, Nam Tau was, once again, besieged, presumably, this time, by Lei Man-wing, somewhen in the period 1656–1657. This extract thus supports the findings of the salt field censuses, and strongly suggests that the plague, the attacks by Chan Yiu, and then the attacks by Lei Man-wing, caused a major disaster in the area around Nam Tau in the years 1647–1657.

The figures from the salt field censuses look very much as if most of them are exact counts.[10] If 64% of the salt workers around Nam Tau were killed or died in the period between 1647 and 1650, with the city besieged both in 1647, and again in 1656–1657, then the devastation of the county by the plague and then by Chan Yiu and Lei Man-wing, must be accepted as being appallingly heavy. It is likely that the devastation was especially severe in the area around Nam Tau, given that the magistrates there were supporters of the Qing, while Lei Man-wing, and probably Chan Yiu, claimed to support the Ming.

As well as the salt workers, probably, as later, living in flimsy huts on the bunds around the salt fields, the poor and landless men trying to open new fields and living on their own on the land they were opening would have been particularly at risk in this period.

By the 1672 salt worker census, there were still 817 salt workers fewer than there should have been "because of the deaths in the evacuation, and by banditry some time ago" (遠年寇亂殺絕) — i.e. there was still a full quarter of the workforce required missing, despite efforts to recruit in the meantime.[11] The salt fields still fell short of the number of workers they should have had by

811 as late as 1688,[12] and the taxes due could still not be levied in full because of this. The reduction in the tax was from a little above 1,769 taels to a little above 1,449 taels, or about 18%.[13] This shortfall was to remain in being throughout the eighteenth century.

San On must, therefore, be assumed to have been in a very poor state in the late 1650s. The 12 years of political instability, plague, famine, widespread devastation, and a heavy death rate, following on from Zhou Xiyao's resignation in 1644, must have left local society in a weak condition, and in desperate need of rehabilitation and recovery.

Unfortunately, before any rehabilitation and recovery could begin, the county was devastated a second time, by the Coastal Evacuation of 1662–1669. The 1688 gazetteer states (see Appendix 2):

> The court became concerned about the traitors active at sea, who were causing trouble to the people. People living beside the sea were required to move inland, and to relocate to places 50 li from the coast (朝廷慮海逆不靖民, 受其毒將濱海之民遷入五十里).[14]

These "traitors" were Ming remnants, who had taken refuge on Taiwan, under Koxinga. Koxinga and his fleet of ships ravaged the coasts of south China as a way of attacking the Qing. The Qing originally had no ships, and thus had no effective way of dealing with the threat from Koxinga. The evacuation of all people living near the coast was the stratagem decided on. The evacuation was probably more trenchantly implemented in San On than anywhere else, because of the strategic importance of the area, controlling the entrance to the Pearl River and the access to Canton: any assistance to Koxinga from this area would have been very dangerous. To ensure that those evacuated could not return, the area cleared was put under strict martial law, and all the houses and other buildings were unroofed, and burnt.

As the description in Appendix 2 makes clear, the evacuation was exceedingly traumatic for the county. The inhabitants were driven away from their homes without preparation, and nothing was done to succour them or to find them work once they had been driven inland. Huge numbers died: the gazetteer in one place says "half died" (丁半死亡), and, in another "more than half died" (死喪已過半).[15] Again, the poor would have suffered particularly seriously.

While the population figures for the county given in the "Population" (戶口) section of the gazetteer are likely to be very much less than exact counts, the numbers there do suggest a catastrophic decline in population between 1642 and 1672. The figures given in the gazetteer were probably drawn from the registers of those required to perform corvée, and as such are likely to represent, at best, the number of households on the corvée registers.[16] Magistrate Li Xuan (1635–1637), as noted above, however, found the corvée registers to be in a deplorable state and incapable of giving accurate figures, and this must call into question the accuracy of these census numbers. However, the figures as they are given show populations of 33,971 and 34,520 in 1573 and 1582. These figures attempt to enumerate both males and females. From 1593 the records are for adult males only (presumably those adult males registered for the corvée), and suggest that this adult male population varied from 16,675 (1593) to 17,871 (1642); in other words they give figures entirely in line with those given for 1573 and 1582.

The equivalent figures for the period after the Coastal Evacuation, which are probably inaccurate to the same degree

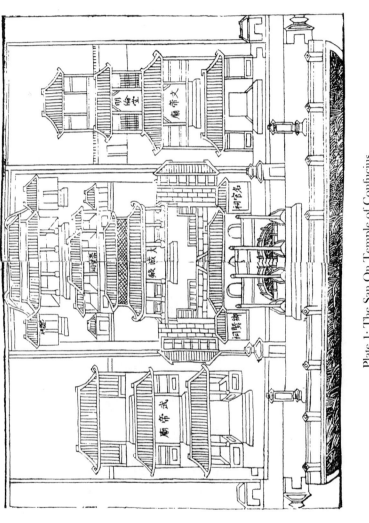

Plate 1: The San On Temple of Confucius

From the 1819 gazetteer, but probably largely as rebuilt by Zhou Xiyao

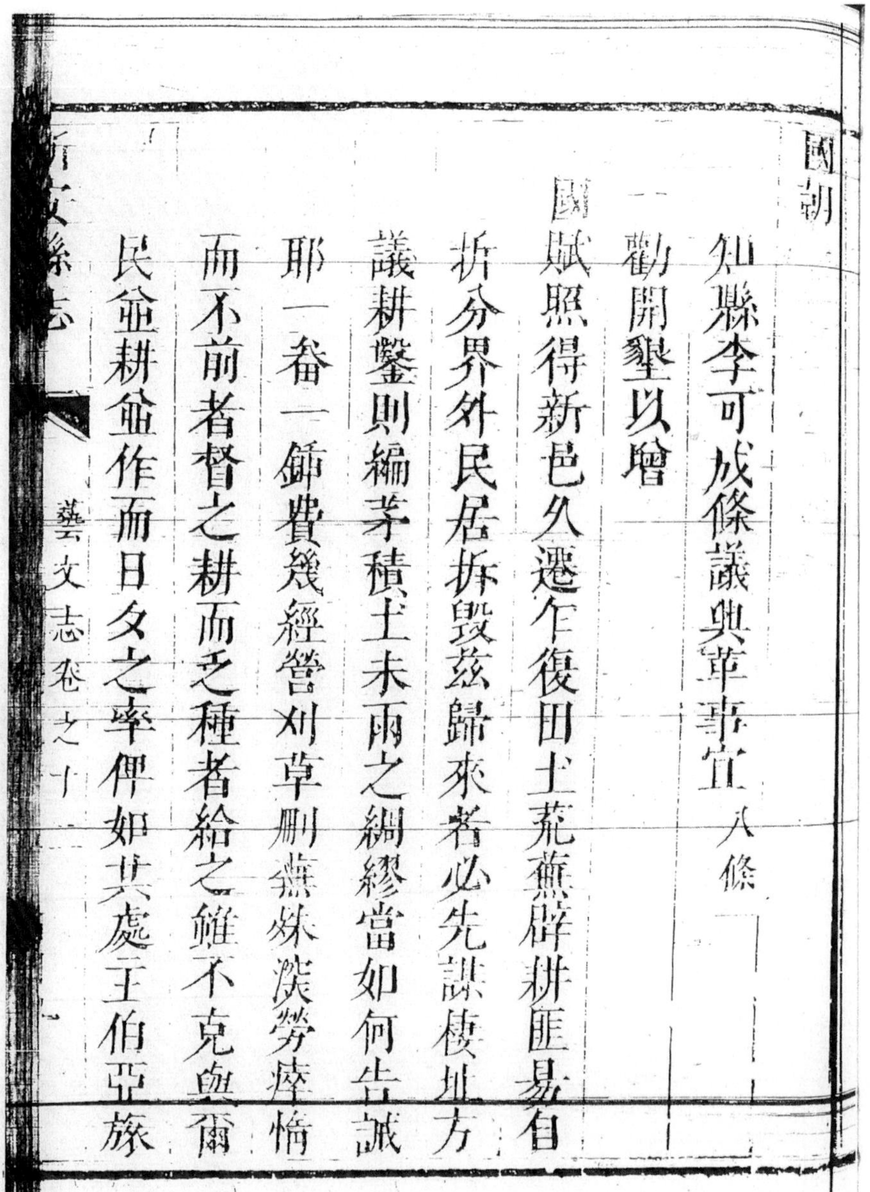

國朝
知縣李可成條議興革事宜八條
一勸開墾以增
國賦照得新邑久遷乍復田土荒蕪辟耕匪易自
折分界外民居拆毀茲歸來者必先謀棲址方
議耕鑿則編茅積土未雨之綢繆當如何告誡
耶一畚一鍤費幾經營刈草刪蕪殊涉勞瘁惰
而不前者督之耕而乏種者給之雖不克與爾
民並耕並作而日夕之率俾如其處王伯亞旅

新安縣志 藝文志卷之十

Plate 2: A Poem by Zhou Xiyao, from the San On County Gazetteer

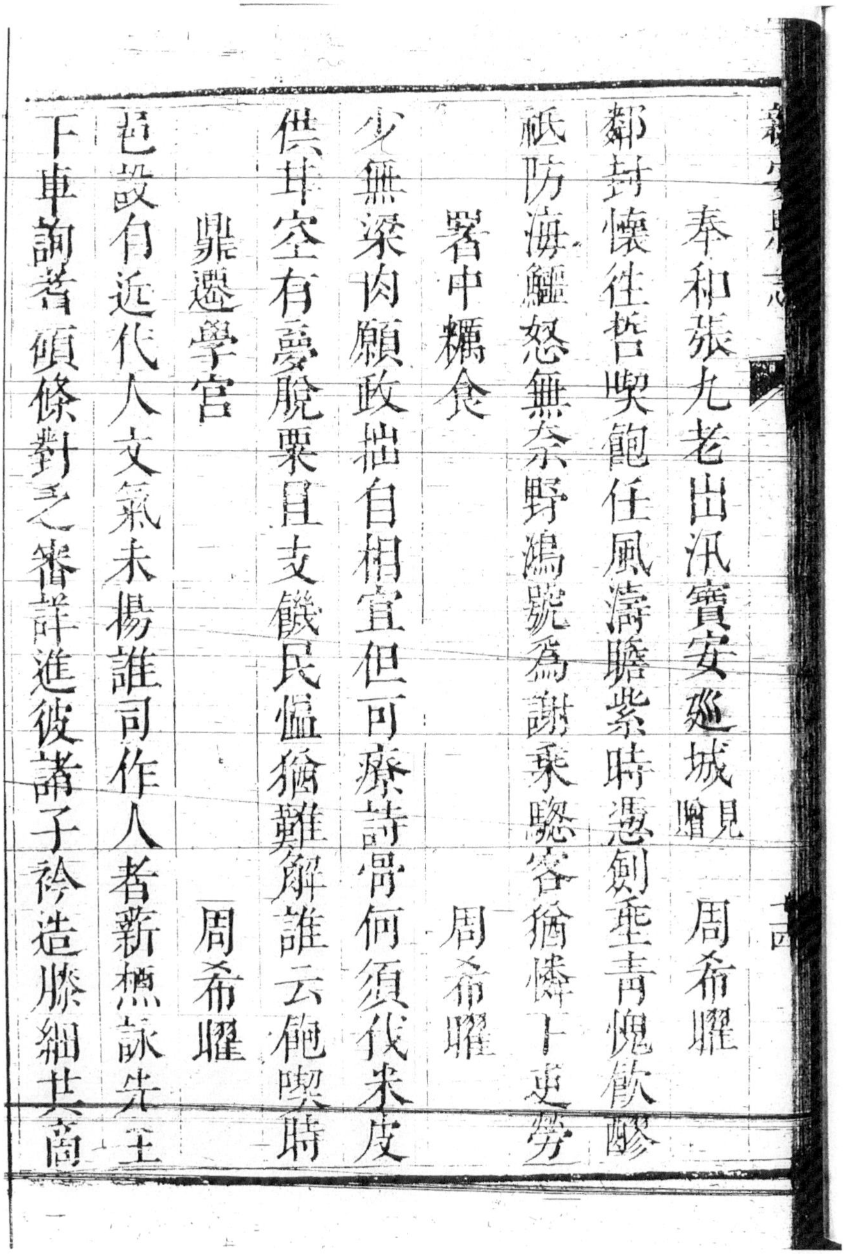

奉和張九老出汛寶安巡城見贈　周希曜

祇防海疆怒無奈野鴻號為謝乘驄猶憐十吏勞

鄰封懷往哲喫飽任風濤瞻紫時恩劍垂青愧歉酬

署中糲食　周希曜

少無深肉願政拙自相宜但可療詩骨何須伐來皮

供其空有夢脫粟且支饑民慍猶難解誰云飽喫時

鼎遷學宮　周希曜

邑設有近代人文氣未揚誰司作人者新構詠先生

下車詢耆頎條對之番詳進彼蕭子矜造滕細其商

Plate 3: An Edict by Li Kecheng, from the San On County Gazetteer

Plate 4: Inscription Against the Four Evils,
in one of the Nam Tau Yamen Gatehouses

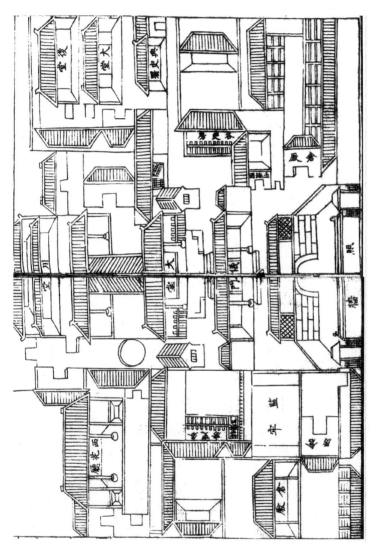

Plate 5: The San On Yamen

From the 1819 gazetteer, but probably largely as rebuilt by Li Kecheng

Plate 6: The Western Nam Tau Yamen Gatehouse

Plate 7: The Eastern Nam Tau Yamen Gatehouse

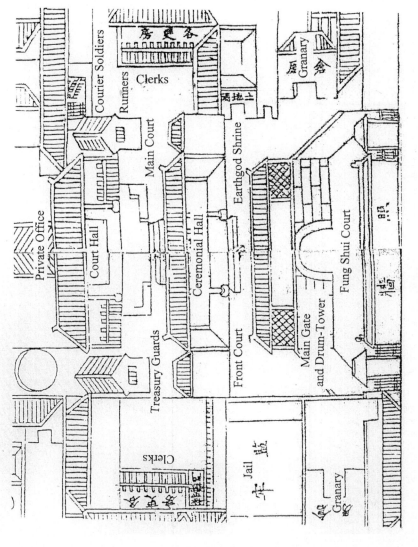

Plate 8: The Nam Tau Yamen, Detail

Plate 9: The Yexian Yamen: Clerks' Fong
The San On Yamen Clerks' Fong were very similar to this

Plate 10: The Yexian Yamen: Court Hall
The San On Yamen Court Hall was very similar to this

Plate 11: The Nam Tau Military Yamen: Gunpowder Store

Plate 12: A Courier Soldier, from the Ha Tsuen Ta Tsiu

A three-quarter size model, one of a pair from the Ha Tsuen Ta Tsiu, 2014:
this courier soldier stands ready to courier messages for the deities, but is a
representation of the courier soldiers of the San On Magistracy as would have been
seen by the Ha Tsuen villagers' ancestors

Plate 13: Eighteenth Century Soldiers' Residences, Tai Pang

Plate 14: Eighteenth Century Soldiers' Residences, Tai Pang

Plate 15: Late Qing Residences of Officials, Tai Pang

Plate 16: Inscription at Shiu Hing
*The inscriptions by Guo Daozian (middle inscription on left of picture)
and Zhou Xiyao (inscription on right of picture)*

Plate 17: Inscription at Shiu Hing, Detail
The inscription by Zhou Xiyao

Plate 18: South Gate, Nam Tau
Recently restored to its condition as built by Li Kecheng

Plate 19: West Gate, Nam Tau
Recently restored to its condition as built by Li Kecheng

Plate 20: The Tung Kwun Meeting House

Plate 21: The Memorial Temple to Man Tin-cheung

Plate 22: Ancestral Hall of the Cheng Clan, Nam Tau Tsan

Plate 23: Nineteenth Century Shops, Nam Tau Tsan

Plate 24: A Well, Nam Tau

Plate 25: Drainage in a Street of Late Qing Official Residences, Tai Pang

Plate 26: South Gate, Tai Pang
Recently restored to its condition as built by Li Kecheng

Plate 27: West Gate, Tai Pang
Recently restored to its condition as built by Li Kecheng

Plate 28: North Gate (Blocked), Tai Pang

Plate 29: Chek Wan Left Fort

The Chek Wan Left Fort was one of two which defended the wide sandy beach of Chek Wan, to the south of Nam Tau. The decision to build the two forts was taken in about 1669, and the work was done by Li Kecheng after 1670

Plate 30: Chek Wan Left Fort: Gun Platform

Plate 31: Nam Shan Beacon Tower
This Beacon Tower transmitted alarms from the Chek Wan Forts to the city of Nam Tau, so that reinforcements could be sent quickly in the event of an attack. It was built at the same date as the Chek Wan Forts

and in the same way as those of the late Ming, show a population (probably, again, in this case, of adult males registered for the corvée) of only 3,972 in 1672, and still of no more than 7,289 in 1731 (probably in fact reflecting the position in 1711, when the corvée ceased to be enforced). The 1672 figures thus suggest a very heavy drop in the population (as they stand, a drop of the order of 78%) between 1642 and 1672. Thereafter the population rose quickly, however, to an estimated 225,979 in 1818.

The same conclusion, of a catastrophic collapse in population, must be drawn from the implications of what is said about the period in various clan genealogies (族譜) and oral history accounts from the area. Only two males of the Chung (鍾, Zhong) clan of Chung Uk (鍾屋, Zhongwu), between Tuen Mun and Yuen Long, returned from the Coastal Evacuation. Chung Uk had been founded about 1450–1475, and, by 1662 there must have been a dozen males in the clan, so the death rate during the evacuation period was very serious.[17] Again, at Nga Tsin Wai (衙前圍, Yaqianwei), just outside Kowloon City, the Ng (吳, Wu) clan, settled in the village from about 1350, only had eight males return from the Coastal Evacuation, from probably about 20 or more in the generation before the evacuation.[18] At Shek Po village (石埗, Shipu), between Yuen Long and Tuen Mun, founded about 1600, only one member of the Lam (林, Lin) clan returned from the evacuation, of about six a decade earlier.[19]

In yet other places, such as Tsuen Wan (荃灣, Quanwan) and Kwai Chung (葵涌, Kuiyang), no-one returned from the evacuation at all. There is a Tsuen Wan village (淺灣) and a Kwai Chung village named in the 1643 list of villages[20] — this is the list of villages copied from the "old gazetteer" into the 1688 version, presumably because so many villages had still not been resettled after the evacuation, that no 1688 list would be of any value.[21] None of the present-day clans of the 12 or 13 villages of the Tsuen Wan area, nor of the three or four villages of the Kwai Chung area believe they settled there until after the Coastal Evacuation. Thus it is likely that none of the original inhabitants returned from the evacuation.[22]

However much these figures are discounted, therefore, they still clearly show that a catastrophic collapse in the population must be accepted as having occurred over the period of the plague, Chan Yiu and Lei Man-wing's attacks, and the Coastal Evacuation.

* * *

Once the decision was taken to rescind the Coastal Evacuation edict (for the mainland of San On in 1669, although for Lantau and the islands only in 1681), and to re-establish the county of San On (1670), the new county magistrate, that is, Li Kecheng, was faced with the task of rehabilitating the county. This was clearly a huge, and hugely difficult, task: he had to restore the county following a full 26 years of devastation.

As Li Kecheng said in his account of the evacuation (see Appendix 2), he was:

> greatly affected by the poverty of the people he saw milling around when he arrived, and dying where they stood from hopelessness and despair as much as from privation and hunger (下車伊始, 見遷民未歸者尚眾, 其一二新復殘黎).[23]

He wrote something very similar about his feelings of compassion for the sufferings of the people in his preface to the county gazetteer,

> The bodies of the old and the young were flung into ditches, while the strong fled in every direction: if you climbed up to a high place there was nothing to be seen but weeds and ruined

walls...how could it be that there was no-one left? No matter how much care was given to encourage the people, they were completely overthrown, and it was difficult to keep them alive (老幼委溝壑, 壯者散四方, 每登高一望荒草頹垣...不可得豈無孑遺, 雖加意招徠顛沛難存也).[24]

Li Kecheng wrote a set of eight rehabilitation edicts (條議興革事宜八條) in which he set out his priorities for this work.[25] Some of the problems he faced were similar to those faced by Zhou Xiyao, and some of Li Kecheng's proposals were, therefore, similar to those of Zhou Xiyao.

Li Kecheng could see very clearly that, for an agricultural population, nothing was more important than to get a roof over their heads, the fields re-opened, and crops into the ground. Only this would overcome the hopelessness and despair that he saw. His first priority was, therefore, to get the people to build shelters and restart the work of tilling the ground. As he said in the first of his county edicts (see Plate 3):

> After the long evacuation of San On, now ended, the fields lie waste, and are difficult to till, the homes of the people were all ruined when the people left, and so the first priority for those returning must be to build shelter, before thought is given to tillage, from woven grass mats and mud plaster, before the rains come" (新邑久遷乍復, 田土荒蕪, 辟耕匪易. 自折分界外, 民居拆毀; 茲歸來者, 必先謀樓址, 方議耕鑿. 則編茅積土, 未雨之綢繆).[26]

Once this was done, and the simplest mat-sheds, mud-plastered bamboo huts, erected, then what was needed was to "mow down the weeds, working as hard as possible" (刈草刪蕪, 殊深榮瘁).[27] Li Kecheng himself would go out into the fields on the fifteenth and thirtieth day of every month to encourage the farmers with his presence and to urge them to carry on with all their strength. This initiative is mentioned again in his preface to the county gazetteer,

"Every fifteenth day, one or two survivors are gathered together on some piece of waste land, and we talk together, to encourage them to plough and dig" (每朔望, 集一二遺黎, 最以耕鑿, 荒土立談).[28] At the same time, as well as these moral exhortations, Li Kecheng offered more practical help, "those who work hard but have no seeds will be given seeds" (乏種者給之). He also gave the farmers plough cattle where they had none (see his biography, at Appendix 3). The editor of the gazetteer stresses that the donations of seeds and plough cattle were paid for from Li Kecheng's private funds, and Li Kecheng himself implied this in his preface to the county gazetteer ("Hence I assisted them with cattle and seeds, 於是資之牛種").[29]

Li Kecheng ends this edict with an expression of hope: with good will and hard work, year by year things would improve. Initially, whenever he spoke to the people, they were able only to sigh and weep: "Never anything but sighs and falling tears; gathering food is so difficult, officials and people are equally in deep anxiety" (未嘗不相對欷歔泣下, 蓋手口荼苦, 官民均在況瘁中),[30] but, towards the end of his time in San On, he ended a poem he wrote, ("A gentle, happy rain encourages the farmers, 勸農喜雨"), on a much more hopeful note, "All the worries and anxieties can gradually be forgotten, when the misery ends, there will be no more food shortages" (心勞漸何忘, 應憐瑣尾後, 無復賦羊牂).[31]

Another part of his strategy to get the land back into cultivation was to encourage newcomers to take up empty land in San On, land where no-one had returned from the evacuation. Li Kecheng does not mention this in his surviving edicts, but it is prominently mentioned (in the same words in both places) in the gazetteer account of the evacuation (Appendix 2), and in his biography as a worthy official (Appendix 3): he "devoted all his attention to recruiting new settlers" (悉心招徠). This action involved getting the newcomers easy terms of tenancy, and easing their way in by grants of small payments of cash (presumably from his private funds, as no government money would have been available for such grants, see his biography at Appendix 2, "He gave donations to the people", 民乃多賦).[32]

The gazetteer, in the "Population" (戶口) section, mentions that 526 adult men were added to the registers between 1674 and 1682, and states that these were a mixture of men returning from the evacuation and "newly registered men" (新增人丁): many of these would have been single adult men arriving to try to open land in accordance with Li Kecheng's encouragement.[33] In a number of cases the present-day indigenous clans of the New Territories date their occupation of the land to "when the county magistrate encouraged newcomers to take up land". The process was to be critical in the final establishment of the traditional customary land law in the area.[34]

* * *

The second area of concern to Li Kecheng was education. The local schools in the county would have been closed during the evacuation, had their roofs removed and been burnt, and would have been unusable without considerable expense. As a result, as he said: "Scholarship among the older men is not as it was, and younger men have no interest in study" (父兄之教不先, 子弟之率不謹).[35] Li Kecheng had no concrete proposals to rectify this sad state of affairs, and his edict is essentially just one of moral exhortation, urging those with the money to do so to restart the work of education. This, however, took time: even as late as the date of the gazetteer (1694–1700) none of the intermediate schools near Nam Tau had re-opened: all were still in ruins.[36]

At the heart of the county's educational provision, of course, was the county school and Temple of Confucius. This had not been destroyed at the evacuation, out of respect for Confucius, and Zhou Xiyao's buildings were still standing when Li Kecheng came to the county in 1670. Unfortunately, they were wrecked beyond repair in a terrible typhoon in September 1671, and hence had to be rebuilt.[37] There were no government funds for this restoration, and private donations had to be sought. Li Kecheng gathered funds and began to rebuild, but the work that he had started was utterly destroyed when bandits captured the city of Nam Tau (1676–1677). Work began again in 1679, and was completed in 1682, under magistrate Zhang Mingda (1678–1684) (see Plate 1). Plate 1 is taken from the 1819 gazetteer. However, the temple, despite its many repairs and restorations, seems at all dates following the building by Zhou Xiyao to have used the original foundations, and so Plate 1 probably gives a rough idea of the temple as built by Zhou Xiyao, and as rebuilt by Li Kecheng.[38]

* * *

Li Kecheng's third rehabilitation priority was the restoration of damaged and ruined government buildings, especially the yamen, the city walls and gatehouses at Nam Tau and Tai Pang, and the scattered network of forts and fortlets guarding the roads along with those established for coastal defence. He issued two edicts on this subject.[39]

The first of these is related to the restoration of the city wall and moat at Nam Tau. In it he stresses that San On is the outer defence of Canton, and has to safeguard the whole province, so that strong city defences — high walls and deep moats — were more important than in other counties. Unfortunately, because of the evacuation, the city wall had collapsed, the four gates and the watchtowers had disappeared, the crenellations had fallen in, and the ditches were all silted up. While the work was called restoration, it was, he states, in reality reconstruction from the foundations upwards. Some government money was available for this work, which started as soon as Li Kecheng arrived in San On, and went on well, both on the defences and on the restoration of the yamen.

Unfortunately, a year later (September 1671) the same terrible typhoon which wrecked the county Temple of Confucius destroyed everything that had been done on the restoration of the yamen and the city walls. Since there was no hope of any further government cash assistance, Li Kecheng immediately restarted the work by donating 600 taels of his private money (50 pounds weight of silver) to the restoration of the defences, and convinced other county officials to donate their salaries for that year.[40] Incredibly, in July 1673 another typhoon seriously damaged the work a second time, requiring yet more money. Li Kecheng had to appeal to the gentry of the county for donations: he was able to secure what he needed, and started the work a third time. He was probably unable to complete the reconstruction before he left his post in 1675, and yet another terrible typhoon caused grave damage in 1677, requiring another full-scale restoration, which was undertaken and completed by magistrate Jin Wenmo (1687–1694).[41] Plates 18 and 19 show the remaining parts of the defences of Nam Tau as rebuilt by Li Kecheng and Jin Wenmo.

While the defences of Nam Tau were in need of urgent restoration in 1670, those of Tai Pang were in an even worse condition. The nine years of rule by Lei Man-wing, and the three-month siege of the city in 1657 had left the walls of Tai Pang in a very badly damaged state, even before the destruction caused by the evacuation. Exactly the same story was played out there as in Nam Tau: rehabilitation work started in 1670, assisted by government money, only to have to restart a year later after the typhoon of 1671, and to begin yet again after the typhoon of 1673. Once again, the money for the 1671 redevelopment came mostly from Li Kecheng's private funds (he donated 175.995 taels, while the five senior military officers at Tai Pang between them donated a total of 100 taels), but in 1673 he had to depend on donations from the leading men of the county.[42] The edict on the restoration of the walls of Nam Tau does not specifically mention the concurrent need to restore the walls of Tai Pang. Plates 24 to 26 show parts of the defences of Tai Pang as rebuilt by Li Kecheng.

The rebuilding of the yamen (which is also not mentioned in the edict on the defences of Nam Tau) is yet another case of the same story. Work began in 1670, as soon as Li Kecheng arrived, with some government money, but everything done was wrecked by the typhoon of 1671. In his preface to the county gazetteer, Li Kecheng mentions the extreme destruction of the 1671 typhoon, "Officials and people alike were rendered homeless, it was all extremely miserable" (官民又復露外, 淒其萬狀).[43] As with the Nam Tau and Tai Pang defences, there was no further government money, and Li Kecheng paid for the work to restart in 1671 from his private funds, although the exact sum he donated is not stated in the gazetteer:

> A terrible typhoon struck, the main gate, the drum tower, the residences of the officials and the offices were utterly overthrown: the county magistrate, Li Kecheng, donated the moneys needed for the purchase of the material needed for work to restart (颶風

大作, 頭門鼓樓, 官房衙宇, 又被倒塌, 知縣李可成復捐資買料).[44]
Again, as with the other restoration projects, the typhoons of 1673 and 1677 set the work back.

Li Kecheng wrote a poem trying to express how important it was for the people to support the restoration of the defences by donations, ("Announcing the restoration of the walls and buildings by donations", 捐修城垣告竣), and he said much the same thing in his preface to the county gazetteer,

> It is clear that, unless there are donations to restore all the city walls, the buildings of the yamen, the forts and other military buildings, then how can we defend ourselves from people coming over the sea (爰諏爰度, 凡城垣縣治臺寨營盤, 靡不捐資修葺, 以捍外侮)?[45]

On top of the damage caused by the typhoon of 1677, terrible floods arising from yet another typhoon in 1686 resulted in further serious destruction to the yamen and the defences of Nam Tau in 1686, ("the towers, and the yamen drum-tower, were destroyed, 唯頭門鼓樓尚未葺"), and this required yet another full-scale restoration.[46]

The biography of magistrate Jin Qizhen (1700–1713) states that "in his time the river was silted up, and there were terrible floods, which brought great suffering to the people: he had the river dredged, so that the floods were stopped right down to the present" [meaning 1819] (其時河道壅塞, 水潦大至, 民傷蕩析, 公措理疏導, 水患悉除, 于今賴之).[47] However, it is probable that the floods which the biography of Jin Qizhen states occurred "in his time", were in fact those of 1686, 14 years before he arrived.

The "Disasters" (災異) section of the gazetteer describes these 1686 floods in great detail.[48] The lower parts of Nam Tau city were under more than ten feet of water, and the yamen, although it stood on slightly higher ground, was still inundated, and left in ruins. The city walls were broken through to allow the waters to escape. The two gaps opened through the walls at the lowest points of the circuit were probably left open, as postern gates, to ensure they could be opened again if another flood should come: two postern gates are shown on the map of Nam Tau in the 1819 gazetteer at these points, but not in the map in the 1688 gazetteer, which was probably drawn before the 1686 flood. The account also mentions the huge loss of life in the surrounding villages. The Kap Yat area was, it would seem, particularly hard hit: the floodwaters of the river could not reach the sea because of silting at the river mouth, but probably also because of a storm surge and devastation from the sea. The Kap Yat area must have been ravaged by storm waves, and under many feet of floodwater: the Ming bridge and pier were probably swept away, and Zhou Xiyao's fort wrecked. There must have been serious loss of life there.

After these floods in 1686, repairs to the yamen would have been the first priority since the magistrate's residence and the county offices had been destroyed, and An Yumei (1684–1687), who was magistrate at the time the floods hit, sought provincial funds for this, without success. His successor, Jin Wenmo, spent his efforts in gathering donations to repair the yamen and city walls, eventually successfully, and the yamen was accordingly repaired in his time.[49] Eventually he persuaded all the civil officials (led by his own example) to donate their salaries for a year, and with donations from the elders of the county, he was able to do the work. It was probably at this restoration that a barbican was added to the east gate of the city (barbicans had been built at the south gate and west gate earlier — these are the gates facing the landing place — perhaps by Li Kecheng, as part of his reconstruction of the city walls). The attack by bandits which had captured the city in 1676–1677 had probably been centred on this weaker east gate, since the county Temple of Confucius, which stood immediately outside the east gate, was destroyed in the bandit attack. It was probably also in this restoration that the gaps opened through the walls in 1686 were rebuilt as postern gates.

It is unlikely that any magistrate would have dared to try to get donations for more than one project at a time, unless as an absolute last resort. An Yumei had to secure donations to build the Baoan Academy, and Jin Wenmo had to struggle to raise funds to repair the yamen and the city walls. Ding Tangfa, who followed Jin Wenmo in post, had to concentrate his efforts on the rebuilding of the county Temple of Confucius. It would, therefore, only have been after Ding Tangfa's time that his successor, that is, Jin Qizhen, could think about gathering funds to dredge the river. He tried for provincial funds, but unsuccessfully. Jin Qizhen, as part of the dredging exercise, seems to have rebuilt the bridge over the river, moving it to a new site, a little to the east of the old bridge. The change to the position of the bridge, which is suggested by the maps in the 1688 and 1819 gazetteers, very probably occurred at this period. Jin Qizhen, in all likelihood also rebuilt the pier; perhaps replacing the old pier with two new landing places, one to the south, serving the Nam Tau market, the other to the north, serving the salt fields (none of the maps, in either gazetteer, show the position of the piers). He probably also used the ruins of Zhou Xiyao's fort as the site of a new temple, the Shan Chuen Tan (山川壇, Shanchuantan, "altar to the mountains and streams"). He certainly built a new temple on the other bank of the river, immediately opposite to the Shan Chuen Tan, in 1701. This was the Chiu Yam Nunnery (潮音菴, Chaoyinan, "nunnery of the ocean's roar"). It is probable that these two new temples were a votive offering to the deities to beseech protection against any such devastating storm in the future.[50]

Plate 5 (from the 1819 gazetteer) shows the yamen: the yamen was restored many times after Li Kecheng, but probably always on the original foundations, and so the plate probably shows the yamen more or less as Li Kecheng left it, and, indeed, probably more or less as it had been in the Ming. Li Kecheng also restored the Kwan Tai temple (關帝廟, Guandi), and the Shing Wong (城隍廟, Chenghuang, "city god") temple.[51] There were two Kwan Tai temples at Nam Tau, one inside the walls and not far from the yamen, the other outside the walls and associated with the garrison parade ground and display platform (演武亭); it is not stated which of the two Li Kecheng restored, but it was probably the one near the yamen, since this would have been a temple at which the magistrate would very probably have worshipped (Kwan Tai was the patron deity of the Qing: Qing magistrates would certainly have worshipped here).[52]

Given the devastation of the typhoons of 1671 and 1673, it is not surprising that Li Kecheng did more than merely find the money to restart the work of restoring the yamen and the defences. In 1673 he organised a major sacrifice to the wind gods, writing a long prayer in finely structured rhythmic prose beseeching mercy for the people of San On (祭風文).[53] The core of the prayer is,

> What crimes have the people of San On committed, that they should suffer such disasters? This county by the sea has been

evacuated and broken, then good fortune came again, how could it all be in vain, how could such disasters come so frequently" (新民可辜, 頻罹鞠凶...海濱之邑, 在撤在遷, 道惟致省, 文用申虔, 彼多受社)?

He ends by beseeching the gods, in effect: "Please, no more typhoons, just gentle winds; no more floods, just gentle fertilising rain". However, it would seem the gods did not listen: as another devastating typhoon struck in 1677, and yet another in 1686.

It is probable that the period 1669–1686, with five devastating typhoons within 17 years, was the worst period for typhoons in the history of the San On area.[54]

* * *

In 1672, San On was attacked by another large and dangerous bandit band, led by Lei Kei (李奇, Li Ji). Li Kecheng took vigorous and ultimately completely successful action to eradicate Lei Kei and his band. This is mentioned in one of his edicts, in his preface to the county gazetteer, and in a poem he wrote; it is given a prominent place in his biography as a worthy official, and it is also noted in the "Bandits" section of the gazetteer.[55]

In one place the fighting against these bandits is called "the Battle of Tuen Mun", in another "the Battle of Ho Chung": major fighting took place at both places. Taking all these sources together, it would seem that the bandits attacked and occupied Tuen Mun, thereby threatening the entrance to the Pearl River. Li Kecheng took personal command of the county militia and the county military forces. They took a joint oath to live or die together (誓眾). Li Kecheng then led his forces in a headlong dash to attack the bandits. The attack was entirely successful, a great number of the bandits being killed. The rest fled east to Ho Chung (蠔涌, Haoyong) in today's Sai Kung district; Li Kecheng was able to trap the remnant of the bandit fleet in the bay at Ho Chung, and, in a second battle again routed the bandits, killing a great number.[56] A few fled over the mountains to Lek Yuen (瀝源, Liyuan), in today's Sha Tin district, where Li Kecheng had them all hunted down. Every one of the bandits was killed in these battles, except for 70 taken captive and, presumably, executed after being taken back to Nam Tau.

For Li Kecheng, the importance of this fighting was that it showed him the vital need for the coastal defence forts, and the road forts and fortlets. His second edict for the restoration of damaged buildings was, therefore, designed to urge the restoration of this scattered system of defence points. In this second edict he showed how the system of forts and fortlets was essential to an effective local defence, pointing out how the fight against Lei Kei demonstrated this.[57]

Initially 12 forts were to be restored, at a total cost of 2005.865 taels: half of this sum was donated by the San On civil officials, of which Li Kecheng personally donated 600 taels (see Plates 29–31 for forts restored in this period). In addition, a further nine forts, damaged in the typhoon of 1671, were to be restored, at a total further cost of 255.557 taels. Li Kecheng donated 129.403 taels of this sum from his private funds, and the county military officers a further 120.403 taels.[58] Li Kecheng also provided all the money needed for the restoration of the gun platform to the north-west of Nam Tau after it was damaged by one of the typhoons.[59] This gun platform defended the city from any bandits landing on the shore to the north. This was not the same fort as had been built by Zhou Xiyao (i.e. the pier head fort), which was built to the south-west, and which was to be left in ruins after the 1686 storm, and then used as the site for the Shan Chuen Tan Temple. Li Kecheng may also have been responsible for building the string of forts which protected the road to Tai Pang, along the north shore of Mirs Bay, through what had been Yao territory in the Ming.

Given his problems in restoring the walls and other defences at Nam Tau and Tai Pang, and in restoring the yamen, it seems likely that the restoration of the other forts, beyond these 22, remained as an expression of intent for at least a few years. However, most of these coastal defence forts and other defences were repaired over the next few decades, and seem mostly to have been in usable order by the date the county gazetteer was issued.

Li Kecheng, like Zhou Xiyao, at all stages makes it very clear that his anxiety about the state of the defences of Nam Tau was because of the risk to Canton if Nam Tau fell into the hands of bandits. This nightmare scenario had come close to realisation in 1630, 1634, 1635, and during the Chan Yiu and Lei Man-wing years (1647–1657), but had been avoided. Unfortunately, in 1676, a year after Li Kecheng left San On, Nam Tau, (the walls of which were probably still not by then completely restored), did indeed fall to another large bandit force, showing that the anxieties of Li Kecheng and Zhou Xiyao were not ill-founded.[60] The city was recovered a few months later. The then county magistrate, Luo Mingke (1675–1678) was not captured by the bandits: he was presumably away from the city when the bandits took it. He was removed from his post shortly afterwards, possibly because the city had been lost during his term of office, but the risk had been persistently drawn to the attention of the higher authorities for many years before that.

* * *

When Li Kecheng arrived in San On, he faced a particular problem of poor junior staff. Usually, a new county magistrate would inherit from his predecessor a set of experienced local junior officials (clerks, treasury guards, and runners), but in his case these had all been scattered during the evacuation and he had to hurriedly find new staff. Inevitably, many of those who put themselves forward were crooks, looking to make easy money out of squeezing the local residents, or, to put it more sympathetically, were people desperate for money to restore their villages after the chaos of the bandits and the Coastal Evacuation period. In at least two cases, villages today claim that their rehabilitation was done at the expense of villagers who took office in the yamen in this period: both Tai Long (大朗, Dalang), near Shataukok (沙頭角, Shatoujiao), and Chung Uk (鍾屋, Zhongwu), between Yuen Long and Tuen Mun say that their redevelopment was due to a villager working at this period for the yamen, probably as a runner.[61] In any case, Li Kecheng was obliged to issue two edicts stating that he would thoroughly reform in particular the runners he had employed.[62]

A major duty of these runners was to collect the taxes, but they also worked as police, arresting suspects for trial, and enforcing orders of the magistrate. Li Kecheng found that they were squeezing the people while collecting the taxes. The taxes were assessed in grain, but paid for in cash at a fixed rate of commutation, as had been true also, in large part, in the late Ming, as Zhou Xiyao's edicts show. He found that the runners were charging an additional sum above the cash due in tax as a "meltage fee" (火耗), in theory to cover any impurities in the silver paid in. Li Kecheng said that, in an impoverished place like post-evacuation San On, such additional charges could not be borne: they were to be immediately stopped. The meltage fee was a widely charged fee, and was usually assessed at 10–20% of the sum paid in, although the actual expense of purifying the silver and casting it into standard weight ingots was only 1–2% (the provincial treasurer would only accept payments to him in ingots of a standard weight and a standard degree of fineness, so the silver paid in to the magistracy had to be melted down, purified, and cast into the standard weight ingots before it could be remitted to the provincial treasurer). The money received above the actual cost of the purification process customarily went to the fees received by the junior staff of the yamen. Money had to be found, however, for the purification of the tax silver and for casting it into standard weight ingots: this was not an expense which could be charged against the taxes. Li Kecheng, by banning the meltage fee, was probably committing himself to meeting the actual cost of this work from his own personal income.[63]

More fundamentally, in these edicts Li Kecheng noted that, in the past (presumably following Zhou Xiyao's edict on this subject), runners were not employed by the magistracy: rich families took turns to provide runners to collect the taxes from their own districts, as part of the families' bao-jia and corvée duties. However, over time a system had evolved whereby the families paid a cash sum to allow for the hiring of professional, full-time runners. Li Kecheng felt Zhou Xiyao's system was better: the rich families would be less greedy and would always have to consider the other rich families, who would later take over the work, and would undoubtedly demand payback for any extortion they or theirs had suffered. He wanted to revert to the older system, as put in place by Zhou Xiyao, although it seems unlikely that he had any success in doing so: the rich families were entirely unwilling to cooperate. In the Ming, as Zhou Xiyao's edicts show, the taxes were collected by runners working on their own. At some date in the early Qing it became the local practice for the runners to be accompanied by a clerk and a treasury guard when collecting the taxes. This, while it raised the costs of tax collection substantially, would clearly have reduced the risk of the runners embezzling the taxes. This reform may have been introduced by Li Kecheng, once it became clear that tax collection by rich families as part of their bao-jia duties was not going to eventuate.

Neither Zhou Xiyao nor Li Kecheng left an edict which directly discussed the corvée, although Zhou Xiyao's requirement that the wealthier villagers collect the taxes as part of their bao-jia and corvée obligations, and Li Kecheng's stated desire to do the same, clearly touch on this issue. What were seen as excessive corvée demands on the households of the county had been a problem in San On for a long time, however, and it was to remain a problem: magistrates Qiu Tiqian (1586–1590), Chen Liangyan (1622–1624), Peng Yunnian (1637–1640), An Yumei (1684–1687), and Ding Tangfa (1694–1700), all attempted to restrain excessive corvée, although the gazetteer gives no details as to exactly what the abuses were which they were trying to curtail.[64] The richer families almost certainly would have viewed Zhou Xiyao's handing to them the duty of tax collecting as excessive corvée. It is likely that the corvée was a particularly burdensome imposition after the Coastal Evacuation, since the number of households had dropped so sharply. It is likely that this problem effectively disappeared after 1711, when the corvée was cancelled and replaced with a small cash surcharge on the land tax.

Li Kecheng also ruled in the second of his two edicts on tax collection, that "there should always be someone who takes responsibility" (責有攸歸) for tax payments. Where there was anyone who persistently defaulted on his taxes (leniency was always given at first), then the taxes would be demanded from a guarantor. This was in accordance with the law as formally adopted in 1750, but which was in practice probably considered desirable long before, which required tax payers to be entered onto the land tax register under a "head of household", who would be held responsible in case of default.[65] This rule had not, however, been followed in San On in late Ming times, as Zhou Xiyao's edicts show.

Defaulting tax debtors had been a problem in San On for a long time. Magistrate Chen Gu (1628–1631) was "lenient as to the minor taxes, would not call in mortgages, and cancelled debts for the very poor" (寬里甲, 恤編民, 免緩贖, 清羨余; it would seem that some defaulting taxpayers mortgaged property to the yamen when they could not meet their tax debts). Magistrate Peng Yunnian (1637–1640) was "forgiving towards the people…he forgave debts" (寬厚…蠲緩贖). Magistrate An Yumei (1684–1687) "gave extensions to defaulters" (而里排各遵限赴納), and repeated Li Kecheng's refusal to allow the meltage fee to be charged; he also tried the experiment of allowing the taxes to be paid in four installments over the year, instead of the two which were standard in San On, to see if this made it easier for poorer taxpayers to meet their obligations.[66]

In most cases, if there was to be a guarantor, then the guaranteeing head of household would be the clan ancestral trust for the clan in question, and any tax in default would be taken from the ancestral trust's funds. This was very unpopular with the wealthy villagers who managed the major ancestral trusts, and this ruling of Li Kecheng's was cancelled by magistrate Jin Qizhen (1700–1713), presumably after pressure was exerted by the wealthy village leaders who were bearing the burden of any defaults. Jin Qizhen's biography in the gazetteer thus states:

If anyone failed to pay taxes, his whole clan was held responsible...if someone had accumulated debts which he could not pay, only the one man need be held guilty, so that the people could go about their occupations with a quiet mind (一姓同戶, 逋 稅者, 合族株連...有稅欠不清者, 罪止一人, 民皆蕩安業).[67]

In the meantime, Li Kecheng's ruling must have been effective in reducing defaults.

Li Kecheng's edict on the abolition of the meltage fee also covered another improper practice, which had been forbidden by Zhou Xiyao, but which had crept back in, that is, the provision of daily necessities like vegetables to the magistracy at below market prices. This, Li Kecheng, like his predecessors, utterly banned, "the merchants must not be allowed to bear this" (並無行戶承值). Li Kecheng also, like Yu Zhu, had to take steps to eradicate improprieties in the procurement of horses for the courier soldiers.[68]

**

Criminal law was another area which Zhou Xiyao had tried to reform, but where improprieties had reappeared. Li Kecheng issued an edict taking action against certain such abuses.[69] The abuses he tried to deal with were all things Zhou Xiyao had tried to remedy 30 years earlier, and included suspects absconding, giving false names or places of residence, perjury, implicating the innocent in criminal cases and so on, leading to cases which could not be brought to an end, and to huge losses being faced by families involved in criminal cases. A particular problem, as with Zhou Xiyao, was criminal gangs taking dead bodies, giving them false identities, and using them to extort pay-offs from wealthy families. Li Kecheng's response to these abuses was much the same as Zhou Xiyao's had been: questions of identity, residence, etc. were to be dealt with before the substantive criminal case was begun, and any perjury would be investigated fully and punished severely. Extortion using dead bodies would also meet with the harshest punishment.

The final edict of Li Kecheng was a moral exhortation to implement the bao-jia system fully.[70] In the situation of San On after the evacuation, with large numbers of newcomers, single men, cutting fields out of the wilderness, a high percentage of the population would not have been on the bao-jia registers, and this was clearly a matter of concern: "where the bao-jia is ineffectively administered, various abuses will flourish" (第行之不力, 以致弊竇叢生). It is unlikely that Li Kecheng was able to do much; it was to be a generation or so later before the bao-jia was to be effectively enforced within San On.

* * *

It cannot be said that the superiors of the San On magistrates were at all helpful to them and towards San On County in general in this late Ming and early Qing period. Even though Li Kecheng was clearly acceptable to Shang Kexi, nonetheless, no provincial money was found for the second and third reconstructions of the defences of Nam Tau and Tai Pang and the yamen, nor for the rebuilding of the county Temple of Confucius and county school. This was, to say the least, unhelpful. This had long been a problem, and was to remain one. Zhou Xiyao had faced exactly the same impediment of bureaucratic refusal to fund essential public works in the county when the provincial authorities declined to find money for the rebuilding of the Temple of Confucius and county school, for the raising of the height of the city walls, and for the two new forts he considered essential to the defences of the city. Exactly the same problem arose, or was to arise, under magistrates Chen Gu (1628–1631), where no provincial money was given for the two new watchtowers on the north wall; Zhang Mingda (1678–1684), where money was refused for the re-building of the county school and Temple of Confucius, despite repeated requests; Jin Wenmo (1687–1694), who was given no financial aid for essential repairs to the yamen and city walls; and Jin Qizhen (1700–1713), who was denied money for the dredging of the river. These public works were essential for the security and normal administration of the county, and the continual refusal to find any provincial money for them suggests that the provincial authorities rather despised the county magistrates, and dismissed their concerns as of no account. John Watt has shown that such an attitude was not unusual: the provincial authorities were appointed under different rules, and were invariably higher level graduates than the district magistrates, and tended to belittle them and their concerns.[71]

Since no provincial money was found for these public works, the money for them had to be raised by donation drives, but, at the heart of these were gifts from the private incomes of the magistrates. As well as Li Kecheng, magistrates Zhang Mingda (1678–1684), An Yumei (1684–1687), and Jin Wenmo (1687–1694) are all stated to have donated money from their private resources towards repairs and restoration of the yamen:[72] clearly, all the magistrates of the period immediately after the Coastal Evacuation felt this was necessary for the needs of the county.

As the gazetteer clearly shows, Li Kecheng spent very lavishly from his personal funds for the sake of the county. The details of his tenure show how much a conscientious county magistrate might feel obliged to pay out of his private income for county projects. As well as the 600 taels he donated to the restoration of the walls of Nam Tau, the almost 176 taels given to the walls of Tai Pang, and the slightly above 722 taels provided to the restoration of the forts and fortlets, he spent significantly on the reconstruction of the north-west gun platform at Nam Tau, the yamen, and the Kwan Tai Temple. He also probably donated money to the restoration of the Shing Wong Temple, and certainly used his own money to buy seed rice and plough cattle for the recently returned San On men who could not otherwise re-establish themselves, and yet again, probably, on the small cash grants to newcomers wanting to make a start in San On. He probably also helped fund purifying and casting the tax silver into standard-weight ingots. It is unlikely that he spent less than 5,000 taels of his private money, very probably a good deal more. To put this into perspective, 5,000 taels is a little below three and three-quarters hundredweights of fine silver, or nearly a fifth of a ton.[73] He was clearly a generous man. At no point is there any hint that he diverted even a cent to himself: he must have left San On a good deal poorer than he arrived. It may have been, indeed, his wealth, as well as his unquestionable loyalty to the Qing, which led the central authorities to post him to San On, where heavy expenditure was clearly going to be needed. His immediate successors also all donated from their private incomes towards county projects, as noted above. Had a man without private funds, like Zhou Xiyao, been appointed in 1670, or in the next decade or two, he would have been unable to do what was needed.

Similar action by the provincial authorities showing disdain for the county magistrates, their views, and the views of the county community is shown in the cases of magistrates Chen Gu (1628–1631) and Li Jungzhu (1650–1654). Chen Gu "offended a rich and powerful man" (以忤權貴去) (probably in Canton), and was forced out of office, despite the strong support he was given by his county community. Li Jungzhu found that the commander of the city garrison, Wong Sau-tso (王守祖, Wang Shouzu) was far too harsh: he wanted him dismissed, and was supported by the county community in this stance.[74] However, the provincial authorities dismissed his concerns as of little importance, until the matter triggered a mutiny within the garrison in Nam Tau. Li Jungzhu put this down firmly, and the provincial authorities then sent an investigator to look into the matter. The investigator eventually found that Li Jungzhu was in the right, but, in the meantime, a great deal of unpleasantness had been caused. The county magistrates could clearly not depend on support and assistance from their superiors.

In addition to his official duties, Li Kecheng greatly appreciated the beauties of the scenery of San On. He wrote a series of eight poems on sites around Nam Tau: he clearly went on walks into the countryside, climbing up the hills, when he could find the time.[75] Unlike Zhou Xiyao, whose childhood among the beauties of Huang Shan may have led him to look down on the scenery of on the county he had been posted to, Li Kecheng was brought up in the fertile, but flat and somewhat featureless Liao River plains, and he clearly fell in love with San On and its mountains.

Li Kecheng's biography as a worthy official (Appendix 3) stresses his kindness, amiability, and compassion, as well as his honesty and self-discipline. It mentions his care in the matter of the taxes, and in the hearing of lawsuits. As with Zhou Xiyao's biography, Li Kecheng's biography is firmly within the eulogistic tradition, but all of the virtues stressed in it come out in his writings as well. The biography mentions specifically his generosity in donating to the restoration of the walls and defences and of the yamen, his donation of plough animals to poor families, his meticulous care in strengthening the coastal defences, and his vigorous action in quelling Lei Kei. It ends by saying he was widely praised, not only in San On, but in other counties within the broader area. It is clear from the gazetteer that Tang Man-wai, the editor, greatly admired him.

6

Salt and Fish

S alt, and the problem of providing it to the commercial fishing fleet, is not included in Zhou Xiyao's "All the Problems" paper, but it had been a serious issue in San On ever since the county was first established in 1573. At least two of Zhou Xiyao's predecessors as county magistrates had issued edicts designed to deal with the problem, and Zhou Xiyao issued at least two more; it remained a problem until the very end of the eighteenth century.[1]

The underlying problem was that the salt fields were working under rules laid down by the salt monopoly in the Song Dynasty, 500 years and more before Zhou Xiyao's time, and these rules were, by the late Ming, no longer even marginally effective. The rules stipulated that every salt worker had to hand over as tax to the salt monopoly a certain fixed amount of salt without payment, or a slightly larger amount at cost price — the so-called "production quota" (徵鹽額). Each salt field traditionally used either one method or the other. This, with the production quota salt from other salt fields, was then shipped to the great salt depot at Canton, where the salt tax and various other levies were added to it. Every up-country county then had to receive and sell a certain fixed amount of this taxed salt (the "consumption quota", 引額), at a price fixed by the salt monopoly. Usually, the county where the salt fields were located (sometimes several nearby counties) got their salt directly from the salt fields, not from the Canton salt depot, and for this salt the taxes were imposed at the salt field, usually at a lower rate.

The Ming code stated that all salt made had to be handed over to the salt monopoly, and that making any salt which was not handed over to the salt monopoly was a criminal act. Salt made above the production quota would be paid for by the salt monopoly at an agreed "market price".[2] By the late Ming it had become normal, however, to allow salt made by the salt workers above the production quota ("excess salt", 餘鹽) to be sold retail at the market price, free of tax, at the salt fields, so long as this excess salt was not shipped inland through Canton to compete with the salt monopoly's consumption quota salt trade: this was specifically agreed for Tung Kwun ("in accordance with the old rules") in 1510 (at that date this included the later San On area).[3] Wholesale trade in excess salt was considered illegal by the salt monopoly: it was assumed that the amount of excess salt would be low.

In addition, the salt monopoly held a considerable quantity of arable land in San On ("furnace lands", 竈田), over a third of all the taxed arable land in the county, including also fuel lots (山塘). These were held on a hereditable basis from the monopoly by the salt working families. The families had to pay two sets of tax

for this land — the normal land tax paid to the magistracy, and
a further tax, levied in salt, to the salt monopoly. While this land
was, therefore, relatively expensive, it was, in many cases, the only
thing that kept the salt working families from sinking into penury,
as salt working on its own was usually a marginal occupation
in San On. Some salt working families had no furnace land,
and were, as a result, desperately poor. Magistrate Qiu Tiqian
(1586–1590) therefore petitioned the provincial authorities to
redistribute the furnace lands, so that every salt working family
might have access to some, but this was rejected and the poor salt
families stayed poor.[4]

* * *

The underlying problem for salt working in San On, from the
late Ming right through until the end of the eighteenth century,
was that the production quota for the San On salt fields was low,
and the consumption quotas for San On and Tung Kwun, the
two counties adjacent to the salt fields, and which got their salt
directly from the salt fields, were extremely low: by the late Ming
most of the local salt trade was in excess salt. The amount of
excess salt being produced was substantial; the productivity of the
San On salt fields having been greatly improved since the Song,
but without any changes being made to the production quotas.
The local resident population was, in the seventeenth century,
much higher than it had been in the Song, and demand for salt
was far higher than the long-out-of-date consumption quotas
even where the landward population alone was in question.

In addition, the commercial fishing industry demanded
immense amounts of salt, and there had been no quota in the
Song for the fishing fleets. Commercial fishing in the lower Pearl
River area does not seem to have begun before the sixteenth

century (Macao was possibly the first commercial fishing port in the broader area, from the middle sixteenth century, with San On ports following suit in the very late sixteenth and seventeenth centuries). In the Ming, ships were forbidden to sail out of sight of land, on pain of death, for fear the sailors would meet up with foreigners and so compromise the security of the state; that fishermen were included in the ban on sailing out of sight of land was, in fact, confirmed by the Ming government in 1551.[5] This thus made deep-sea fishing illegal.[6]

In the fifteenth century the only fishing known to the Tung Kwun county authorities seems to have been subsistence fishing from sampans in the East River and Pearl River; there is no mention of deep-sea fishing. The 1464 Tung Kwun Gazetteer, in the "Office of the River Trade" (河泊所), section (at that date San On still formed part of Tung Kwun County), mentions an official, the "official for administering the river trade" (河泊所官), this officer was responsible "for administering the Tanka within the county, and collecting the fish tax" (專管邑境蛋戶歲徵魚課). The post had been established in 1381. He had a clerk to assist him ("disbursement and documents", 攢典, — thus a general clerk).[7]

The Tanka within Tung Kwun County in 1464, including the whole of San On, were arranged in "communes" (社). The fishermen paid the "fish tax" (魚課) in their communes. Four of these fishermen's communes, previously under the Tung Kwun river trade supervisor, passed to the new county of San On when it was established in 1573 (the other fishermen's communes were along the East River and within its delta). Three were along the Pearl River coast, north of Nam Tau, and one was on a tributary of the Pearl River, a few miles upstream from the coast. This tributary was the Yeung Chung River (洋涌河, Yangyyonghe) the stream which formed the northern border of San On County. None of the fishermen's communes faced the open sea (see Map 6).[8] It is noticeable that there was no fishermen's commune at Nam Tau, nor in Deep Bay; the open sea, and even the lower Pearl River were clearly not open to fishermen in the fifteenth century, nor indeed in 1573. At those dates fishing would seem not to have been permitted south of a limit a little south of Nam Tau: the fishermen were thus all then clearly part of the "river trade". Given the arrangement of these four fishermen's communes, there can be no doubt that the fishermen in question were subsistence fishermen, fishing from sampans and selling only a few fish, fresh, to villagers living along the shore. Such fishing would have used very little salt.

The gazetteer suggests that the first commercial fishermen appeared in San On at the end of the sixteenth century, probably shortly after the county was established. A special tax was paid by 126 fishermen at the end of the sixteenth century.[9] This is the tax Zhou Xiyao called the "going-out-to-sea tax" (出海税).[10] This tax, originally levied at the rate of one tael per family, was probably a permit fee to allow the fishermen paying it to fish at the mouth of the Pearl River, and around the islands, below the old fishing limit just south of Nam Tau. Magistrate Yu Zhu (1594–1599) reduced the tax to 0.8 tael in 1595, in order to ensure that the fishermen "had enough to buy rice". Magistrate Li Xuan (1635–1637) cancelled this tax altogether for very poor families: 23 families benefitted from this cancellation.[11] When the people were allowed to return to San On after the Coastal Evacuation (1669), fishing was initially only permitted above the old fishing limit just south of Nam Tau. However, in 1686 magistrate An Yumei (1684–1687) sent a petition to the emperor beseeching permission to reopen the seas below this limit to the fishermen since Taiwan had now been pacified.[12] Following agreement to this petition 136 fishermen paid the 0.8 tael going-out-to-sea tax, plus those who had the tax cancelled because of poverty: over the next generation the number of deep sea commercial fishermen soared.

The 1688 gazetteer, after noting the four fishermen's communes, contains an impassioned paragraph on the hardships of the fishermen's life (which few, it states, would dare to try): defended from the heaving waves only by flimsy hulls and sails, at the mercy of typhoons, in constant danger and risk. At the end of autumn, the fisher people paid the going-out-to-sea tax and went out to fish for yellow croaker (黃花魚), to gain income to meet their taxes and to provide for their families. And yet yamen people (衙官) were arresting them and prosecuting them — presumably because they were breaching the law about going out of sight of land: the going-out-to-sea tax doubtless allowed fishermen to fish south of the old fishing limit, but not out in the deep sea. This paragraph is certainly an extract from an edict of Zhou Xiyao. It goes on to say that Zhou Xiyao "strictly forbade action to be taken against the fishermen (going out into the deep sea to fish for yellow croaker): they were only trying to make a living", (and, therefore, were not interested in treasonable contact with foreigners, which was the context of the prohibition in the Ming code) "and anyone taking action against them would be punished" (知縣周希曜嚴禁侵奪, 將投獻者, 經置之法, 海濱之民, 得以守嘗利矣).[13]

The yellow croaker live in vast shoals. It is particular as to the temperature of the water in which it lives. In midwinter they can be found in the gulf of Tonkin, off the Red River: as the water warms up with the coming of spring, the shoals move north, until, at midsummer, they are off the mouth of the Yangtze. The shoals move north and south about a hundred miles offshore. The shoals are at their densest in late autumn, when they appear off the mouth of the Pearl River, and, at that time, San On fishermen could make very large catches. Catching yellow croaker thus required larger boats, able to stay at sea for weeks at a time, as the fishermen followed the shoals well out of sight of land. The fish caught had to be salted on board, and were then landed at specialist commercial fishing ports, where there were merchants who could buy a whole catch and then export it inland in bulk, where the salt fish became a mainstay of the inland farming people, for whom it quickly became a cheap and dependable source of protein. This was a development essentially of the late seventeenth and eighteenth centuries. The yellow croaker fishery, therefore, required deep-sea fishing, and was thus clearly opposed to the letter of the Ming law, but this did not stop Zhou Xiyao explicitly giving approval to the yellow croaker fishery, and to fishermen going out to the deep sea. This edict by Zhou Xiyao can, therefore, fairly be called the foundation document of the commercial fishing industry of the Hong Kong area.

In 1880, in response to a petition from the fishermen of San On, the viceroy issued a viceregal edict on the question of how much salt a deep-sea fishing boat reasonably required. He employed experts who sent him detailed reports, and he eventually ruled that a small fishing boat (capable of carrying at most fifteen tons of fish) would have to carry 135,000 catties of salt, or a little below five tons: he ruled that no fishing boat carrying that amount of salt was to be proceeded against as a suspect salt smuggler.[14] Each boat of the San On commercial fishing fleet would have needed to carry this amount of salt, therefore, every time it went out to sea to fish for yellow croaker. The San On commercial fishing fleet thus clearly required an enormous amount of salt, which would initially have had to be bought from the excess salt available for sale in San On. This would have become significant during the seventeenth century, as the trade became established, and certainly from the time Zhou Xiyao specifically approved the deep-sea yellow croaker fishery. Eventually, a quota for the fishermen was agreed, in the early eighteenth century, initially of 300 tau (道: this was a unit of weight used in the salt trade in the San On area: one tau equalled ten yan, 引, or something over 4,000 catties, or a little below two and a half tons). This initial quota thus represented a weight of about 750 tons. This quota was then raised several times until, by 1819, it had reached 6,148.687 tau, or a little over 15,000 tons. However, it is entirely unlikely that this quota was sufficient to provide for all the needs of the fishermen at any date.[15]

* * *

The original rule for excess salt, as noted previously, was that it all should be sold at an agreed market price to the salt monopoly, who would then sell it on. However, this rule broke down in San On under the pressure of the large amount of excess salt being handled. The salt monopoly was extremely bureaucratic, and was not able to respond to the commercial demands this active involvement in the excess salt trade implied. Something closer to a commercial salt market was needed. Such a salt market was locally called a fau (埠). This initially, it would seem, meant "pier", but it came to mean "port of trade", and then, more specifically, "free market salt port".[16] Salt was exported from the salt fields from a pier owned by the salt monopoly. If that pier was leased to a merchant, then that merchant could make of it a port of trade, and take on the active commercial trade in excess salt as a monopolist, leaving the salt monopoly its production quota tax salt (or, more usually, paying the salt monopoly its expected tax income in a single lump sum, and then handling all the salt as if it were excess salt). This was a development essentially of the later Ming. Existence of a fau made life easier for fishermen in particular, as there would be a place where salt could be purchased legally without quota problems, but arrangements such as these were extremely open to abuse.

Magistrate Yu Zhu (1594–1599) discovered that the coastal defence fort garrison at Mau Chau (茅洲, Maozhou, near the Kwai Tak (歸德, Guide) salt fields in the north of San On) was extorting squeeze from the Kwai Tak trade in excess salt by arresting any of the salt workers who did not pay them off and confiscating their salt, presumably on the ground that the salt sales breached the salt monopoly's control on the trade in excess salt. The salt monopoly was not, however, buying the salt. The salt workers could not, therefore, sell their excess salt legally. The salt workers were selling the excess salt at the salt fields to anyone who came to buy. Since this trade was strictly speaking, illegal, the salt workers were only able to do this after the bribe was paid. Yu Zhu was "deeply hurt" (本縣實切痛心). He ordered that salt from the Kwai Tak salt fields should be freely traded, and ordered the soldiers not to impede this. The salt makers were given a communal licence, for which they paid a fee, paid on all salt exported, and from then on the trade was under the control of the salt makers as a single communal body.[17]

These licence fee payments to the magistracy would doubtless have been much lower than the payments previously extracted by the Mau Chau garrison. While his edict does not say so explicitly, it seems likely that Yu Zhu effectively cancelled the responsibilities of the salt monopoly at the Kwai Tak salt fields: the county magistracy would pay the salt monopoly its expected tax income from the licence fee it received from the salt makers, and the salt monopoly would not have any further direct contact with the salt makers there. Any income from the licence fee beyond the annual sum paid to the salt monopoly would become excess tax income available for the magistrate to spend on county projects. Yu Zhu was thus establishing a fau, a free market in salt, at the Kwai Tak salt fields, where the salt makers could sell their salt freely to all comers, subject only to the licence fee. However, Yu Zhu was not able to make any reforms in the salt field areas near Nam Tau. (These were, in the late Ming, known as the Tung Kwun salt fields, formed in the Ming from amalgamation of the older Wong Tin, 黃田, Huangtien, and Tung Kwun salt fields).

Magistrate Li Xuan (1635–1637) noted in 1635 that the salt trade in the north of the county (i.e. the salt trade of the Kwai Tak fields) was in a satisfactory state, presumably following Yu Zhu's reforms, but that the position at the Tung Kwun salt fields near Nam Tau was then still very poor. An "evil official" (宦棍) had procured a salt monopoly document leasing the Nam Tau pier to him, and had thus been granted a fau by the salt monopoly, with monopoly rights to trade in excess salt there. He then used his power over the only available landing place to force the salt makers to sell their salt to him at far below the market price. All the salt available for sale was thus in his hands. He could then sell the salt at a high price to consumers, especially to the deep-sea fishermen, who were, by that date, desperate for salt (the Kwai Tak fau was too far upriver to be useful for the deep-sea fishermen). It is probable that the salt monopoly had commuted its production quota from the Tung Kwun salt fields to a cash payment as part of this arrangement. The cash would have been paid to the salt monopoly by the lessee of the pier from the income he received from the use of the pier. As Li Xuan noted, this effectively meant the salt makers were paying two loads of tax: their production quota salt (handed over to the fau merchant either free or at cost price), and then the difference between the price they were actually receiving and the true market price for excess salt for the rest of their salt. They were also being forced to do corvée duties, although salt workers were, by law, exempt from this.[18] The salt workers were being pushed close to starvation as a result.

Li Xuan proposed to make reforms along the same lines as Yu Zhu's earlier reforms in the north of the county. He specifically proposed that the operations of the salt monopoly be cancelled in the Nam Tau area. A fau should be set up, under the communal control of the salt makers. The salt monopoly official post for the area should be cancelled forthwith. The county administration would assume responsibility for paying the tax due for the salt (1333 taels, taking into account the savings from cancelling the post), which would be met from a levy on salt leaving the pier, to be gathered by the salt workers themselves. The gazetteer includes an impassioned section which is without doubt an extract from the petition submitted on this occasion by Li Xuan: it speaks of the "bullies" (異棍) who were terrorizing the salt workers, to the point where the salt workers were abandoning their homes and fleeing — the situation was "disastrous for the salt districts, and unbearable" (捺之四鄉, 已不堪矣). The "gentry and elders of the county had strenuously raised their concerns about the unacceptable position" (士民力陳疾苦, 及局害情事). This extract ends by saying that "the poor salt people were unable to support their families, their situation would make anyone weep, and for him, as the only local administrator, it was heartbreaking" (夫少民之身家; 固不足惜: 倘有不測, 而治城孤立, 豈不寒心. 嗚呼! 此亦當事者之懼也).[19] His biography in the gazetteer summarises his actions in the salt fields as "sympathizing with the hardships of the salt workers, he proposed to set up a salt fau" (恤竈丁之難, 詳立鹽埠).[20]

These proposals were sent to the provincial authorities for agreement, but, despite the passion with which they were expressed, they were not, it would seem, approved. Zhou Xiyao in 1640 found the same problems still in existence as Li Xuan had five years earlier. The pier was, by then, under the control of a Shun Tak (順德, Shunde) businessman, Lei Yat-pun (李日搬, Li Riban, also called in another place Lei Yat-shing, 李日成, Li Richeng), who had a lease of the pier, issued, presumably, by the salt monopoly. This is probably not the same man as the "evil official" of Li Xuan's time: that official may have divested himself of his lease after Li Xuan started to investigate him.

Zhou Xiyao's proposals were the same as Li Xuan's: set up a communally managed fau, and pay the salt monopoly the annual cash payment due, through the county magistracy, by way of a levy on salt sold at the pier, with any surplus becoming excess tax income available to the magistracy to spend. This, his first set of proposals, were, like Li Xuan's, not agreed upon by the provincial authorities. In a second proposal, sent to the provincial authorities immediately after the first one had been turned down, and after he had received a petition on the subject from the local people (1641, 知縣周希曜屢文申請兩院鹽臺),[21] Zhou Xiyao repeated his proposal:

I propose that the people of Tung Kwun and San On, the two counties, should each look after their own sea, their own salt market, and their own salt tax, so that Tung Kwun people should take responsibility for Tung Kwun affairs, and San On people for San On affairs, so that strong-arm men cannot interfere and take over control, and thus the fisher people and the farming people can really be benefitted (曉諭莞新兩邑諸民, 各管各海, 各阜各稅,莞民供莞之捕, 新民供新之捕, 不許勢豪占冒侵奪, 則漁蛋細民受惠多矣).[22]

Zhou Xiyao's proposals were eventually implemented, following consideration of his second proposal by the provincial authorities. Li Xuan, as intendant of the coastal region, would have been Zhou Xiyao's superior at this date, and can be assumed to have supported him.

The 1688 gazetteer refers to four salt fau in existence in the Nam Tau area at the date the gazetteer was issued: that is, at Pak Shek, (白石, Baishi, a little north of Sai Heung, 西鄉, Xixiang); at Sai Heung; at Kwu Sut, (固戍, Guxu, a few miles north of Pak Shek); and at Nam Tau; as well as the fau for the Kwai Tak. The gazetteer states that these four fau were established "of old" (舊有) which implies they were already in existence when the Qing came to power (1647 in San On).[23] The 1819 gazetteer quotes "the old gazetteer" for these four fau: the wording used in this 1819 quote differs significantly from the wording in the 1688 gazetteer, and thus this 1819 entry must reflect an entry in the gazetteer issued by Zhou Xiyao in 1643, which no longer survives (references in the gazetteer to the "old gazetteer" seem all to refer to this 1643 version).[24]

These fau were thus not in place in Li Xuan's time, but they clearly were by the end of Zhou Xiyao's time. Not only were they, it would seem, mentioned in the gazetteer published in his time (1643), and in place by 1647, but, furthermore, Zhou Xiyao states in one of his edicts that "it is at the Pak Shek Fau near Nam Tau that the salt makers and the fisher people meet for trade" (南頭白石一埠乃灶民漁蛋貿易), so that fau, and presumably the other three, were in existence by then. The gazetteer puts it, in the "miscellaneous taxes" (雜餉) section, that the fishermen "went to the fau to buy salt to preserve fish" (買還生鹽回埠, 資給魚戶腌魚).[25] These fau must, therefore, have been established late in Zhou Xiyao's tenure as county magistrate, probably in 1643.

The fishermen had petitioned the county magistrate in 1634 and 1635 to get better access to salt, and county magistrates Wu Wenming (1631–1635) and Li Xuan had attempted to do something about the problem, including Li Xuan's attempt to set up a salt fau,[26] but it was only with Zhou Ziyao's establishment of the new fau, and his clear approval of deep-sea fishing, that the fishing trade in the area was put onto a firmer basis.

These arrangements did not, however, survive for very long. Two-thirds of the salt workers died in the troubles of the period 1647–1669 (as mentioned in the previous chapter), and, after 1669 the salt monopoly had to take back control and management of the San On salt fields. The salt monopoly tried to find and bring back those salt workers who had survived the evacuation, and to recruit new salt workers, not very successfully; the numbers were to remain, throughout the eighteenth century, far fewer than there had been in the Ming. In fact, the San On salt fields did not fully recover from the disasters of the Coastal Evacuation until the nineteenth century.

Since the salt fields were in so fragile a state in the post-evacuation period, the salt fau had to be once again leased to merchants. Wong San-man (王新民, Wang Xinren) leased the San On fau in 1668, and another merchant, Cheng Kwing-tsun (鄭迵

珍, Zheng Jiongzhen) took over the lease in 1671. The shortage of workers, and the inability of the salt monopoly to get enough salt to meet the quotas, led to great pressure being put on the salt workers; their hardships were, doubtless, a major reason why the salt monopoly found it so difficult to recruit new salt workers.

Furthermore, the huge increase in the number of deep-sea fishing boats at the beginning of the eighteenth century put the system under ever greater strain: there was not enough salt to go round, the few salt workers could not make enough, and the people who needed salt were quarreling over who should get it. In particular, the county of Tsang Shing (增城, Zengcheng) which had traditionally bought its salt in San On was finding it impossible to buy enough.[27]

To add to the problems, the central imperial authorities tended to take the view that the salt merchants were wealthy, and that the central authorities were not getting a fair share of this wealth. However, this seems to have been far from the truth in San On, where dealing in salt seems always to have been a rather marginal commercial undertaking. In the middle Ming, in accordance with this belief, the local salt taxes were raised sharply (1542: all excess salt was to be taxed before sale), causing "hardship to the salt workers" (竈民受困矣), but these additional taxes were "little by little" removed: by the later sixteenth century things were back to the earlier situation, when excess salt was sold untaxed.[28] The reason these higher taxes caused hardship at the grass roots salt worker level was that no increase was permitted in the price to be paid for the consumption quota salt by the end consumer: the extra taxes were to be met by the salt workers and salt merchants, mostly by the salt workers.

In the period immediately after the rescission of the Coastal Evacuation edict, the Kang Xi central authorities tried to do the same thing. In 1681–1682, the tax paid to the salt monopoly for the fau by the salt workers was doubled, and certain other imposts on the salt workers were raised. As in the Ming, however, no increase was permitted in the price for the consumption quota salt, so causing "distress throughout the salt making areas" (四鄉苦之).[29] This led the magistrate (either An Yumei, 1684–1687 or Jin Wenmo, 1687–1694, or possibly Ding Tangfa, 1694–1700) to send a very impassioned petition to the high provincial authorities begging that the taxes be lowered, as the tax rises were harsh, and discriminatory, affecting only the poor salt workers. Anyone could see that the salt workers were "poor and weak, and in desperate need of assistance" (少為清豁, 其于貧竈, 豈曰小補之哉).[30] However, nothing came of this petition. Indeed, the taxes on the salt fields were raised again, and very sharply, in 1717, and once again the price the end consumer was to pay for the consumption quota salt was not raised.[31] As a result, the local salt trade ceased to be even marginally profitable, and the local salt merchants, facing bankruptcy, all retired from the business, forcing the government to run the salt fields directly, using government boats to transport the salt.

This unsatisfactory situation seems to have continued until 1737 when the viceroy dropped the salt taxes within Kwangtung by 40%, thus allowing salt merchants to come back into business. The viceroy achieved this, it would seem, by formally dropping the salt tax paid for the furnace lands by 40–60% (this was a provincial tax, and could be dropped without reference to the central state authorities), and by increasing the weight of the

Kwangtung bau (包, the unit of weight used in the salt trade), so that the state salt taxes, paid on the bau, dropped sharply when calculated against the previous weight of the bau.[32] The viceroy ordered that the "Swatow bau" was to be used throughout Kwangtung: this was the bau traditionally used in Swatow (汕頭, Shantou) for the salt trade; it was made up of catties weighing 18 standard taels, and was thus about an eighth larger than the standard catty. These actions allowed the viceroy to drop the salt taxes, without drawing the attention of the central authorities to what he was doing.

Even after 1737, however, the salt taxes were still high, even if they had been dropped back to a level which allowed merchants to re-enter the trade: the action taken by the viceroy brought the taxes back to the levels they had stood at the end of the seventeenth century, when the impassioned appeal against them noted above was presented. Another appeal seems to have been made for a further reduction in the taxes. There is a comment in the 1819 gazetteer to the effect that the level of taxes after 1737 made the quotas "difficult to meet, and that a further reduction would be a very welcome thing" (酌盈劑虛, 撫恤鹽賈, 可謂法良意美矣). This is probably an extract from something written by one of the magistrates, perhaps Tang Ruoshi (1744–1745) or Wang Dingjin (1746–1751).[33]

The fau set up by Zhou Xiyao were to be re-arranged in 1749, with the Pearl River fau centralised at Pang Shing (彭城, Pengcheng, just outside Nam Tau) and with two major new "subordinate fau" (子埠) established, at Cheung Chau (長洲, Changzhou), in today's New Territories, and at Sha Yue Chung (沙漁涌, Shayuyong), near Yim Tin (鹽田, Yantian), on Mirs Bay, for the greater convenience of the fisher people, supported by a fleet of six vessels to counter smuggling (巡船六隻查緝走私). The Pang Shing Fau was designed essentially for sale of salt destined for the rural populations of San On and Tung Kwun (山埠), and those at Cheung Chau and Sha Yue Chung predominantly for sale of salt to the fisher people (海鹽).[34] At Cheung Chau a "salt market" was set up, at the southern end of the town, where the salt merchants stored their salt and sold the salt to the fishermen. The county stipulated that the salt sold there, and at Sha Yue Chung, was to be sold to the end consumer at 0.007 taels a catty (12½ cash), a reasonable figure.[35]

* * *

These constant changes in the way the San On salt fields were run caused long-term problems, throughout the late seventeenth and eighteenth centuries. Salt output started to decline, and the local salt fields became steadily less and less efficiently run. By the later eighteenth century, many of the salt workers "existed in name only" (有名無實) — they had become either full-time farmers (by this date the furnace lands, originally probably rather poor-quality single-cropping arable land, after several centuries of work, were doubtless much more fertile double-cropping land), or they had become artisans. These nominal salt workers were paying their taxes in purchased salt.[36] By the end of the eighteenth century the San On salt fields were seen as a hopeless case. In 1789, the viceroy ordered them all closed down. He ordered that the taxes previously received from them be cancelled (taxes were raised slightly from the other Kwangtung salt fields to offset the loss), and that the salt monopoly posts for them be abolished, and ordered that "the salt fields be converted to rice fields" (鹽田池漏拆毀淨盡淡改作稻田).

Unfortunately, the salt field sites were mostly far too saline to be used for arable. The viceroy sent experts to report, and had eventually to accept that only a minority could be converted as he wished.[37] He insisted, however, on cancelling the taxes and abolishing the salt monopoly posts (1801). He then leased the remaining salt field areas at a high annual rent (1,000 taels a year), but zero tax, as salt fields, to merchants who were given a free hand to sell their salt as they wished within San On County. They were not, however, permitted to sell it inland through Canton, or along the coast. The leases were issued by the provincial treasurer for ten-year terms. The lessees were to bring in gangs of salt workers from other salt working areas down the coast for the term of their lease — there were to be no more permanently resident salt workers. Existing salt working families were amalgamated with the general village communities of the areas where they lived, and their holdings of furnace lands were converted to standard taxed arable land, paying only the standard land tax to the magistracy. The salt monopoly was to have no further supervisory contact of any kind with these salt fields — it would seem that the viceroy was entirely exasperated with the salt monopoly.

This system remained in force throughout the nineteenth century, and was kept in being by the Hong Kong government for the New Territories salt fields until they ceased to operate in the 1960s (apart from disallowing the lessee the local monopoly he had previously enjoyed).[38] This free market high rent but zero tax system worked well: it would seem that output rose sharply, and the efficiency of the salt fields improved markedly. However, the abolition of the salt taxes and the salt monopoly posts meant that the San On salt fields disappeared from the central government notice: the great 1906 summary of the salt trade in China thus ignores them.[39] The system as finalised in 1801 was able to work because of the huge local market for salt implied by the large local fishing fleet, and, after 1841, by the new city of Hong Kong.

It would thus seem that Yu Zhu, Li Xuan, and Zhou Xiyao's proposals, that the salt monopoly be left basically powerless in San On, and that the local salt trade be conducted at communally operated licensed fau, once implemented, went a long way to solving the salt trade problems of the area at that date, even if problems arising from the Ming-Qing handover bedeviled the local salt trade for the following century, until the viceroy's root and branch reforms of 1789–1801.

7

Corruption

Confucianism was the Chinese imperial state philosophy. All officials in the empire were expected to conduct themselves and the business of state they were involved with in accordance with the precepts set down by Confucius and elaborated by his followers; the precepts which form the Confucian way. Officials of the state were expected at all times to conform with this Confucian way, and to act at all times as Confucian superior men (君子), committed to giving everything they had to the service of the people: they were to be not only men of integrity, efficient and intelligent, but also hard-working, frugal, and utterly dedicated; men who would never dream of corruption. They should at all times be "close to the people", full of concern for their problems, affectionate and understanding towards them, while at the same time being awesome figures, who would discipline the people for any infraction of the right way of life: in short, true "father and mother officials".[1] Such an official would be respected, the state believed, even revered, by the people, who would live lives of virtue thanks to his example and leadership. The Chinese imperial state tried to ensure that all its officials were Confucian superior men. By appointing graduates of the imperial examinations as officials, Kui Yan or Tsun Sz, the state could at least be sure of the officials' intelligence and their grasp of Confucian ethics and principles.

Prospective officials, often only appointed when they reached the age of 50 or even 60, would have started to study the Confucian classics from the age of about 5, so that, by the time they were appointed county magistrates they would have spent about 50 or 55 years in which a good deal of their waking hours had been spent reading and thinking about the Confucian way, and so they would have been thoroughly imbued with the ethics of Confucianism.

Unfortunately, stories abound from the last thousand or so years of the Chinese imperial period of county magistrates who were far from righteous and benevolent, who did not do everything they could for the good of the people, but who were venal and corrupt and self-serving, and who made little or no attempt to ensure that their junior staff behaved properly. As is so common, reading these stories led many people to tar all county magistrates with the same brush, and assume they were all as venal and corrupt as the men portrayed in the stories.

If the magistrates have, over the last thousand years, received something of a poor press and given fuel to the public perception of them as disreputable, this is, however, nothing in comparison with the extremely poor reputation that persists of the magistracy underlings, who were, almost universally, considered utterly corrupt. Huang Liu-hung said that a magistrate of integrity would have to spend a great deal of his time supervising his underlings, to stamp out any corruption among them as it arose. His manual for local magistrates, was, to a large extent, a discussion of commonly found corrupt practices by magistracy underlings, with suggestions as to how they could be dealt with, although he stresses that magistrates would always be able to find dependable and uncorrupt clerks and runners within his staff.[2] Bradly Reed's book also shows how easy it was for magistracy underlings to slip into corruption, although there were nonetheless plenty of magistracy underlings in Ba County who were reasonably uncorrupt and dependable.[3]

In part, this public perception of the magistrates and their staff as unscrupulous was because the system was dangerously open to corruption, with corrupt acts subject to few restraints except the consciences and moral sensitivities of the county magistrates.[4]

* * *

At the heart of the problem was that the county magistrates and their staff were not paid a realistic wage. In the late Ming and early Qing, a San On magistrate was paid only 45 taels a year.[5] This is only 220 cash a day. Since the average daily wage of a coolie (an unskilled labourer) in Hong Kong was between 35 and 230 cash a day in 1867, and 200 cash a day in the 1890s,[6] even assuming a substantial inflation over the preceding 200 years, the pay given to a late Ming or early Qing San On magistrate was clearly extremely low. From the Yongzheng period (雍正), 1723–1735, county magistrates were paid a much more realistic wage: in Kwangtung, 500–600 taels a year. The additional salary was specifically designed to reduce the risk of corruption: this additional salary was called "preserving virtue in office money" (養廉錢); the cash for this extra salary was found by making the meltage fee a legal surcharge, requiring it to be accounted for, and then redistributing it to the magistrates as additional salary. But for most of the magistrates under discussion here, who were in post before this reform, the pay was totally inadequate.

What is more, a late Ming or early Qing magistrate could not expect to enjoy his salary, minimal though it was, without cutbacks. Every magistrate, on appointment, had to send "gifts" to all his senior officers; that is, to the sub-prefect, prefect, taotai (intendant), provincial governor, provincial treasurer, provincial judge, and viceroy. They then had to send further gifts, every summer and winter (冰敬, "a gift to buy ice" in the summer, and 炭敬, "a gift to buy charcoal" in the winter). These "gifts" were prescribed, and the levels fixed, and were not open to negotiation: they were extra-legal, but were fixed and hallowed by long tradition. If any of these senior officers was replaced, then another gift had to be sent to both the outgoing and the incoming official.[7] The newly appointed magistrate would in turn receive "gifts" from his official assistants, from his clerks and other underlings, and from all the county graduates.[8] A late Ming or early Qing magistrate's first year salary might well have been taken up entirely with these expenses.[9]

It was, furthermore, very common that the provincial authorities, in the execution of their policies for the province, found themselves short of money to undertake them. The usual response was to demand special assistance from the county magistrates (a practice known as tan kuen, 攤捐, "spread out donations, Tanjuan"), in addition to the routine "gifts" which were demanded.

The clearest example of a tan kuen demand about which we have evidence from the San On Gazetteer is the demand for 1,500 tam of grain which Zhou Xiyao received in 1643, to help the provincial authorities pay the salaries of their soldiers in the fight against the Yao people. It seems that all the Kwangtung County magistrates were faced with a demand for assistance on this occasion (the "donation" was thus "spread out"). While these demands were called "donations", the county magistrates were not given any discretion in the matter: the provincial authorities required this grain to be sent, and the magistrates had to find what was demanded. As mentioned in Chapter 4, Zhou Xiyao wrote saying that the 1643 demand was quite impossible and could not be met, but the response from the provincial authorities was unhelpful: the grain had to be found. This sort of demand was extra to the taxes, and had to be met from extra-legal sources. Magistrates always had to be ready to respond to such demands, which at times were frequent, and could come without warning.[10]

In addition to this, a county magistrate had to pay substantial sums to entertain any of his senior officers (together with their accompanying staff) when they visited his county, for instance, for a routine check on the work of the magistracy.[11] He had to fund all maintenance work on government buildings in his county, and to pay for the cleaning, repairs, and servicing of the yamen buildings and offices, as well as to fund all public works in his county, without any income to allow for any of this.[12] He also had to find funds for any emergency or special expenditure in his county, again without any funds to cover such expenses.

On top of this, the magistrate, as the leader of the community, the "father and mother of the people" (父母官), was always expected to take the lead in any county donation drive. A magistrate could scarcely expect the leaders of the county community to be generous if he did not head the donation list himself. Such donation drives, to fund important public works, or to provide assistance to those suffering from some natural disaster, were a common occurrence, and would have led to a significant cutback in the magistrate's income.

* * *

The Chinese imperial authorities were conscious that, if they did not keep taxes low, there would be unrest. As a result, the imperial taxes were mostly paid on a fixed and unchangeable quota basis. The county magistrates were required to send set sums to the provincial authorities each year as their tax quotas. The two major taxes were the land tax and the salt tax. The land tax for San On was set at a fixed sum in about 1582, and was to remain effectively unchanged until the end of the imperial period, and the salt tax was prescribed from the early southern Sung (in the twelfth century).[13] Even the fish tax was paid by way of an unchangeable annual sum, and had been since before the establishment of the county of San On in 1573.[14]

This meant the taxes were not increased with the steady increase in population from the early eighteenth century, which in effect meant that the real burden of the taxes decreased, since the fixed amount due was divided among ever more households. In the late eighteenth century Lord Macartney, an acute observer, was sure that China was taxed at rates very much lower than Ireland, which was the lowest taxed area of Europe at that date, even allowing for bribery and extra-legal surcharges.[15] While this freezing of the taxes was certainly effective in reducing unrest, it meant that the Chinese imperial government never had enough cash to fund its bureaucracy adequately, and no Chinese government office ever had enough cash from state sources to function effectively.

At the very least, the chronic and systemic shortage of cash within the magistracies made corruption a more attractive option than it otherwise would have been.[16]

In sophisticated, modern territories, what the government can charge is carefully and clearly set out in the law, individual government offices do not have to find the cash they need to function, and there can be no question as to what is, or is not, within the scope of the law. But the situation was nothing like so clear in traditional China.

To traditional Chinese Confucian scholars, what a modern lawyer would consider corruption consisted of two separate things. On the one hand, there was the case where a government official would take money to turn a blind eye to a criminal breach of the law, or would commit a crime himself. Examples would include, for instance, having a criminal released for a consideration; having the criminal punished as if for a less serious crime than the one he was guilty of; accepting payment to issue a biased judgement in court; or taking a cut from the income his junior staff were getting for doing some similar illegal act. For this sort of act, Chinese scholars were as unanimous as western scholars in castigating them as utterly unacceptable in every circumstance. The Chinese imperial law code, both the Ming and the Qing code, punished such acts very seriously, even with capital punishment in some circumstances.[17]

There are no cases within the San On Gazetteer where such serious acts of corruption are mentioned involving any magistrate. At the least, no San On magistrates are recorded as having been dismissed from their posts for such acts.

The gazetteer does, however, record many places where magistrates did not commit such acts when the opportunity to do so came their way. Magistrate Yu Zhu could thus easily have overlooked the improprieties he discovered in the procurement of horses, for a consideration, and even more easily he could have ignored, for a share in the illegal income, the corruption in the county granaries. He might similarly have left the Mau Chau garrison extorting the salt workers, and profited from doing so. Magistrate Li Xuan could just as easily have ignored the payoffs forced from the salt workers by the lessee of the Nam Tau pier. Zhou Xiyao equally could have turned a blind eye to the problems at the Nam Tau pier. He could similarly have very easily ignored the problem of false government patrol vessels for a share of the profit. He could even more easily have "failed to notice" the activities of the wealthy clans of the county in forcing newcomers to become their tenants. He wanted donations from those clans for his many public works projects, and quietly letting the wealthy clans have their way would clearly have made such donations easier to get. Had he "overlooked" their actions, he would have been allowing corrupt considerations to bias his actions, even if he did not profit personally. Just as with Yu Zhu, Zhou Xiyao could very easily have overlooked corruption in the county granaries. In all of these cases, and many others recorded in the gazetteer, the magistrates did not accept corrupt money to ignore the illegalities, but took action to reform the position and eradicate the criminal acts. They were not always successful in eliminating such crimes in the long term, but, at the least we can see that they did not themselves take money to ignore the situation. In all of these circumstances actions which were criminal under the Ming code had taken place.

* * *

The second area of corruption was far less clear-cut. Clearly, magistrates had to find some other source of income apart from their salaries. They and their staff had to eat, feed, house, and clothe their families, and to educate their sons. The magistrates had to repay debts amassed before they became magistrate — Du Fengzhi worked for the viceroy for four years as an expectant official before being posted to Kwong Ning; he received no salary, and consequently amassed large debts, which were increased by the very stiff fee he had to pay for the posting.[18] Somehow, essential public works had to be funded, and the yamen and other public buildings maintained and, where necessary, renovated. The traditional gifts to the magistrates' senior officers had to be found, and tan kuen demands for assistance from the province had somehow to be met.

The sources of additional income were excess tax, customary fees, and donations. All these were extra-legal, and were contrary to the letter of the law.[19] In the late Ming and early Qing, the law stated that no charges other than those stipulated in the law code were legal, but, at the same time, the imperial authorities set up a system in which additional charges could not be done without since the magistracies could not possibly meet their responsibilities on salary alone. Unless the imperial authorities were willing to increase taxes, and this they steadfastly refused to do, then the only alternative available to the magistracies was extra-legal income. In each of these three sources mentioned, the additional income was not in itself generally regarded as improper by Chinese scholars or by the local county community, but only the abuse of it. Excess tax was thus an acceptable form of income, but it could easily become "squeeze" (撝詐) which was unacceptable: customary fees were acceptable, but they could easily drift into "evil customs" (陋規), which were not; donations were acceptable, but similarly could easily be abused.[20] Huang Liu-hung was fully aware of the fact that magistrates could not function without receiving customary fees and surcharges: these "could not be done without", but he goes on to show how they could be abused.[21]

What Confucian scholars said was necessary was for magistrates to draw a clear and firm line between the acceptable and the unacceptable, and only use the acceptable forms of extra-legal income. Unfortunately, there was no agreed place where the line should be drawn: this was left to the moral sensitivities of each individual magistrate, and, to some extent, to the customs which had developed over time in that particular magistracy. There was, therefore, a broad grey area between the acceptable and unacceptable, and some magistrates could very easily accept forms of income which more stringent moralists would reject as "evil customs" or "squeeze".

If the tax income of any county was higher than the annual tax quota required to be sent to the provincial authorities, then the magistrate could spend the excess, to a large extent, as he wished. Despite the fact that excess tax was, strictly speaking, illegal under the Ming code, nonetheless, so long as the tax quota was duly remitted, there was no control by provincial authorities as to whether there were any excess taxes collected, and there was no audit by senior provincial organs on expenditure of excess tax income. Furthermore, the county magistrates were not required to account for such expenditure. It was assumed that any surplus tax income there might be would be spent on worthy projects, and that the magistrate, the man on the spot, would know best what those were. If there was little surplus tax income, however, then, unless the county magistrates had substantial private income, it was difficult for them to cover their office expenses, to meet tan kuen demands, or, still less, to initiate public works projects in the county, no matter how desirable.

T'ung-tsu Chü suggests that very few magistrates were able to meet their tax quotas in the nineteenth century,[22] but his examples are all drawn from heavily-taxed areas in central China: in Kwangtung, which was much less heavily taxed, it seems certain that the county magistrates were usually able to collect all the taxes due under their quotas in the middle and late Qing, and, indeed, to gather excess tax as well, often in substantial amounts.[23] Even in the late Ming and early Qing, as Zhou Xiyao's writings make clear, the magistrate was usually able to collect the taxes, albeit with difficulty.[24]

Not surprisingly, county magistrates were always on the lookout for acceptable ways to increase tax income above the quota. This system clearly made corruption easy. Spending tax income which was in excess of the tax quota was not seen by Confucian scholars or the county community as corruption in any sense, but squeezing the inhabitants for tax income that was clearly excessive was, as was pocketing large amounts of excess tax income for self-enrichment. There was, clearly, a broad grey area between the acceptable, and the utterly unacceptable.[25]

The gazetteer gives a number of examples of actions by San On magistrates which brought in some morally acceptable excess tax. The setting up of salt fau by magistrates Yu Zhu and Zhou Xiyao set up a free trade in the salt fields. This involved issuing communal licences to the salt workers, who thereafter paid a small sum to the magistracy on all salt exported, and the magistrate paid the salt monopoly their expected income from the sums paid by the salt workers. This reduced sharply the amount the salt workers had to pay: before these reforms they had been subject to squeeze by corrupt merchants and local military garrisons. There can be little doubt, however, that the income from the salt export fee paid to the magistracy was more than the amount paid to the salt monopoly by the magistracy, so that there would have been some excess tax.

Another similar case seems to have been the "going-out-to-sea tax", which was charged in San On from the late sixteenth century. It seems probable that this was an extra-legal tax charged by the San On magistracy, without formal approval from the imperial or provincial authorities, with the income from it kept by the magistracy. This at least is the implication of the fact that magistrate Yu Zhu was able to reduce the sum paid from one tael to 0.8 tael, and magistrate Li Xuan was able to cancel the tax for impoverished fishing families, without, it would seem, seeking any approval from Canton.[26] This tax would not have been considered extortion as the fishermen were getting a very real benefit in the right to fish in the open sea for very little expenditure.

Another major source of morally acceptable excess tax was land tax charged on newly reclaimed land. Where anyone opened new arable land from the waste by their own labour, and at their own cost, then it was open to them to register the newly reclaimed land for land tax at the magistracy. While most such land was not registered, some was, since there were advantages in having land which paid land tax, especially since it was, in effect, only land tax payers who could sit the imperial examinations.[27] However, any such additional land tax would be extra to the quota, and could be kept back by the magistracy as excess tax.[28] There were doubtless other sums of morally acceptable excess tax received and kept by the San On magistracy.

"Squeeze", however, did occur as well, since several magistrates are said to have eradicated it, including Li Kecheng (1670–1675), and Li Dagen (1784–1788). This is also one possible meaning of the "leniency in the taxes" spoken of about magistrates Chen Liangyan (1622–1624), Chen Gu (1628–1631), Li Xuan (1635–1637), Ding Tangfa (1694–1700), and Duan Yangsheng (1724–1725): these magistrates were, clearly, rejecting morally unacceptable excess tax income.[29]

* * *

Clerks and runners were paid only a pittance (supernumerary clerks and runners were not paid any salary),[30] certainly less than a coolie, and the wages of the clerks were cancelled in 1662 altogether.[31] Extra-legal customary fees brought in most of the income of the magistracy staff, and, indeed, of the magistrate himself. "Fees were collected on every conceivable transaction".[32] These customary fees were mostly fixed and known, and were not negotiable. Yamen staff were expected to charge only the fixed, customary sum: if they tried to squeeze more, then this would be widely condemned. In some provinces, these customary fees were published in the Qing by the viceroy or provincial governor as an edict, and so enjoyed a semi-legal status: in other provinces they were fixed and known, if not formally published in a schedule.[33]

The most important of these fees were those for allowing a document or person into the yamen, for writing a document, for fixing the seal of the yamen onto a document, and the fee for closing a case, together with the fees charged for work undertaken outside the yamen.[34] No-one could enter the yamen without paying the "gate fee" (開門費), except where they wanted to attend a court hearing, or to report a crime; if they wished to report a crime they could demand to speak with the magistrate, or whoever was in charge of the magistracy at the time. As noted above, a crime could be reported by "raising a clamour", and so interrupting the magistrate in his court, or by beating a drum or gong hung at the main gate: anyone striking the drum or gong would be conducted by a clerk to the magistrate. If the magistrate found a crime had indeed been committed, and initiated action to investigate it, then the person reporting the crime paid nothing. However, if the magistrate found the report frivolous, then the person reporting it would be beaten, and would have to pay the "gate fee".[35]

When a piece of land paying land tax was sold, and the land tax had to be transferred to the purchaser, the purchaser had to bring the land deed issued by the vendor to the yamen, paying the gate fee for bringing the document into the yamen. Paying this fee had the effect of initiating action in the yamen. The yamen clerks had to issue a kai mei (契尾, qiwei, "memorial"), in duplicate, a chap chiu (執照, zhizhao, "certificate"), again in duplicate, and two pairs of tax receipts for the first year's taxes as paid by the purchaser (one pro forma, showing the nominal grain paid in, the other showing the silver actually paid), both in duplicate. For each of these eight documents an "ink and paper fee" (墨紙費) had to be paid. The original land deed required four yamen seals to be impressed on it, marking the stages of its process through the yamen, the kai mei had the seal impressed across the two copies, as did the two copies of the chap chiu, and across each pair of tax receipts. A fee had to be paid for each of these eight seal impressions. Finally, all the documents in the case had to be passed to the magistrate in person, who checked them, and impressed his own seal on the original land deed. This marked the formal closure of the case, and allowed the yamen copies of the documents to be filed away.

The fee paid for the impression of the magistrate's seal was more substantial than the fee paid for the magistracy seal. Most of these fees were small (three to five cash) but the total paid might well come to a relatively significant sum, especially if the land being transferred was low in value. No receipts were issued for these fees. In addition to these, there was an ad valorem (4%) transfer tax on land transfers which had to be paid before the case could be closed and the documents filed away (3% was a state tax, and 1% was a Kwangtung provincial levy paid to the viceroy; both had to be accounted for: ink and paper fees and seal impression fees were also charged on the processing of this tax).

Another important customary fee was the meltage fee, as explained in chapter 4. In San On, the land tax was paid in silver from the late Ming or very early Qing, often very tiny amounts of silver, and not always in the same degree of fineness.[36] However, the provincial treasurer would only accept payments in silver of a standard degree of fineness, and presented in ingots of a standard weight. This requirement was stipulated, in fact, in the Ming code.[37] The silver received in tax, therefore, had to be melted down, purified to the standard fineness, and then cast into standard-weight ingots. This was usually done by a silversmith under contract to the magistracy.[38] To cover the costs of this, every payment of silver received by the magistracy had an ad valorem meltage fee surcharge placed on it. If taxpayers paid in copper cash, then a further fee was charged to convert the copper cash into silver, plus the meltage fee. The meltage fee charged, however, was higher than the actual costs of the purification process, and thus brought in some customary fee income. This was authorized by the emperor in 1724, after which date it became a legal surcharge: before that date it was universally imposed, even if not yet formally approved.[39] Other customary surcharges were also routinely added to the taxes: while the gazetteer does not mention any as being charged in San On, they may well have been.

Li Kecheng banned this meltage fee from being charged in San On, because, he said, following the Coastal Evacuation, San On was just too poor to bear this extra expense at that time. But this was a temporary ban, and San On certainly charged this fee most of the time. It is likely that Li Kecheng paid from his private income for the actual cost of purifying the tax silver and casting it into ingots, since someone had to bear this expense, and it could not be offset against the taxes. Magistrate An Yumei (1684–1687) also ordered this fee not to be charged.[40] However, there can be no doubt that the fee was usually charged, and it certainly was after the county settled down from the chaos of the mid-seventeenth century devastations. In the case of a transfer of land, a meltage fee surcharge would also have been added to the transfer tax.

If any yamen staff had to do work outside the yamen, a fee (the "sandal fee", 草鞋費) was charged for every hour they spent outside the yamen, plus fees to cover meals, and for quarters for the night. If the yamen staff travelled by horse, fees were paid for every hour spent, both for the man and the horse. Expenses met by the travelling yamen staff (for instance, ferry fees, and the costs of meals) had to be reimbursed. When yamen staff went out to collect the taxes, it was, in the Qing, usually a party of at least four or five: a clerk, one or two treasury guards, and one or two runners. Each would expect to be paid his fees for travel and subsistence.

In the event of a criminal case, the yamen would issue summonses to witnesses, and an arrest warrant for whoever was suspected of the crime. Serving such a summons or warrant would usually require two runners, and a treasury guard or two. Each would expect a fee for his travelling expenses, as well as the ink and paper fee for drawing up the document served. The witness or the suspect had to pay these fees as soon as the runners arrived. If they were too poor to pay, the runners would demand payment from the village community in question: someone would have to find the money.

Usually, when runners came to serve a warrant for the arrest of a suspect, they would also arrest everyone else from the community, as possible witnesses: for all such arrests there would be fees charged. The runners would hold hearings. When it was clear that a potential witness knew nothing, they would be released, but usually only after further fees were paid. There were also payments for slackening the chains which were used to bind prisoners, so that they could, for instance, eat on the journey (witnesses in serious criminal cases were also often chained unless they were clearly unlikely to abscond, and were able to pay the fee demanded for being left unchained). This was all usually demanded up front, as were the fees, ostensibly for other expenses that would have to be met en route back to the yamen (payment for food to be given to the witnesses and suspect, for instance, and the gate fee to be charged at the entrance to the yamen). In practice they were charged at a premium above the likely actual expenses. If the community from which the suspect came was poor, the arrival of runners with a warrant could be a financial disaster. Given the ease with which magistracy underlings serving summonses could demand money in excess of the customary fees during the process of serving a summons, Huang Liu-hung stated that the magistrate should take great care in ensuring that any runner ordered to serve a summons was honest and dependable. However, this was not usually possible, because of the need to ensure runners all had an income on which they could live, and this meant they all needed to have the opportunity to carry out such tasks.[41]

Serving arrest warrants was by far the most profitable action for a runner. In fact, they often could not get enough from the fees they received to keep their families unless they were able to serve at least one arrest warrant during the year. There was always a risk that senior runners would take all these plum jobs, causing the other runners to be unable to support their families unless they drifted into serious corruption. In San On, magistrate Qiu Tiqian (1586–1590) therefore ensured that warrants were distributed fairly amongst the runners so that each got a fair crack of the whip. Magistrate Yu Zhu (1594–1599) similarly took care with the allocation of work, especially in poor years, when food rose in price.[42]

When suspects arrived at the yamen and were put in the jail, there were further fees. There was a daily fee for looking after those incarcerated, a fee for relaxing the chains so that the prisoners could eat, and fees for food. Rice and tea were a charge on the taxes, and the magistrate was required to check that they were provided at full weight, and in a fit state to consume, but any other food had to be paid for, plus a fee to the runners for going and getting it and bringing it into the jail. The longer people were held in the jail, the more fees that would be charged. As a result, the better magistrates would ensure that cases were heard as quickly as possible, so that people did not languish in jail, if necessary rising early in the morning to hear them. Rising early to hear cases and so get people out of jail is said of magistrates Zeng Kongzhi (1576–1579), Li Kecheng (1670–1675), An Yumei (1684–1687), Jin Wenmo (1687–1694), and Li Wenzhao (1771).[43]

There were many other customary fees for less routine duties. If a man wanted to establish a "heading" and "entry" in the county land tax register, so that he could pay land tax, then, according to a late nineteenth-century source from Hong Kong, the fee was at that date the huge sum of 100 Hong Kong dollars, which was enough to buy a whole farm.[44] If a man lost a land deed and wanted to take out a certificate of title issued by the magistrate after a search of his records, then this, too, would trigger a substantial fee.[45]

The magistrate himself was not immune from this requirement to pay fees. If he ordered a document to be prepared, then he would have to pay his clerks for doing so, if there was no member of the public who could be required to front the payment, and the same payment to the clerks or copyists would have to be made by the magistrate if he ordered the clerks to draw up a clean copy from a draft prepared by him. The magistrate also had to ensure that his staff, when they carried returns or other documents to Canton, to his superiors, had the cash needed to get the document through the gate and into the yamen of those superior officers.[46]

All of these fees were "customary fees", and were not generally seen as corruption. In those provinces where the governor or viceroy had issued a schedule of acceptable customary fees, it was these which were usually included. Even the most morally inflexible of magistrates would accordingly let them stand, since, without them, the work of the magistracy would immediately come to a complete stop. Thus Li Kecheng, when he expressed his concern about witnesses and suspects absconding over the border of the county, said that it made criminal cases very difficult to close and caused huge financial losses to the families involved. The reason for the huge financial losses would have been that the yamen would have had to issue many summonses and warrants; one set first, and then another after it was shown that someone had absconded rather than respond, and so families would have to find the money to pay the fees repeatedly.[47] There can be no doubt, therefore, that Li Kecheng considered that the fees charged by runners when they went to serve summonses or warrants were acceptable customary fees.

* * *

The practice of the yamen being provisioned at the cost of the merchants in the Nam Tau Market was, however, considered an "evil custom" by a number of magistrates. Zeng Kongzhi (1576–1579) "absolutely eradicated" (警栗税驱) this practice,[48] Li Xuan (1635–1637) eliminated some "small taxes" (集餉) which probably included this practice, Zhou Xiyao (1640–1644) forbade it, as did Li Kecheng (1670–1675) a generation after Zhou Xiyao, as also did magistrate An Yumei (1684–1687), and magistrate Jin Wenmo (1687–1694).[49] In the gazetteer, a number of magistrates are credited with doing away with "evil customs", without specifying exactly what these were. This is said of magistrates Zeng Kongzhi (1576–1579), Chen Gu (1628–1631), Li Xuan (1635–1637), An Yumei (1684–1687), Jin Wenmo (1687–1694), and Ding Tangfa (1694–1700).[50]

Two magistrates, An Yumei (1684–1687) and Wu Yi (1780–1784) are recorded as having considered the practice of their official assistants, clerks and other underlings, and the county graduates, giving presents to every incoming magistrate, and then again every summer and winter thereafter, as improper. An Yumei gave all the money he thus received to the infirm and needy in Nam Tau, while Wu Yi rejected the presents entirely.[51] Probably most of the other magistrates considered these gifts as being hallowed by long tradition.[52]

Another clear case of an evil custom being abolished by the magistrate in San On is the "shue leung tax" (薯莨餉). Shue leung is a wild plant which, when macerated, provides a potion which waterproofs rope. All the nets and cordage of fishing boats had to be regularly treated with it, usually twice a year. Villages which had stands of shue leung would take care to preserve them: sale of shue leung to the fisher people was an important source of villager income.[53]

The fisher people paid the fish tax communally, not boat by boat. The communal organisation of the fishermen was called, according to the 1819 gazetteer, the Wan Tung Heung, (溫同鄉, Wentungxiang). At some stage, a "vicious and treacherous" yamen underling (豪猾) named Wang Ning (王寧), instituted a tax on shue leung: the fisher people would communally pay eight taels a year for a permit to allow them to buy this essential material, effectively as an addition to the fish tax. The fisher people petitioned the magistrate, Wu Wenming (1630–1635), against this additional tax, and the magistrate, having looked into it, abolished the requirement to pay this money. The fisher people then came forward with a free will gift of eight taels (five taels for the magistrate in person, and three for the clerks of the magistracy) to recognize the trouble this had caused the magistracy. It was offered to the magistrate by the fisher people leaders, a group of about a dozen, led by four men. The magistrate (by then Li Xuan, 1635–1637) refused the money and returned it to the fisher people leaders: Li Xuan, clearly, was not prepared to accept money for doing away with an evil custom, no matter how much the money was offered as a free will gift.[54] The Wan Tung Heung was called upon by magistrate An Yumei (1684–1687) to repay the arrears of taxes (presumably the fish tax), uncollected since the Coastal Evacuation. The Wan Tung Heung fell into long-term financial problems as a result of this: despite some of the arrears being remitted in 1724, it remained in debt right through until 1819.[55]

It is probable that the fight against evil customs was almost perpetual. When a reforming magistrate was in post, the yamen staff would behave properly: this is specifically recorded of magistrates Li Xuan (1635–1637), An Yumei (1684–1687), and Wang Dingjin (1746–1751),[56] but when the reforming magistrate was posted away, then, very often, the old bad practices were quietly brought back in, until another reforming magistrate noticed what had happened. In the case of San On, this is particularly clear for the evil custom of requiring merchants to provision the yamen for free, which was banned by at least five or six magistrates in turn, and for the extortion involved in underpaying for the courier soldier horses which was outlawed by at least three.

Sometimes corrupt junior officials were thrown into jail. Magistrates Li Xuan (1635–1637) and An Yumei (1684–1687) are both recorded as having jailed corrupt junior staff. An Yumei is said to have felt as much heartache when he found a corrupt junior official as he would have done if his parents had died.[57]

* * *

Despite the customary fees the magistrate could expect, his total income from salary and customary fees together, before the addition of the "preserving virtue in office" money in the Yongzheng period, was still quite inadequate. A magistrate could survive on this income, but only if he was extremely careful with his expenditure, and if he lived a very circumscribed life. Not surprisingly, therefore, the biographies of late Ming and early Qing illustrious magistrates in the gazetteer almost all stress that the magistrate lived a very simple, frugal life, and thus sought no extra income to support a more lavish private lifestyle. At the very least, the biographies stress that the magistrate "carefully distinguished public and private" (公私便之, Yu Zhu, 1594–1599), was "clean and not corrupt" (潔已奉公, Li Jungzhu, 1650–1654), or "was rigid in taking no money for his private life" (冰心鐵面不可干以私, An Yumei, 1684–1687).[58]

Comments of this general character, that the magistrate was frugal, and careful with money, are made of magistrates Chan Liangyan (1622–1624), Chen Gu (1628–1631), Li Xuan (1635–1637), Peng Yunnian (1637–1640), Zhou Xiyao (1640–1644), Li Jungzhu (1650–1654), Jin Wenmo (1687–1694), and Duan Yansheng (1724–1725), as well as Yu Zhu, Li Jungzhu, and An Yumei. After the introduction of the "preserving virtue in office" money, frugality was less frequently mentioned among the virtues of the magistrates, but it was said at least of magistrates Wang Dingjin (1746–1751), Wu Yi (1780–1784) and Li Dagen (1784–1788).[59] Some of the magistrates whose biographies in the San On Gazetteer do not stress their frugality were men with substantial private incomes and therefore not dependent on their salaries and customary fees for their lifestyles, and who thus had no reason for frugality. This is certainly the case for Li Kecheng, and probably for most of the other Kang Xi appointees. However, in the case of Li Kecheng, at least his biography in the Canton prefectural gazetteer, which is not taken from the San On Gazetteer, does say he was "frugal and clean" (廉潔),[60] and it would, therefore, seem that, even though he had substantial private income, he was still careful not to be seen to spend lavishly.

Perhaps the clearest expressions of frugality as a virtue of the magistrates are made in the biographies of magistrates Chen Gu (1628–1631) and Peng Yunnian (1637–1640). Of Chen Gu it states that "he was extremely frugal, and had no clothes-boxes other than the simplest, and, in the Summer his clothes would get sweaty, but he was not able to change them, even when there were visitors" (正直廉平, 笥無廉衣, 夏日衣污而解客至),[61] and of Peng Yunnian it states, "he was frugal...and had very little luggage when he left" (質儉寬厚...瞻之去日行李蕭然).[62]

Alongside the expressions of frugality many of the magistrates are recorded as having worked hard: diligence was another virtue worthy of recording. Many magistrates are spoken of as hard-working: typical are Jin Wenmo, who was "diligent in his duties, rising early and going to bed late" (勤於政事夙興夜寐),[63] or magistrate Wang Dingjin (1746–1751), who died of overwork.[64]

If excess tax could be used to pay for the routine running expenses of the yamen, and customary fees for the living expenses of the yamen staff, public works in San On usually had to be funded by donations from the leaders of the county community. The magistrate did not have the powers that the provincial authorities had to demand tan kuen support. The magistrate had to convince the leaders of the community that the public works in question were vital, and get their support. The magistrate, therefore, had to "call the gentry together" (集紳士,

Ding Tangfa), "appeal to the gentry for donations" (乃倡率紳士捐助鳩工, Zhang Mingda), or "solicit donations of salaries" (乃設法捐, Jin Wenmo).[65] Once the support of the leaders of the county community was secured, however, the magistrate could probably "lean" on those of the wealthy members of the community who were less enthusiastic. These "donations", therefore, while not being quite forced donations, were still probably not entirely free will.

If there was some essential public work in the county, the magistrate could petition the provincial authorities to grant some money to fund the work, but this was usually, as we have seen, unsuccessful. Thus magistrate Chen Gu was refused provincial money for the construction of the two new watchtowers he wanted to improve the defences of Nam Tau. Zhou Xiyao was denied funds to raise the walls of Nam Tau, to build his two new forts, and to rebuild the county Temple of Confucius and county school. Li Kecheng arrived in San On with provincial money to restore the fortifications of the county, and to rebuild the yamen after the devastation of the Coastal Evacuation, but, when the work he had started was destroyed in typhoons and had to be restarted, twice, he was refused any additional money. He also was not granted provincial money for the essential reconstruction of the county Temple of Confucius and county school.

Similarly, magistrate Zhang Mingda (1678–1684) failed to get any financial aid to restore the county Temple of Confucius and county school after the buildings were leveled in a bandit attack; magistrate Jin Wenmo (1687–1694) was refused money to rebuild the drum tower of the yamen and to restore the city walls after they were destroyed or badly damaged in a typhoon; magistrate Ding Tangfa (1694–1700) was denied funds to build a county free school, despite "repeatedly" begging for help (these three magistrates, like Li Kecheng, as noted above, donated money from their own resources towards these public works). Jin Qizhen was similarly refused cash for the essential dredging of the river, despite several requests for help.[66] It was assumed that the county magistrates would make and keep savings and would thus have cash in hand for any such essential public work: this, however, assumed that there were savings. In the late Ming and early Qing the San On magistracy never had savings sufficient to undertake these public works projects: the only way out was to seek donations from the wealthy of the county.

As the table below shows, the gazetteer includes references to some 16 public works projects between 1620 and 1785 funded from donations from the county community, nine from the period 1670–1713.

Table 2
Donations for Public Works and Destructive Events in San On

Magistrate	Date	Public Work Undertaken	Destructive Event
Chen Gu	1629		Plague
	1630		Siege of Nam Tau
	1631	Two watchtowers	
	1633		Bandit attack
Wu Wen-ming	1634		Siege of Nam Tau
	1635		Siege of Nam Tau
Li Xuan	1636		Famine

Magistrate	Date	Public Work Undertaken	Destructive Event
Zhou Xiyao	1640	Raising walls of Nam Tau	
	1641		Bandit attack
	1641	Pier-head fort built	
	1641	Rebuild of county school	
	1641	Lotus Path Fort built	
	?1643		Plague
	1643		Typhoon
Zheng Wenhuang	1647		Siege of Nam Tau
	1648		Plague and famine
Ma Yimao	1656/7		Siege of Nam Tau
-	1662/9		Coastal Evacuation
-	1669		Typhoon
Li Kecheng	1671		Typhoon
	1671	Rebuild of county school	
	1672		Bandit attack
	1673		Typhoon
	1673	Second rebuild of Yamen	
	1673	Second rebuild of walls of Nam Tau	

Magistrate	Date	Public Work Undertaken	Destructive Event
	1673	Second rebuild of walls of Tai Pang	
Luo Mingke	1676		Siege of Nam Tau
	1677		Typhoon
Zhang Mingda	1679	Repair yamen	
	1679	Rebuild of county school	
	1680		Bandit attack
An Yumei	1686		Typhoon and flood
Jin Wenmo	1687/94	Repair of yamen and walls	
Nam Tau			
Ding Tangfa	1694	Repair county school	
Jin Qizhen	1700/13	Dredge river	
Duan Yansheng	1724/25	Building of Wenkang Academy	
Wu Yi/Li Dagen	1784/85	Repair of Wenkang Academy	

It can be seen from Table 2 that donations were sought from the wealthy of the county on a very regular basis, especially between 1631 and 1713.

Many of the wealthy families from whom these donations would have been sought were from the Nam Tau mercantile community. However, that community was centred in the commercial suburb of the city (南頭鎮), outside the safety of the city walls. This commercial suburb had been repeatedly ravaged by siege, plague, flood, and the Coastal Evacuation between 1630 and 1686, as Table 2 shows. It is, in fact, surprising that the merchants had any spare cash to donate to the magistrate's public works projects in these years, when they would have had to rebuild and rehabilitate their business premises anything up to eight times in the same period.

There is some suggestion, particularly in the period 1687–1713, that magistrates, where this was feasible, would collect money for only one project at a time, but Zhang Mingda collected for two projects, and Zhou Xiyao and Li Kecheng for four each. Given that, in Li Kecheng's time, as well as a devastated mercantile community, the rural population may have been barely a quarter of what it had been in Zhou Xiyao's time, and given that every rural family in the county would have been strapped for cash for the rebuilding of their homes, and the rehabilitation of their fields, it is amazing that he was able to find as much as he did. It is probable that Li Kecheng collected for some of his projects in only one part of the county (e.g. donations for the walls of Tai Pang may well only have been sought from the Tai Pang part of the county). Despite this, and even taking into account Li Kecheng's moral authority as a major donor himself from his private income, nonetheless, he must have been pushing the wealthy of the county to the limit of their capacity to respond.

All the projects which were funded by donations from the county community were entirely desirable and, in most instances, absolutely essential. However, the magistrate's dependence on the leaders of the county community for the cash to fund essential public works, meant that the magistrates, particularly the better, more public-spirited magistrates, were dependent on the county elders, and could not function without their support and backing. The magistrates had to get agreement from the county community before they could move. It is no surprise, therefore, that the Tung Ping Kuk (東平局, "council for peace in the east") became, in practice, more powerful than might have been expected. Magistrate Chen Gu (1628–1631) might have tried to "avoid too much close association with the rich and influential" (不避權貴),[67] but such aloofness could not stand in the face of the relentless year-on-year need for donations from them.[68]

Local government in traditional China always depended on a workable cooperation between the magistrate and the county elite. Over time, however, during the middle and late Qing, the balance of power in the local areas of Kwangtung seems to have shifted more and more towards the local elite. The increase in the power of the elite and their council in San On in this late Ming and early Qing period because of the ever-present need to get donations from them was thus a portent of things to come. In many Kwangtung counties by the 1860s the magistrates had become rather weak in the face of what had evolved into, by then, entrenched gentry power.[69] In the 1850s, the almost total failure of the imperial armed forces against the Taiping meant that, by the 1860s, the army had effectively ceased to function in many Kwangtung counties, and only the gentry-run local militia were available to keep the peace.[70] The high provincial authorities were, by that date, riven with corruption and factionalism. In San On in this period the magistrate was, therefore, entirely unable to stop inter-village wars, of which there were several dozen.[71] Stewart Lockhart believed that, in San On in this general period, no inter-personal civil case could go to the magistrate (unless one or both of the parties to it were gentry) unless it had been before the gentry for arbitration at the local, district, and county levels, thus reducing the magistrate's powers as judicial arbiter sharply. Du Fengzhi also noted that most civil cases arising were being considered firstly by gentry bodies.[72]

In Kwong Ning at the same date, Du Fengzhi found he could not collect the taxes without gentry help, which was only given if the taxes due from the gentry were left uncollected.[73] The only armed forces he could access were the gentry-run militia, the money for which was collected by the gentry, who had set up an extra-legal county likin station to tax all tea, timber, and bamboo leaving the county, and collected and disbursed the income so gained without any input from the magistrate. The magistrate found himself effectively having to rubber stamp gentry decisions in many of his court cases. His senior clerks had been "recommended" by the gentry, and were out of the magistrate's control. Du Fengzhi fought a very fierce battle with his gentry to try to improve the magistrate's power over tax collection, with some success (he eventually managed to collect the taxes due from the gentry leaders), but his weakness in the face of the county gentry is very clear from his diary.[74] In the late Ming and early Qing the balance of power between the magistrates and the county gentry seems to have been much less tilted towards the gentry, but the need for regular donations had started to tip the scales even then.

* * *

It is, nonetheless clear that, although the dividing line between "excess tax" and "squeeze", and between "customary fees" and "evil customs" was not at all clear, and not at all easy to draw, nevertheless, the leaders of the county community felt that many of the San On magistrates did draw the line appropriately, and did administer the county without what the county community considered corruption, despite the constant disasters and pressures the county had to face. The gazetteer also shows how easy it would have been for donations to be abused, although it is clear that the county community considered the 16 cases noted above to have been appropriate, reasonable, and properly spent. That the magistrates were considered generally clean and uncorrupt is particularly clearly shown for the period 1628–1713, when 13 of the 22 magistrates are specifically stated in their biographies in the gazetteer as having been incorrupt, while others of them, like Li Kecheng, whose biography in the San On Gazetteer does not say specifically that he was incorrupt, had substantial private income, and was clearly equally clean, (as, indeed, his biography in the provincial gazetteer specifically states). Huang Liu-hung notes that the magistrate was not all-powerful: it was always open to the senior gentry of the county to petition the high provincial authorities against him if he was seen as seriously corrupt, and there was always the risk of anonymous denunciations of a magistrate's misgovernance being posted up on the walls of the county city — something which would be a major black mark against the magistrate.[75]

Finally, it must be said once again that the biographies in the gazetteer are eulogies, recording only what was good about the magistrates in question. The question must remain open, therefore, as to the character of those administrations in particular about which the gazetteer is silent. The question as to what degree those administrations which are invisible in the records as we have them were as clean as those discussed cannot be answered.

At the least, however, it is clear that many of the San On magistrates were seen by the leaders of the county community as having been clean, uncorrupt, frugal, and careful: this doubtless also implies also that these magistrates were seen as keeping their underlings in line.

The question needs to be asked, if San On was a normal rural county, and if so many of its magistrates were Confucian superior men, acting in accordance with the Confucian way of dedicated, intelligent, and efficient public service and selflessness, and seen as such by the county community they administered, then why do the majority of the people today assume that all imperial county magistrates were corrupt and self-centred? This view has, in fact, become a truism which can be stated in newspapers or novels without needing to be justified. Even today, children leave school in Hong Kong with a fixed idea that imperial county magistrates were all, or almost all, corrupt and that there is nothing positive which can be said of them.

Many people say that their view of the imperial county magistrates was formed by Cantonese opera, either as seen on stage, or on television, in their childhood. In Cantonese opera almost all county magistrates depicted, other than those portrayed as marvellously acute criminal judges, such as Judge Dee or Judge Bao, are shown as being corrupt, cruel, and self-centred, and often as being consumed with lust and greed. Some say that this attitude was reinforced at school, when teachers said that it was a historical fact that few if any imperial county magistrates were anything other than corrupt. Later, many people had this negative view of the imperial county magistrates reinforced when they read classical Chinese fiction, like *Strange Stories from a Chinese Studio* (聊齋誌異)[76] or *The Scholars* (儒林外史).[77] In these books, and many others, county magistrates are usually depicted as corrupt and evil hearted. It is scarcely surprising that a prejudice has arisen, a fixed idea that the magistrates were all corrupt.

A major component of the common view of the magistrates and their staff as corrupt is the heavy fees that were required to be paid when a suspect was arrested, or a summons issued. These fees could easily beggar a poor family, or reduce a whole poor village to penury, and could be a serious burden even to relatively wealthy households. It is clear that these fees were a serious problem to anyone faced with them.

There can be no doubt that runners could be merciless in levying these fees, and that those called on to pay felt the system was cruel. A poor fishermen's village in Hong Kong petitioned the magistrate for assistance in 1803: a totally false accusation had been raised that the villagers had refused to pay their rents, and, as a result, the village had been devastated by runners arriving with summonses; "A gang of runners like tigers, came and disturbed us with their brutal extortion, all very emotional" (串差如虎, 擾詐靡寧, 情極).[78] Doubtless, these views would have been widely held by those who suffered having to meet these fees, no matter how "customary" and "essential" they were.

While these fees were "customary fees", and while collection of them was not usually considered at the time as corruption, nonetheless many people think of them today as extortion or as an evil custom because of the merciless way in which they were exacted and the social devastation they could cause — rather unfairly, since they were essential to the operation of the local government. However, it is very easy from the perspective of today's practices to call all these fees "evil customs", without considering the background which made their collection essential. Cheung Yin, for instance, castigates these payments as both "extortion" and an "evil custom", and Liu Pangjiu similarly calls them all "evil customs".[79]

This, however, seems to be viewing these fees in accordance with today's practices, not those of the seventeenth and eighteenth centuries. It is essential, when looking at magistracy practice in traditional China, to view it as the scholars and gentry of the time did, and not to view them as being unacceptable then, since they would be unacceptable today. These fees were a harsh imposition on those who had to pay them, and they had heavy and serious effects on the households paying them, but they could not be done without while the system stayed as it was, and cannot realistically be called either corruption or extortion. At the same time, the collection of these fees provided abundant opportunity for the appropriation of extra levies, thus leading to the universal belief of the better magistrates that great care had to be taken as to which runners were selected to issue summonses or arrest suspects, and that they should never go out to do so on their own.

8

Conclusions

The area which was to become the county of San On seems to have had, before the eighteenth century, a violent and dangerous history. After a thousand years during which the area is believed to have been under martial law, the establishment of normal Chinese civil law and civil administration, led, in particular in the middle Ming, not to the quiet, rural life its inhabitants can be assumed to have wanted, but to an endless series of attacks by bandits and pirates, taking advantage of the defencelessness of the new settlers, and the absence of any effective military garrisons. The establishment of the new county of San On, in 1573, did lead to a period when bandit attacks were effectively contained, but the increasing decadence and degeneration of the Ming caused the local garrisons to become corrupt and ineffective, and, from 1630, bandits and pirates again dominated the local scene.

The half-century from 1630 to 1686 brought San On to the brink of annihilation. Eleven major bandit attacks, including six sieges of the county city (one of which was successful, in 1676) and a siege of Tai Pang City leading to that city falling to the bandits for nine years, three major attacks of plague (1628, 1643, 1648), famine (1636 and 1648), five ruinous typhoons (1669, 1671, 1673, 1677, 1686), devastating floods (1686), and, on top of everything else, the Coastal Evacuation of 1662–1669, brought the county to its knees. The population collapsed: the figures in the gazetteer suggest that the collapse was, between 1630 and 1670, perhaps something between 64% and 78%. While these figures are not certain, they are probably not too far off the reality. All the public buildings of the county had to be rebuilt several times over. No wonder magistrate Li Kecheng said, in 1670, "if you climbed up to a high place there was nothing to be seen but weeds and ruined walls…how could it be that there was no-one left" (每登高一望荒草頹垣…不可得豈無子遺?).

However, less than 30 years later, at the end of the magistracy of Jin Qizhen (1713), the county was back on track. The population was growing steadily, the public buildings were all rebuilt and in good shape, banditry was under control (there are no recorded bandit attacks between 1680 and 1804), and normality had returned. Famines came no more frequently than was to be expected: about once a generation (1708, 1777–1778, 1786–1787, with a less severe famine in 1757); serious typhoons also came only occasionally (1760, 1761, 1791, 1797); and floods also (1768, 1770). Public works were very few: mostly repairs to the Man Kong Academy in 1724–1725, and 1784–1785.

How had the county managed to weather this terrible time, and return to rural normality, in only one single generation? There can be little doubt that this was due above all to the county magistrates.

In the first 50 years of the county's existence, between 1573 and 1622, there were a handful of magistrates who left good reputations behind them: Wu Daxun (1573–1576), Zeng Kongzhi (1576–1579), Qiu Tiqian (1586–1590), and Yu Zhu (1594–1599). This small number does not necessarily imply that the other magistrates of the period were corrupt and ineffective: the county was running as it should, and there were few crises which might have disturbed the routine of the yamen, and thus have allowed the magistrates to show their mettle. When everything in the county was functioning properly, the magistrates only needed to act in accordance with precedent and practice to keep things as they should be, and the county in this period seems to have been functioning quite normally.

A string of outstanding county magistrates in the late Ming, including Chen Liangyan (1622–1624), Chen Gu (1628–1631), Li Xuan (1635–1637), Peng Yunnian (1637–1640), and Zhou Xiyao (1640–1644), however, can be seen working to try and fend off the ever-growing decadence of the period, as the Ming floundered towards its final collapse. We know most about Zhou Xiyao, but it seems likely that, if we knew more about these other magistrates, we would see similar commitments to dedicated service to the people of the county, similar attempts at reform and similar heartfelt hard work as the details of Zhou Xiyao's administration show so clearly. The collapse of the Ming state, and the ever-growing degeneration of state organs was too great a problem for the magistrates of any one county to withstand, but, nonetheless, these magistrates tried as hard as they could to keep the floodwaters back. Certainly, the county community felt all these magistrates were honourable, hard-working, and incorrupt.

After the coming of the Qing, San On was, for most of the period 1646–1663, in a state of perpetual tension. Bandits, led by Chan Yiu and Lei Man-wing, ravaged the county throughout much of this period. The fortress-city of Tai Pang fell to the bandits in 1647, and was to be held by them until 1657. The county city was under siege in 1647 and again in 1656–1657. Between 1647 and 1656 the constant attacks by the bandits made life in and around Nam Tau very difficult, even when the city was not formally under siege. The country people must have pressed inside the safety of the city walls as refugees, abandoning their fields and homes. Hunger and deprivation would have been, to a greater or lesser degree, perpetual. The soldiers inside the city were quivering on the edge of mutiny because of the lack of food. To top all this, in the middle of this difficult time came the most serious of the three outbreaks of plague that the county was to suffer (1648).

Again, during this strained time there were a string of magistrates who left a very good reputation behind them: Zhang Wenxing (1646–1648), Li Jungzhu (1650–1654) and Ma Yimao (1656–1661). These magistrates were not remembered as reformers, but they were remembered as managing to keep the people alive during the sieges, maintaining morale, and preventing the soldiers from mutinying: acting truly as "father and mother officials". The biography of Ma Yimao makes the endeavours of this string of magistrates very clear:

> He regarded the sufferings of the people as if they were caused by him: in his time, warfare was constant, the fields were abandoned, there was frequent confusion, and the people had no food, but he sorted it all, keeping up the spirits of the people (愷悌成性, 軫恤民難, 有如己饑己溺, 時兵燹多事, 田地荒蕪, 開多混淆, 民苦虛粮, 悉為清出, 以免賠累).[1]

From 1670 to 1713, after the Coastal Evacuation, the county was in desperate need of rehabilitation. Every public building was in ruins: the walls of the two cities, the road forts and fortlets, the yamen, the county school and Temple of Confucius, and the temples of the city. The remnant population was starving, the fields were just weeds and wild things, none of the houses were usable.

The Qing authorities must have considered the rehabilitation of San On a priority, and they seem to have posted to the county men whose loyalty to the Qing was not in question, who had close personal connections with the Qing, and who were highly competent. Most left excellent reputations behind them, especially Li Kecheng (1670–1675), Zhang Mingda (1678–1684), An Yumei (1684–1687), Jin Wenmo (1687–1694), Ding Tangfa (1694–1700), and Jin Qizhen (1700–1713). It was these magistrates who saw to the reconstruction of the public buildings, encouraged the returning people to resume farming, restarted education, and generally got the county back on its feet. Most of these magistrates, but especially Li Kecheng, poured out their own private money to help the county restart and rebound to a state of vigour. The Kang Xi emperor would have had every reason to be pleased with the magistrates his advisors chose for San On. They were a fine group of men: it is a great pity we have so few of the documents of the magistrates, apart from Li Kecheng, especially unfortunate is the relative lack of information on An Yumei, Ding Tangfa, and Jin Qizhen.

After 1713, San On once more became a normal county, quiet and rural: the disasters of the period 1630–1686 were well behind it, and life once again moved into a period of rustic peace and quiet. As with the period 1573–1622, there were few crises, and little opportunity for magistrates to become outstanding. There are a smattering of magistrates in this period who left particularly good reputations behind them; Duan Yansheng (1724–1725), He Mengzhuan (1730–1741), Tang Ruoshi (1744–1745), Wang Dingjin (1746–1751), Li Wenzao (1771), Wu Yi (1780–1784), and Li Dagen (1784–1788), but the other magistrates of the period may well have been just acting in accordance with precedent and practice, and need not have been corrupt or ineffective.

The county gazetteer shows that the late Ming and early Qing San On magistrates constantly had to face huge administrative problems, terrible shortages of money, constant irruptions of banditry and piracy, often ill thought-through interference or lack of support from the magistrates' superiors, to say nothing of dubious support from their junior staff. Nevertheless, many of them clearly struggled to react appropriately to their problems, while preserving their Confucian standards, and to provide to the people of the county an administration which was indeed dedicated to their good, as well as one which demonstrated loyalty and commitment to the imperial state as a whole.

Peter Ng and Hugh Baker speak of "the fewness of the really able men who had ever been set in charge of" San On, but this is a less than charitable judgement. The county was, in fact, administered by a substantial number of genuinely able, honest, hard-working, and decent men. None of them went on to achieve high office, but this was mostly because of the practice of the imperial authorities of posting to San On mostly elderly men in their fifties or even sixties, who retired after this single posting, or perhaps after two or three postings, and who had no chance of showing what they could have done in high office. The magistrates who might have gone on to have a full career, Li Xuan (1635–1637) and Jin Wenmo (1687–1694) began promising careers which were abruptly and prematurely ended, in the one case by the coming of the Qing, and, in the other, by an early death. But the fact that they were not promoted to high office after their time in San On cannot be taken as implying any lack of ability in the San On magistrates.

It is doubtless because of the fixed idea that there is nothing positive to be said of the imperial county magistrates that almost nothing has been done to study them at the local level in recent years, nor to consider their achievements and work within their counties, nor their relationships with their county communities. However, this short study of the San On magistrates shows that this prejudice is not based on very much evidence: many of the San On magistrates in the late Ming and early Qing did give a great deal of thought and effort to the problems of their county.

Appendix 1[1]
Biography of Zhou Xiyao

Zhou Xiyao (周希曜, Chau Hei-yiu), courtesy name Daosheng (道 升, To-shing), was a native of Jingde in Jiangnan Province (江南 旌德). He was the holder of a Kui Yan degree, and was appointed county magistrate in 1640. Methodical in all his administration, he was skillful in managing the economy, and was greatly concerned with the suffering of the people and with providing encouragement for the training of men of ability. He dealt with the evils of the day by such measures as reviving the fishing and salt industries in order to give local people a livelihood again. He stabilised prices out of compassion for the merchants. He coordinated the granaries to stop abuses (併倉儲以革陋規). He forbade extortion in order to root out corruption (禁投獻以絕擄 詐). All of these were examples of good government. Seeing that very few men from San On passed the civil service examinations, he used the large site of the old academy at Man Kong (文 崗) outside the east gate, facing Pui To Mountain (Castle Peak Mountain), and, regardless of the difficulties, built a new school there. Thereafter generations of good scholars were produced, and benefitting the whole county.

Appendix 2[2]
The Evacuation

In the latter half of the seventeenth century, the court became concerned about traitors active at sea, who were raiding the shores and causing trouble. They decided to combat this problem by removing the people: those living beside the sea were required to move inland, and to relocate to places 50 li from the coast. When Taiwan was pacified, and the pirates there put down, the provincial governor, Wang (撫院王, Wong), petitioned that the people be allowed to return to their old homes. The hardships of the evacuation and the inspiration of the return, are worth recording.

The Initial Evacuation

In January, 1662, brigadier-general Zhang (總鎮張, Cheung) came and surveyed the coast. In March 1662 the grand commissioner (大人科) settled the boundary of the area to be evacuated, which amounted to two-thirds of the county. In April 1662 brigadier-general Cao (總鎮曹, Tso), general commandant Ma (總統馬, Ma), and a force of regular troops (營兵) were sent to secure the new boundary, and to drive the inhabitants inland. At first, the people did not understand what the evacuation meant, even though proclamations had been posted up. Only when the soldiers arrived did the meaning become clear. They had to abandon their property, and set off to unknown destinations inland with their families. Some died sleeping in the open. Others sought refuge in Tung Kwun (東莞), Kwai Shin (Guishan, 歸善, today called Huizhou, 惠州) and yet others moved on further still and were scattered in many places.

In 1663 His Excellency, Hua (大人華, Wa), the viceroy, Lu (總督盧, Lo), and the high official, Shang (公府尚, Sheung: this is Shang Kexi), inspected the boundary.

The Second Evacuation

In September, 1663, the grand commissioners Yi and Shi (大人伊, 石; Yi, Shek) surveyed the seacoasts of Kwangtung (廣東, Guangdong) again and decided that the whole county should be evacuated. However, viceroy Lu noted that most of the county had already been emptied and so he ruled that only 24 village areas in the eastern roads and western roads parts of the county (東西二路二十四鄉) should be evacuated. In March 1664 military commandant Jiang Hongrun (城守蔣弘閏) and county magistrate Zhang Pu (知縣張璞, Cheung Pok: county magistrate of San On 1663) expelled the people of the 24 village areas. Thereafter, the grand commissioners (大人) inspected the boundaries once every quarter.

At first those expelled had high hopes of returning. However, after they had spent much time wandering with no way of making a living, husbands abandoned their wives, fathers left their children, and elder brothers their younger brothers. Husbands wept and said to their wives: "Go off as a maidservant: take service with some other family in order to preserve your life" (汝

且跟他人為婢以免死). Fathers and elder brothers with tears in their eyes ordered their sons and younger brothers, saying: "Go off and work as a servant in some other family to keep your life" (汝且傭工于他族, 以養汝生). Many wealthy families even took the sons and daughters of those evacuated, without making any payment: many thousands were treated in this way (時豪民富, 客常有不用貲買, 而拾養遷民子女者, 奚啻千百焉). Young men went to military camps to find food. Others begged for food in whatever places they found themselves, beseeching assistance along the roadsides. Yet others, men who valued their dignity and could not bear the shame of begging, but could find no solution, took poisonous plants, squeezed out the juices, and drank them, dying together with their families.

The court, and the county magistracy, tried to find ways of dealing with the problem, but the numbers were too great, and nothing could be done.

The Return

In February 1668, the governor, Wang (巡撫王, Wong), petitioned that the evacuation be rescinded.

He petitioned the higher authorities to rescind the evacuation, the coasts being now secure. He acted together with the prince of Pingnan (平南王: this is Shang Kexi), and the viceroy, Zhou (總督周, Chau). The local people were filled, one and all, with joy. They rejoiced no matter how far away they were. In November 1668, the viceroy, Zhou, petitioned that the evacuation be rescinded first, and later that the closure of the sea be lifted. The evacuated people were desperately eager to come back, being overjoyed at the mere rumour of what was in the wind.

In February 1669, the evacuation was finally rescinded, and the people were permitted to return to their property, the traitors having finally been overcome. The people came back, leaping for joy, as though they had been released from prison.

In August 1669, by imperial command, the county was re-established. In the meantime, as a temporary measure, county affairs were dealt with by the assistant magistrate of Panyu (番禺縣丞, Pun Yue).

In August, 1670, Li Kecheng (李可成, Lei Ho-shing) the county magistrate took up his post. As soon as he arrived, he saw those who had been driven out and who had not yet returned to their homes milling around aimlessly. One after another the newly returned died where they stood, for they had not so much as a hut to shelter in (其一二新複殘黎, 亦無廬舍棲止). There were no sounds to be heard but wailing and sobbing, for they had gathered together in great crowds from many places (欷歔久之, 因而多方招集). He tried to offer them comfort. He gave donations to the people (民乃多賦) as they returned: as it says in the Return (歸來): "the people could now till their fields and peacefully live in their homes" (且畋厥田, 寧厥居). For several years, these praises were the sole subject of the songs the people sang.

As the Analects say, the evacuation was so bitter, with the abandonment of houses and land, that the people were forced to move from ruined homes into new houses of mats and wild grasses. For a long time it was impossible to get rid of vagrants and beggars. What is more, in the poorer families which had lost their livelihoods and were facing total destitution, often fathers would not care for their sons, and husband and wife would no longer care for each other. The rejected came to the army camps, and tried to be taken on as slaves (奴), so difficult it was to keep body and soul together. By the time they returned, more than half had died (及復歸, 死喪已過半). Those lucky enough to survive and return found themselves without plough cattle or the cash to buy them, were thus incapable of clearing away the weeds, and found great difficulty in merely keeping themselves alive. Li Kecheng eventually donated plough equipment and devoted all his attention to recruiting new settlers (李侯給其動耕, 悉心招徠). He vexed himself attempting to find sustainable policies, for the most part with excellent success, each year proving an improvement on the previous one. However, as the fishing and salt making trades had been bankrupted, and it was difficult to import goods, it was impossible to see a happy ending.

In 1681, with Taiwan being now at peace, the islands around Lantau were opened so that people might regain their property, live there, and farm. At the same time, the prohibition on using the sea was lifted, so that people might use their boats to fish and gather prawns as before, by a special edict.

Appendix 3[3]
Biography of Li Kecheng

Li Kecheng (李可成, Lei Ho-shing), courtesy name Jiyou (集又, Tsap-yau), was a native of Tieling (鐵嶺) in Liaodong Province. He was a guansheng (官生), that is, a man appointed to office because his ancestors had been high officials of the Qing in Manchuria before they became emperors of China. He took up the post of county magistrate in the ninth year of Kang Hsi. He was a man with a kind and loving heart, self-disciplined, and honest. He came to the county during the early period after the restoration of the county, when unsettled grievances were many. He devoted all his attention to recruiting new settlers (悉心招徠). He donated cattle and seeds (給以牛種) and personally supervised the ploughing work. The city wall and the yamen had been abandoned, and he donated money of his own to the repair work, since he did not wish to burden the people. He was meticulous in strengthening and repairing the coastal defences. This he did solely to defend the people for the future. He oversaw the work of the yamen underlings and carefully supervised the collection of the taxes, both in silver and in grain, and absolutely forbade the practice of bao (包), that is, the practice whereby poor families paid their taxes through the agency of a rich family, a practice fertile in abuse. Many other abuses and bad practices were also ended. This brought great happiness to the people. He

gave earnest attention to the hearing of lawsuits: he would rise
early in order to hear them expeditiously. Although the prison
was usually empty in his time, this was because people, when
arrested, were always dealt with immediately and summarily. In
his time, crooks were driven out, and local bullies were expelled.
Half the men of the people, enfeebled by starvation, had died,
many by violence (有孱弱之民, 丁半死亡, 素被狼戾), and those who
had fled far away were unwilling to return until they were sure
that they could return in safety to resume their property. Upon
learning of the outrages committed by the notorious bandit Lei
Kei (李奇, Li Ji), he immediately and in person led the militia of
the villages, together with the government soldiers, and captured
all the bandits. When he received the students of the county
academy (諸生), the candidates for the imperial examinations, he
was kindly and amiable, although he would never offer any sort
of preferential treatment. He was kind and caring, but was, at the
same time, of sound judgement. He was honest and cautious, but
was, at the same time, diligent and restrained. He was not only
praised within the county, but was widely admired within all the
neighbouring counties.

Endnotes

Preface

1 T'ung-tsu Chü, *Law and Society in Traditional China*, Paris, Mouton, 1961; *Local Government in China under the Ch'ing*, Harvard University Press, 1962.

2 John R. Watt, *The District Magistrate in Late Imperial China*, Columbia University Press, 1972.

3 Philip C. C. Huang, *Civil Justice in China: Representation and Practice in the Qing*, Stanford University Press, Stanford, 1996; and *Chinese Civil Justice, Past and Present*, Bowman and Littlefield, 2010.

4 Linxia Liang, *Delivering Justice in Qing China: Civil Trials in the Magistrate's Court*, Oxford University Press, for the British Academy, 2007.

5 In this article, pinyin is used for the names of all non-local persons and places (especially the county magistrates), with characters and Cantonese transcription given also on first appearance (the Chinese characters and Cantonese transcription of the names of the magistrates are at Table 1). Local placenames within San On, and the names of local Cantonese people are given in Cantonese transcription, with characters and pinyin on first appearance.

6 Bradly Reed, *Talons and Teeth: County Clerks and Runners in the Qing Dynasty*, Stanford University Press, 2000.

7 Huang Liu-hung (黃六鴻) (1984), *A Complete Book Concerning Happiness and Benevolence: A Manual for Local Magistrates in Seventeenth-Century China* (福惠全書), translated and edited, Djang Chu (章楚), University of Arizona Press.

8 A few passages are not included in the translation, mostly on the grounds of duplication.

9 Djang Chu, in the Introduction to Huang Liu-hung's *A Complete Book Concerning Happiness and Benevolence*, *op.cit.* p. 2. It is these handbooks, however, which are the main source for T'ung-tsu Chü's work.

10 For Du Fengzhi's career, see Yau Tsit, (邱捷, Qiu Jie), 知縣與地方士神的合作與衝突: 以同治年間的廣東省廣寧縣為例 ("County magistrates and local elites; their co-operation and their differences: examples from Kwong Ning County in Kwangtung in the Tongzhi period"); and 同治光緒年間廣州的官紳民: 從杜鳳治日記所見 ("Officials, gentry, and people in Kwangtung in the Tongzhi and Kuangxu period, as seen from the diary of Du Fengzhi"); reprinted in Yau Tsit (2012), 晚清民國初年: 廣東的士神與商人 ("Kwangtung gentry and merchants in the late Qing and early Republic"), Guangxi Normal University Press, pp. 2–10, 34.

11 As of 清代稿抄本 ("Ching Hand-written Texts"), 廣東省立中山圖書館, Canton, 廣東人民出版社, Vols. 10–19, 2007.

12 The work by Cheung Yin is included in 清代縣級政權控制鄉村的具體考察: 以同治年間廣寧知縣杜鳳治日記為中心 ("A study of Qing County authority and the villages: centred on the Tongzhi period diary of Kwong Ning magistrate Du Fengzhi") (Cheung Yin, 大象出版社, 2010). Yau Tsit's work has been gathered together and reprinted in Yau Tsit (邱捷, Qiu Jie), 晚清民國初年: 廣東的士神與商人 ("Kwangtung gentry and merchants in the late Qing and early Republic"), Yau Tsit (邱捷, Qiu Jie), Guangxi Normal University Press, 2012. Included in this book are a number of essays, including 知縣與地方士神的合作與衝突: 以同治年間的廣東省廣寧縣為例 ("County magistrates and local elites; their co-operation and their differences: examples from Kwong Ning County in Kwangtung in the Tongzhi period"); 同治, 光緒年間廣州的官, 神, 民: 從杜鳳治日記所見 ("Officials, graduates, and the people in Canton in the Tongzhi and Kuangxu periods, from the diary of Du Fengzhi"); 關于康有為祖輩的一些新史料: 從杜鳳治日記所見 ("New material on the early family of Kang Yuwei, the diary of Du Fengzhi"); and 晚清廣東的 "公局": 士神控制鄉村基層社會的權力機構 ("Councils in the late Qing in Kwangtung: a discussion of elite control of basic rural society") respectively, pp. 1–33, 34–58, 59–74, and 75–89. I am indebted to Mr Tim Ko Tim-keung for drawing my attention to these books.

13 I have found *The Cambridge History of China*, Vols. 7–11, *The Ming Dynasty, 1368–1644*, *The Early Ch'ing, 1644–1800*, and *The Late Ch'ing*; F. Mote (1999), *Imperial China, 900–1800*, Harvard University Press; Ray Huang, *1587, A Year of No Significance: Ming China in Decline*, Yale University Press, 1982 particularly useful. For the eulogistic nature of much Chinese historical writings, I have used C. S. Gardiner, *Chinese Traditional Historiography*, Harvard University Press, 1938, as re-printed 1961. Many other works have also contributed to my understanding of the period.

14 Among many other works, I have found T. A. Wilson (2002), *On Sacred Ground: Culture, Society, Politics, and the Formation of the Cult of Confucius*, Harvard University Press; T. A. Wilson and M. Nylan (2010), *Confucius through the Ages: The Many Lives of Civilizations Greatest Sage*, Doubleday, New York; R. Johnson

(1934), *Confucianism and Modern China*; Victor Gollancz (1962), *Confucian Personalities*, Stanford University Press, ed. A. F. Wright and D. C. Twitchett; D.S. Nivison (1959), *Confucianism in Action*, Stanford University Press; D.S. Nivison (1996), *The Ways of Confucianism: Investigations in Chinese Philosophy*, Open Court Publishing; Tu Wei-ming (1993), *Way, Learning and Politics: Essays on the Confucian Intellectual*, State University of New York Press; Tu Wei-ming (1985), *Confucian Thought*, State University of New York Press; and Tu Wei-ming (1985), *Humanity and Self-Cultivation: Essays in Confucian Thought*, Berkeley: Asian Humanities Press, particularly useful.

15   The San On Gazetteer has been recently edited by Cheung Yat-ping (張一兵, Zhang Yibing), 深圳舊志三種 (*Three Ancient Gazetteers of Shenzhen*), 海天出版社, Shenzhen, 2006. This edition covers what survives of the Tung Kwun (東莞, Dongguan) County Gazetteer of 1464, the San On County Gazetteer of 1688, and the San On County Gazetteer of 1819. References in this study to this 1688 gazetteer are to the 卷 of the original, and to the pages in the Cheung Yat-ping edition. Many of the references in the 1688 gazetteer were carried over into the later gazetteer, of 1819: where this is the case the appropriate pages of the Cheung Yat-ping edition of the 1819 gazetteer are also referred to, following the reference to the 1688 gazetteer. If the reference has been translated in Peter Y. L. Ng and Hugh D. R. Baker, *New Peace County: A Chinese Gazetteer of the Hong Kong Region*, Hong Kong University Press, this is referenced as well.

16   See Table 1 for the Chinese characters and Cantonese transliteration of the names of the county magistrates.

1   Introduction: The Origins and Early Years of the County of San On

1   See Wang Gungwu, "The Nanhai Trade: The Early History of Trade in the South China Sea", *Journal of the Malayan Branch of the Royal Asiatic Society*, Vol. 31, No. 2, 1958, reprinted 2003.

2   For the early history of the San On area, see 張一兵, 深圳古代簡史 (Cheung Yat-ping, "A Brief History of Shenzhen in Ancient Times"), 深圳博物館, 文物出版社, 1997.

3   See the 1464 Tung Kwun Gazetteer, 卷2, Cheung Yat-ping, *op.cit.* pp. 76–78, for an essay on the early administrative history of the wider Tung Kwun area.

4   See below for references in the gazetteer to Yao people in the county in the first half of the 17th century.

5   There is, as yet, no adequate history of the salt trade in the Hong Kong area.

6　1464 Tung Kwun Gazetteer, 卷3, Cheung Yat-ping, *op.cit.* p. 171. The implications of "the Canton area" must be the Pearl River area, i.e. the Tung Kwun salt fields.

7　See 林天蔚, "南宋時大嶼山為傜區之試證" and 林天蔚, "論香港地區的族譜與方志及其記載的輋字" in 香港前代論集, ed. 林天蔚; and 蕭國健, 臺灣商務印書館, 1985, pp. 49–51, esp. p. 50, pp. 80–83, for a discussion of these state bond-slaves.

8　See 林天蔚, *loc.cit.* The reference to the "half-garrison" of troops at Kwun Fu is at p.114 and 117. For the "water-borne soldiers" see 蕭國健, "香港之海防歷史與軍事遺蹟", 中華文教交流服務中心, 2006, pp. 17–18. The order for the massacre was given by the governor of Kwangtung, Qin Zhiwang, 錢之望 (tsin Chi-mong).

9　See 林天蔚, "南宋時大嶼山為傜區之試證" and 林天蔚, "論香港地區的族譜與方志及其記載的輋字", *loc.cit.*

10　See 羅香林, "一八四二年以前之香港及其對外交通", Hong Kong, 1959, ch. 3, 大埔海與其地自五代至明之採珠. See gazetteer, 卷12, Cheung Yat-ping, *op.cit.* pp. 494–495, 1819 gazetteer, 卷22, Cheung Yat-ping, *op.cit.* pp. 1006–1008, partially translated in Ng and Baker, *New Peace County*, *op.cit.* p. 121. This is the petition by Cheung Wai-yan (張惟寅, Zhang Weiyin) which led to the closure of the pearl fishing. It gives a good deal of information about the pearl fishery.

11　See 羅香林, "一八四二年以前之香港及其對外交通", Hong Kong, 1959, ch. 2, 屯門與其地自唐至明之海上交通; and Wang Gungwu, *The Nanhai Trade*, *op.cit.* reprinted, 1998.

12　For Lu Xun see Cheung Yat-ping, "深圳古代簡史", *op.cit.* pp. 70–71; and 林天蔚, "論香港地區的族譜與方志及其記載的輋字", *op.cit.* p. 82. For the sack by the Arabs and Persians, see the Tang Dynastic History, "Persians", 波斯 section (sec. 258b), and in the biography of Emperor Su Zung (肅宗) (sec. 10), where it merely says that "the Arabs and Persians sacked the city, 攻城": see E. Breitschneider, *On the Knowledge Possessed by the Ancient Chinese of the Arabs and Arabian Colonies: and Other Western Countries, Mentioned in Chinese Books*, Trübner, London, 1871, pp. 10–11.

13　For Huang Chao see Cheung Yat-ping, "深圳古代簡史", *op.cit.* pp. 93–95, and D. Twitchett, *The Cambridge History of China*: Vol. 3, Sui and T'ang China, 589–906, Part 1, pp. 738–747.

14　Most is known of this system from later periods, but it was probably much the same at all dates. This system tended to break down in periods when the imperial central authorities were weak, but the system was re-established whenever new dynasties tightened up control.

15　The references are taken from the Han Dynastic History: the 220 reference being a mention of the existence of the salt superintendency here, the 265 reference to a change in title, and the 331 reference being to a rebuilding of the offices of the salt superintenency.

16 The Nanhan emperors were very interested in the coastal area of Tung Kwun. It was the Nanhan who increased the number of salt field areas from one to six (as a southern kingdom they needed to get as much salt from the area as possible), and doubtless greatly extended the area being used for salt working. They also proclaimed Castle Peak as the holy mountain of their empire, and were very interested in the effectiveness of the garrison at Tuen Mun, which the Nanhan emperor visited at least once. See also fn. 10 above.

17 See 蕭國建, "屯門考", in 香港前代史論集, ed. 蕭國建; and 林天蔚, 臺灣商務印書館印行, 1985, p. 73.

18 See 羅香林, "一八四二年以前之香港及其對外交通", Hong Kong, 1959, ch. 2, 屯門與其地自唐至明之海上交通; and 蕭國健, "屯門考", in 香港前代史論集, op.cit.; and 劉智鵬 and 劉蜀永, "屯門", Joint Publishing, Hong Kong, 2012. There is no adequate study of the history of Pui To's two monasteries yet published.

19 See 羅香林, "一八四二年以前之香港及其對外交通", op.cit. p. 82, n.14.

20 See P. H. Hase, "Beside the Yamen: Nga Tsin Wai Village", *Journal of the Hong Kong Branch of the Royal Asiatic Society*, Vol. 39, 1999, pp. 1–78.

21 See 蕭國健, 宋季名臣李昴英與大嶼山梅窩發現之 "李府食邑稅山" 界石, in 蕭國建, 香港前史論集, Taiwan, 1985, pp.123–205.

22 The date of foundation of Tai Wai is taken from the Wai (韋) clan geneaology of Tai Wai: the first ancestor of that clan being the first to settle in the Sha Tin area. A copy of the genealogy is in the library of New Asia College, Chinese University of Hong Kong. For the early settlement of Sai Kung, see P. H. Hase, *Hatred and Enmity: Settlement and Politics in Early Sai Kung, 1550–1850*, forthcoming.

23 See the biography of Ho Chan at 卷10, Cheung Yat-ping, op.cit. pp. 422–523, 1819 gazetteer, 卷19, Cheung Yat-ping, op.cit. p. 947.

24 Gazetteer, 卷8, Cheung Yat-ping, op.cit. p. 382.

25 卷11, Cheung Yat-ping, op.cit. pp. 442–443, 1819 gazetteer, 卷13, p. 870, Ng and Baker, op.cit. pp. 106–107, and biography of Wang Hong, 1819 gazetteer, 卷 10, p. 878.

26 卷10, Cheung Yat-ping, op.cit. p. 421, 429; 1819 gazetteer, 卷19, pp. 947, 954–955. In the Tang Hung-lun biography an impossible date is given (Wanli Gengwu Year 萬曆庚午), which should be Longqing Gengwu Year 隆慶庚午, which is 1570. There was no Gengwu 庚午 year during the Wanli 萬曆 reign.

27 Details of the move into the walls of Tai Wai are given in the Wai, 韋, Wei, clan genealogy, of Tai Wai and elsewhere (copy held at New Asia College Library, Chinese University of Hong Kong)

28 The date of the Tai Wai walls is taken from a dated inscription on the earth god shrine of the newly walled village: the Tai Wai villagers used the same feng shui

specialist who had already set out the walls of Nga Tsin Wai to set out their walls, and so the Nga Tsin Wai walls are slightly earlier than those of Tai Wai. The Tin Sam date is from the oral information given to the author by the Tin Sam elders.

29 卷10, biographies of Liu Wen and Ng Tso, Cheung Yat-ping, *op.cit.* pp. 409, 428–429, 1819 gazetteer, 卷14, pp. 878–879, 956.

30 For Shang Kexi and the Rebellion of the Three Feudatories, see Jonathan Spence, *The Search for Modern China*, 2nd Ed. W. W. Norton, 1999, pp. 49–53, and *The Cambridge History of China*, Vol. 9, Part 1, "The Ching Empire to 1800", ed. Willard J. Peterson, 2002, ch. 3 "The K'ang-his Reign", Jonathan Spence, p. 159.

31 So called because the last Ming emperor had granted him the honour of using the imperial surname, to recognise his loyalty to the Ming.

2   The San On Gazetteer: The Magistrates and the County Community

1 The best modern edition of the 1688 San On County Gazetteer is that of Cheung Yat-ping, *op.cit.* at pp. 205–547. The provincial gazetteer is [道光] 廣東通志, (photoreproduction of the 1934 reprint of the 1822 original), 續修四庫全書, 史部地理彙, Vol. 674, 上海古籍出版社, 1995.

2 卷4, Cheung Yat-ping, *op.cit.* p. 297.

3 卷12, Cheung Yat-ping, *op.cit.* pp. 513–515.

4 卷5, Cheung Yat-ping, *op.cit.* p. 326.

5 卷4, Cheung Yat-ping, *op.cit.* pp. 295–298, 1819 gazetteer, 卷5, pp. 720–726.

6 Between 1755 and 1758, and again between 1771 and 1774, when the county was in dire straits, with ephemeral magistrates posted there for just a few weeks or months, no records of the dates were preserved. In some cases no record was preserved even of the magistrates' full names.

7 For Tang Man-wai see 1819 gazetteer, 卷19, Cheung Yat-ping, *op.cit.* p. 958, and 卷15, Cheung Yat-ping, p. 891, see also Chan Wing-hoi, "The Dangs of Kam Tin and their Jiu Festival", *Journal of the Hong Kong Branch of the Royal Asiatic Society*, Vol. 29, pp. 302–375, especially pp. 313–314. It is unlikely that Tang Man-wai was a personal secretary, or paid for his advice: his advice seems to have been offered on an unofficial basis, arising from Tang Man-wai's position as the dominant figure among the San On graduates, and as the only San On Kui Yan active in public life in the county at the time.

8 The best description of the county temple of Confucius is in the 1819 gazetteer, 卷7, Cheung Yat-ping, *op.cit.* pp. 785–787, *New Peace County*, *op.cit.* p. 88–89, see also the 1688 gazetteer, 卷7, p. 381. A drawing of the county school and

temple of Confucius is in the 1819 gazetteer, with the 名官祠 ("shrine of famous officials") clearly marked (see Plate 1). The shrine is called 名宦祠 at Cheung Yat-ping, *op.cit.* p. 788.

9   卷10, Cheung Yat-ping, *op.cit.* pp. 408–410 (崇祀名宦), and pp. 411–420 (宦績列傳).

10   卷14, Cheung Yat-ping, *op.cit.* pp. 878–880, 880–888.

11   The provincial gazetteer, *op.cit.* pp. 230–231, 375.

12   卷10, Cheung Yat-ping, *op.cit.* pp. 408–419, 1819 gazetteer, 卷7, p. 788, 卷14, pp. 880–883.

13   1819 gazetteer, Cheung Yat-ping, *op.cit.* 卷7, p. 788, 卷14, p. 880.

14   卷10, Cheung Yat-ping, pp. 408–410, 1819 gazetteer, 卷14, pp. 878–880. A partial translation of three of these biographies can be found in *New Peace County*, *op.cit.* pp. 114. (those of Wu Daxun, Ding Tangfa, and Jin Qizhen). That the biographies were reworked is shown by the fact that the 1819 gazetteer gives slightly different wordings to the 1688 gazetteer, and the provincial gazetteer, which must have got much of its information, in the last resort, from the same source, has significantly different wordings.

15   卷10, Cheung Yat-ping, *op.cit.* pp. 408–420, 1819 gazetteer, 卷14, pp. 878–888 (section 宦蹟略: only some of the information in the 1688 gazetteer is transcribed to the 1819 gazetteer).

16   These 13 include Zhang Mingda, magistrate 1678–1684, An Yumei, magistrate 1684–1687, and Jin Wenmo, magistrate 1687–1694. In these cases, at least, the tablets are likely to have been placed in the shrine before the death of the magistrate.

17   卷10, Cheung Yat-ping, *op.cit.* pp. 411–420, 1819 gazetteer, 卷14, pp. 880–888.

18   卷10, Cheung Yat-ping, *op.cit.* pp. 420–431, 1819 gazetteer, 卷19, pp. 946–963 (with more divisions of the worthy residents).

19   For the biography of Ho Chan see 卷10, Cheung Yat-ping, *op.cit.* pp. 422–423, and for Ng Tso, 卷10, Cheung Yat-ping, *op.cit.* pp. 428–429; 1819 gazetteer, 卷 19, Cheung Yat-ping, *op.cit.* p. 947, 956.

20   The list of magistrates is taken from the "文官表, 知縣" section of the gazetteer; 卷 4, Cheung Yat-ping, *op.cit.* pp. 295–298, 1819 gazetteer, 卷5, pp. 720–726. For a partial list of the magistrates from 1819 to 1871, and of those from 1912 onwards, see 深圳市志, 社會風俗卷 (*Shenzhen City Gazetteer, Society and Customs Volume*), 深圳市地方志編纂委員會, 方志出版社, 2014, pp. 96–98.

21   This middle Qing period includes the decade 1771–1780, when the county had 14 magistrates in ten years, none of whom were honoured: during this period the county administration must have been close to being in a state of collapse.

22   The characters used for the names differ in some respects in the lists in the two gazetteers.

23   See Huang Liu-hung (*A Complete Book*, ed. Tsang Chu, *op.cit.* pp. 73–80 and 83–88) for a detailed description of the rules governing standard appointments, including the drawing of lots.

24   In the 19th century, expectant officials sent to the viceroy had to work, at least occasionally, without pay, board, or lodging, for anything up to four or more years. Du Fengzhi mentions his four years of unpaid work for the viceroy as an expectant official before he was posted to Sze Wui, and the huge debts he contracted at this time to pay for his daily expenses. See fn. 44 below.

25   On the sending of expectant officials down to the viceroy, see John R. Watt, *The District Magistrate*, *op.cit.* ch. 3.

26   1819 gazetteer, 卷14, Cheung Yat-ping, *op.cit.* p. 885.

27   The registers of the board of civil appointments survive, in part, from 1722, see 中國第一歷史檔案館藏清代官員履歷檔案全編. References to Chao Chongmin are in Vol. 16, pp. 537下 and 547下.

28   As was Ba County, 巴縣, about which Bradly Reed writes in, *Talons and Teeth*, *op.cit.* which included within it the whole city of Chungking (重慶, Chongqing) and its suburbs.

29   See the "Bandits", 寇盜 section of the gazetteer, 卷11, Cheung Yat-ping, *op.cit.* pp. 442–445, 1819 gazetteer, 卷13, pp. 870–873. Ng and Baker, *New Peace County*, *op.cit.* pp. 106–111.

30   Biography of Zhang Wenxing, 卷10, Cheung Yat-ping, *op.cit.* pp. 414–415, 1819 gazetteer, p. 883.

31   卷11. Cheung Yat-ping, *op.cit.* p. 444, 1819 gazetteer, 卷13, p. 872, Ng and Baker, *New Peace County*, *op.cit.* p. 110.

32   See 卷11, Cheung Yat-ping, *op.cit.* p. 439, 1819 gazetteer, 卷13, p. 867, Ng and Baker, *New Peace County*, *op.cit.* p. 123.

33   However, while the attacks by the bandit chiefs Chan Yiu, (陳耀, Chen Rao) and Lei Man-wing (李萬榮, Li Wenrong) in 1647–1656 are mentioned in the "Bandits", 寇盜 section, the fact that these bandit chiefs besieged the county city is only mentioned in the biographies of the then county magistrates, Zheng Wenxing (1647–1648) and Ma Yimao (1656–1661), 卷10, pp. 414–415, 1819 gazetteer, 卷14, p. 883. The gazetteer says of the bandit attack in 1676 that the bandits were "pirates who came from Waiyeung (Huiyang, 惠陽) to plunder, looting and slaughtering in all the villages they passed through, and finally taking the county city, which was only regained the following year (海氛自惠陽入寇, 所過鄉村, 盡行屠掠, 遂踞縣城, 次年始克恢復), (卷11, Cheung Yat-ping, *op.cit.* p. 444, Ng and Baker,

New Peace County, op.cit. p. 110), but there must be some suspicion that this attack on the county city was in fact by forces of Shang Zhimin, who had gone into rebellion against the Qing at precisely this time, and who might well have been intent on taking a county still holding out for the Qing. There is, however, no proof of this, nothing but suspicion that this might have been so.

34   Zhou Xiyao's statement is at 卷12, Cheung Yat-ping, pp. 457–459, 1819 gazetteer, 卷22, pp. 1019–1020, and Li Kechang's is at 卷11, Cheung Yat-ping, p. 440, 1819 gazetteer, 卷13, p. 868 (greatly shortened: *New Peace County, op.cit.* p. 104 translates this shortened version).

35   Gazetteer, 卷4, Cheung Yat-ping, *op.cit.* p. 296, "Civil Officials: Magistrates", 文官表: 知縣 section. This comment is not carried over into the 1819 gazetteer.

36   The 1819 gazetteer says he was from Fengtien (卷5, Cheung Yat-ping, *op.cit.* p. 722). The 1688 gazetteer says he was from 盛京 (an alternative name for Fengtien) in the "Civil Officials: Magistrates", 文官表: 知縣 section (卷4, Cheung Yat-ping, *op.cit.* p, 296), but says he was from 北京 in Zhang Wenxing's biography (卷10, Cheung Yat-ping, *op.cit.* p. 414). "北京" is clearly an error for "盛京", and Fengtien should be taken as the native place.

37   See Jonathan Spence, *The Search for Modern China*, 2nd Ed., *loc.cit.* and *The Cambridge History of China*, Vol. 9, Part 1, "The Ching Empire to 1800", Jonathan Spence, *loc.cit.*

38   See the biographies of these officials, in 1688 gazetteer, 卷4, Cheung Yat-ping, *op.cit.* pp.295–298, 1819 gazetteer, 卷5, Cheung Yat-ping, *op.cit.* pp. 295–297, 720–724.

39   John R. Watt, *The District Magistrate in Late Imperial China*, Columbia University Press, 1972, p. 30.

40   Biography of Jin Qizhen, 1819 gazetteer, 卷14, Cheung Yat-ping, *op.cit.* p. 880.

41   1819 gazetteer, 卷5, Cheung Yat-ping, *op.cit.* pp. 722–724.

42   The surviving records of the board of civil appointments in Peking as printed (中國第一歷史檔案館藏清代官員履歷檔案全編) are unhelpful as to where San On magistrates were appointed from. The 30 volumes of the published records from the period 1722–1820 only mention San On twice, with regard to magistrates Duan Yanshang (1724–1725) and He Mengzhuan (1730–1741). Duan Yanshang, after being dismissed from a post as county magistrate in Fukien for loosing his temper with his subordinates, was appointed to San On by nomination by the viceroy. He Mengzhuan was appointed to Fung Chuen (封川, Fengchuan) county in the north of Kwangtung by casting lots, and was then transferred to San On by the viceroy.

43   The ethnicity of Na Yu, Fu Senbu, and Shu Minga is stated to have been Manchu in the 中國第一歷史檔案館藏清代官員履歷檔案全編, *op.cit.* The other magistrates who may be Manchu share with these three entries in the "Civil Officials: Magistrates", 文官表: 知縣 section omission of information as to province of birth and graduate status, see 1819 gazetteer, 卷5, Cheung Yat-ping, *op.cit.* p. 723.

44   See 中國第一歷史檔案館藏清代官員履歷檔案全編, *op.cit.* for the payments made by Shen Yongning and Gao Zhijing. Du Fengzhi was also a Kui Yan by examination who paid a "donation" to be appointed magistrate. In his case part of this "donation" seems to have been a requirement that he work for the high provincial authorities for four years (1862–1866) to prove himself, without pay, before his appointment as district magistrate. By 1866 he was accordingly in debt to the tune of 9,000 taels.

45   John R. Watt, *The District Magistrate*, *op.cit.* pp. 51–52.

46   See the "Civil Officials: Magistrates", 文官表: 知縣 section, 卷4, 5, Cheung Yat-ping, *op.cit.* pp. 295–298, 1819 gazetteer, 卷5, pp. 720–726.

47   See J. W. Hayes, "Purchase of Degrees, Rank, and Appointment in Late Qing China: Some Impressions from Contemporary Sources", *Journal of the Hong Kong Branch of the Royal Asiatic Society*, Vol. 53, 2013, pp. 31–89.

48   See 中國第一歷史檔案館 藏清代官員履歷黨檔案全編, *op.cit.*

49   See the Linzhou Gazetteer, 中國地方志集成, 江西府縣志, Vol. 48, 同治臨州縣志, 江蘇古籍出版社, 上海書店, 巴蜀書社, photoreproduction of 同治九年 (1870) original, 1996, p. 518.

50   See the Xinjian Gazetteer, 中國地方志集成, 江西府縣志輯, 同治新建縣志, 1871, photo-reproduced 江蘇古籍出版社, with 上海書店 and 巴蜀書社, Vol. 1, 卷31, p. 331.

51   See the gazetteer of his native place (永新, Yongxin; in Jiangxi (江西) Province), 中國地方志集成, 江西縣志輯, Vol. 71, 同治永新縣志, 江蘇古籍出版社, 1996, p. 233. The Yongxin Gazetteer has a note to the effect that his name should be 時階, and not 時偕, as in the San On Gazetteer, and the Kwangtung Provincial Gazetteer (廣東通志).

52   See the Shiqian Gazetteer, 中國地方志集成, 貴州府縣志, Vol. 47, 同治石阡縣志, 江蘇古籍出版社, 上海書店, 巴蜀書社, photoreproduction of 1922 original, pp. 480, 537.

53   See their biographies in the 1688 gazetteer, *loc.cit.*

54   See the Jinxian Gazetteer, 中國地方志集成, 江西府縣志輯, 同治進賢縣志, 江蘇古籍出版社, 上海書店, 巴蜀書社, photoreproduction of 同治十年 (1871) original, 1996, p. 474. A Zhou county is one graded higher than a standard county: they were usually counties in remote areas. The three counties involved, 合浦, 瓜州, and 有傳 I have not been able to locate.

55 See the Tong'an Gazetteer, 中華民國拾捌年刊, 同安縣志, 廈門市同安區方志編纂委員會辦公室整理, 方志出版社, 吳錫璜著, 2007, p. 848. *loc.cit.*

56 See the Tong'an Gazetteer, *loc.cit.*

57 See the record of his posting to San On, 卷4, Cheung Yat-ping, *op.cit.* p. 296; 1819 gazetteer, 卷 5, p. 721.

58 See his native-place gazetteer, Jingde County Gazetteer, 旌德縣志, 1808, reprinted 1925. 成文出版社: 中國方志叢書, no. 227, reprinted 1998. 南京: 江蘇古籍出版社:中國地方志集成, Vol. 53.

59 See his biography in the provincial gazetteer, op.cit. p. 375, taken from the Po Ning County Gazetteer.

60 See the Jiashin Gazetteer, 中國地方志集成, 浙江府縣志輯, Vol. 19, 乾隆桐盧縣志, 光緒重修嘉善縣志, 校勘光緒嘉善縣志箚記; 江蘇古籍出版社, 上海書店, 巴蜀書店, 1993, p. 551, p. 588.

61 See John R. Watt, *The District Magistrate*, *op.cit.* ch. 4.

62 See the Hoi Fung County Gazetteer, 廣東省海豐縣志, 1750, photo-reproduced, 中國方志叢書, 第十號, 成文出版社, Taipei, 1966, p. 21. In the Hoi Fung Gazetteer, Li Xuan's name is given as 李炫. See also the Zhangping (漳平, Tseung Ping) Gazetteer, 中國方志叢書, 第九十三號, 福建省漳平縣志, 1935, photo-reproduced 成文出版社, Taipei, 1967, pp. 265–266. In the Zhangping Gazetteer, Li Xuan's name is given as 李佷.

63 See the Kaizhou (開州) Gazetteer, 清光緒開州志, 濮陽縣地方史志辦公室校注, 中州古籍出版社, 1995, p. 398, pp. 488–489.

64 See the provincial gazetteer, *op.cit.* p. 375.

65 See John R. Watt, *The District Magistrate*, *op.cit.* p. 32 et seq. for a discussion on the age of magistrates on appointment, and the problem of dealing with elderly men coming up for appointment.

66 All the quotes in this section, unless otherwise noted, are taken from the biographies of the magistrates in the 1688 gazetteer (卷10, Cheung Yat-ping *op.cit.* pp. 410–417, 1819 gazetteer, 卷14, pp. 879–885).

67 Provincial gazetteer, *op.cit.* p. 220, biography drawn from the Fujian Provincial Gazetteer.

68 Provincial gazetteer, *op.cit.* p. 220: the provincial gazetteer states that this comment is taken from the San On Gazetteer, but it is not included in the text of that gazetteer as we have it. It is likely that the comment was in the 1643 gazetteer, now lost.

69 Biography repeated in the provincial gazetteer, *op.cit.* p.220.

70   中華民國拾捌年刊, 同安縣志, 廈門市同安區方志編纂委員會辦公室整理, 方志出版社, 吳
      錫璜著, 2007, p. 848. The biography of Chen Gu in this gazetteer is, in part, a
      copy of the biography in the San On Gazetteer, and it is likely that this remark was
      present in the 1643 San On Gazetteer, now lost, from whence the biography in
      the Tong'an Gazetteer must have taken the San On section of its biography, and
      then dropped by a copying error from the 1688 gazetteer.

71   Comment repeated in biography in the provincial gazetteer, *op.cit.* p. 221.

72   中國地方志集成, 江西府縣志輯, Vol. 59, 同治進賢縣志, 江蘇古籍出版社, 上海書店, 巴蜀
      書社, photoreproduction of 1872 original, 1996, p. 537. The comment is in the
      provincial gazetteer, *op.cit.* p. 221.

73   Provincial gazetteer, *op.cit.* p. 375. The comment was taken from the biography
      in the Canton Prefectural Gazetteer. The county gazetteer says: 功噴噴口碑矣, with
      much the same meaning, gazetteer, 卷10, Cheung Yat-ping, *op.cit.* p. 415.

74   Provincial gazetteer, *op.cit.* p. 375.

75   Provincial gazetteer, *op.cit.* p. 375. Huang Liu-hung (*A Complete Book*, ed. Djang
      Chu, *op.cit.* pp. 231-232) notes how important it was to control the census
      takers.

76   Provincial gazetteer, *op.cit.* p. 375.

77   Provincial gazetteer, *op.cit.* p. 375.

78   The comment is repeated in the provincial gazetteer, *op.cit.* p. 375. The inscription
      does not survive today.

79   Comments from entries in the county and provincial gazetteers, *op.cit.*

80   卷12, Cheung Yat Ping, *op.cit.* pp. 449–543. Not all of these writings were
      transcribed into the 1819 gazetteer, 卷22–24, pp. 997–1094.

81   卷12, Cheung Yat-ping, *op.cit.* pp. 451–457, 1819 gazetteer, 卷22, pp. 1014–
      1019.

82   At 卷6, Cheung Yat-ping, *op.cit.* p. 373.

83   卷12, Cheung Yat-ping, *op.cit.* pp. 457–459, 459–460, 483–484, 485–486, 486–
      487; 1819 gazetteer, 卷22, 23, pp. 1019–1023, 1056–1058.

84   卷12, Cheung Yat-ping, *op.cit.* pp. 519–522, 523, 527, 528. Only two of these
      poems are included in the 1819 gazetteer, at pp. 1073–1074 and 1083.

85   卷12, Cheung Yat-ping, *op.cit.* pp. 481–485, 1819 gazetteer, 卷22, pp. 1023–
      1026.

86   卷12, Cheung Yat-ping, *op.cit.* pp. 506–510, 1819 gazetteer, 卷23, pp. 1058–
      1062.

87 卷12, Cheung Yat-ping, *op.cit.* pp. 529–533, only two poems are included in the 1819 gazetteer, at 卷24, pp. 1075, 1084.

88 卷12, Cheung Yat-ping, *op.cit.* pp. 449–450, 1819 gazetteer, 卷22, pp. 1012–1013.

89 卷12, Cheung Yat-ping, *op.cit.* pp. 450–451, 483, 1819 gazetteer, 卷22, 23, pp. 1013–1014, 1054–1055. The excerpted text is at 卷6, Cheung Yat-ping, *op.cit.* pp. 371–372.

90 卷12, Cheung Yat-ping, *op.cit.* p. 470, 1819 gazetteer, 卷23, pp. 1052–153.

91 This is the preface to the county gazetteer, and is in the preliminary section of the 1688 gazetteer (Cheung Yat-ping, *op.cit.* pp. 221–223), and at 卷23, pp. 1064–1066 in the 1819 gazetteer.

92 卷12, Cheung Yat-ping, *op.cit.* pp. 513–515: the excerpted text is at 卷6, Cheung Yat-ping, op.cit. p. 375.

93 卷12, Cheung Yat-ping, *op.cit.* pp. 510–513; only one is included in the 1819 gazetteer, at 卷23, pp. 1062–1064.

94 卷12, Cheung Yat-ping, *op.cit.* pp. 468–470, 479–480, 1819 gazetteer, 卷23, pp. 1047–1048. However, the poem of Qiu Tiqian is only in the 1819 gazetteer, 卷14, Cheung Yat-ping, *op.cit.* pp. 1092–1093. This probably implies that this poem was in the now lost 1643 gazetteer, and omitted from the 1688 gazetteer by an oversight.

95 1819 gazetteer, 卷23, Cheung Yat-ping, *op.cit.* pp. 1066–1067. He does, however, include three poems written by San On natives who had gone on to become magistrates elsewhere (these are on local beauty-spots, and on the pleasure of travel in autumn, 卷14, Cheung Yat-ping, *op.cit.* pp. 1081, 1085, 1091) and two poems written by Yuan Jiayan, 袁嘉言, Yuen Ka-yin, a magistrate, but not of San On, on the Tin Hau Temple and the Nam Shan fort at Chek Wan, presumably written while on a visit to San On (卷14, Cheung Yat-ping, *op.cit.* pp. 1085, 1091).

3 The Work of the County Magistrates and their Magistracies

1 For the imperial examination system, see in particular Benjamin A. Elman, *A Cultural History of Civil Examinations in Late Imperial China*, University of California Press, 2000, and *Civil Examinations and Meritocracy in Late Imperial China*, Harvard University Press, 2013.

2 The sons and grandsons of convicted criminals, prostitutes, and of a few other groups, were ineligible.

3 Several times a month, indeed, according to Du Fengzhi, see Yau Tsit, 知縣與地方士紳, *op.cit.* p. 6.

4 For Chen Gu, see his biography in his native place gazetteer, *op.cit.* For Zheng Sangui and Wu Yi, see 中國第一歷史檔案館 藏清代官員履歷黨檔案全編.

5 1688 gazetteer, 卷3, Cheung Yat-ping, *op.cit.* p. 287.

6 *A Complete Book*, ed. Djang Chu, *op.cit.* pp. 215–217. For the administrative duties of the magistrates in general see especially John R. Watt, *The District Magistrate, op.cit.*

7 Djang Chu, introduction to Huang Liu-hung, *A Complete Book, op.cit.* p. 32.

8 Huang Liu-hung, *A Complete Book*, ed. Djang Chu, *op.cit.* pp. 65, 181, 220.

9 1819 gazetteer, 卷13, Cheung Yat-ping, *op.cit.* p. 869. The "locusts" may have been an attack of blast.

10 1819 gazetteer, 卷14, Cheung Yat-ping, *op.cit.* p. 885, biography of Li Dagen. Huang Liu-hung noted that "setting up rice gruel kitchens" was a useful thing to do when a magistrate was faced with immediate and overwhelming famine, see Huang Liu-hung, *A Complete Book*, ed. Djang Chu, *op.cit.* p. 558.

11 Biography of Ma Yimao, 卷10, Cheung Yat-ping, *op.cit.* p. 415, 1819 gazetteer, 卷 14, p. 883.

12 Du Fengzhi, in Kwong Ning, also had to deal with a serious outbreak of banditry in 1866, which caused him a great deal of difficulty. See Yau Tsit, 知縣與地方士紳, *op.cit.* and Cheung Yin, 清代縣級政權, *op.cit.* pp. 206–213.

13 Huang Liu-hung considered this aspect of the magistrate's duties to be more important than usually believed, see *A Complete Book*, ed. Djang Chu, *op.cit.* 卷 25, pp. 525–541.

14 Huang Liu-hung, *A Complete Book*, ed. Djang Chu, *op.cit.* 卷25, pp. 525–541, felt this duty to be of great social significance.

15 Huang Liu-hung, *A Complete Book*, ed. Djang Chu, *op.cit.* gives integrity, frugality, loving the people, and diligence as the most vital virtues of a magistrate, see *A Complete Book*, ed. Djang Chu, *op.cit.* pp. 72, 141–142, 525, 547.

16 Philip C. C. Huang, "Civil Justice in China: Representation and Practice in the Qing", *op.cit.* and "Chinese Civil Justice", *Past and Present, op.cit.* John R. Watt, *The District Magistrate, op.cit.* Bradly Reed, *Talons and Teeth, op.cit.* 2000, Linxia Liang, *Delivering Justice in Qing China: Civil Trials in the Magistrate's Court, op.cit.*

17 See Philip C. C. Huang, *Civil Justice in China*, ch. 5, for a very lucid description of civil process in traditional China.

18 It is abundantly clear from Du Fengzhi's cases that perjury, wild exaggeration, fake or tampered-with deeds and so forth were extremely common, and hence many plaints could be dismissed out-of-hand. It would seem, from Du Fengzhi's cases, that little if any action was taken against people exaggerating or lying in the plaints submitted: see Cheung Yin, 清代縣級政權, *op.cit.* Table 6–3, 6–4, and 6–5, and the discussions of these cases.

19 See Philip C. C. Huang, *Civil Justice in China*, *loc.cit.*

20 A tael is one-and-a-third English ounces: a silver dollar was 72% of a tael.

21 Huang Liu-hung, *A Complete Book*, ed. Djang Chu, *op.cit.* p. 261, roundly states that all civil cases should be settled "between the parties themselves".

22 Cheung Yin, 清代縣級政權, *op.cit.* Table 6–3 and 6–4, pp. 202–206, 209–213, *A Complete Book*, ed. Djang Chu, *op.cit.* p. 255. Du Fengzhi considered a delay of 24 hours in initiating a complaint of crime a suspicious circumstance, see Cheung Yin, *op.cit.* Table 6–4,8.

23 See Philip C. C. Huang, *Civil Justice in China*, *op.cit.* Table 18, and pp. 176–178.

24 The Kwong Ning Magistracy had been vacant for some months before his arrival to take up the post.

25 See Cheung Yin, 清代縣級政權, *op.cit.* p. 7, pp. 187–190.

26 Cheung Yin, 清代縣級政權, *op.cit.* p. 232, 案件詞訟只有區區不到50件.

27 See Cheung Yin, 清代縣級政權, *op.cit.* pp. 195–226, and see Tables 6–3, 6–4, and 6–5.

28 Table 6–5 in Cheung Yin, 清代縣級政權, mentions only ten "mountain cases", but case 7 is in fact two cases.

29 "Subsoil" and "topsoil" landholdings were land rights under the local Kwangtung customary law. The "topsoil" landholder held the right to till the soil and take its products, subject to the payment of a rent charge to the "subsoil" landholder, who had the right to receive the rent charge, but had few other rights over the soil. The "subsoil" land holder, however, also controlled all the waste land around the arable land which paid him a rent charge. The "subsoil" landholder paid the land tax (if any was paid — only about a fifth of the arable land in San On paid land tax in the later 19th century), and was the only landholder registered in the magistracy. See P. H. Hase, *Custom, Land and Livelihood in Rural South China: The Traditional Land Law of Hong Kong's New Territiories, 1750–1950*, Hong Kong University Press with the Royal Asiatic Society, Hong Kong Branch (Hong Kong Studies Series), 2013.

30 Several cases of exactly the same character arose in the area of the New Territories in the late Qing, see P. H. Hase, *Custom, Land and Livelihood in Rural*

South China, op.cit. pp. 195–214 (pages 206–214 discuss a "mountain case" very similar to those in Kwong Ning). See also *op.cit.* pp. 239–243.

31 A Ta Tsiu (打醮, more properly 太平清醮) is the occasional ritual put on by groups of villages, usually once every ten years, usually lasting five days and nights, and always requiring very substantial expenditure.

32 Huang Liu-hung, *A Complete Book*, ed. Djang Chu, *op.cit.* pp. 251–464: the passage on civil cases is at pp. 446–454.

33 See T'ung-tzu Chü, *Local Government in China Under the Ch'ing, op.cit.* ch. 7.

34 Djang Chu, Introduction to Huang Liu-hung, *A Complete Book, op.cit.* p. 37.

35 He would probably take a more proactive approach if the case had a criminal tinge, e.g. if, in attempting to secure the return of moneys lent, the lender had been seriously beaten by the borrower, or vice versa.

36 See both Cheung Yin and Yau Tsit, *passim*, for Du Fengzhi's use of the gentry as arbitrators in civil cases.

37 HK Public Records Office, document CSO 807, quoted in Michael J. E. Palmer, "The Surface-Subsoil Form of Divided Ownership in Late Imperial China: Some Examples from the New Territories of Hong Kong", *Hong Kong Law Journal*, Vol. 21.1, 1991, pp. 45–77. Here "obliged" is being used in its normal 19th century meaning, "forced".

38 J. H. Stewart Lockhart, *Report on the New Territory during the First Year of British Administration, in Papers Laid before the Legislative Council of Hong Kong, 1900* (Sessional Papers, 1900), Hong Kong, Government Printer, 1901, No. 15/1900, p. 256.

39 J. H. Stewart Lockhart, *Extracts from a Report by Mr Stewart Lockhart on the Extension of the Colony of Hong Kong*, in *Papers Laid before the Legislative Council of Hong Kong, 1899* (Sessional Papers, 1899), No. 9/99, Hong Kong Government Printer, 1900, p. 192, "Local Government in the Villages".

40 Huang Liu-hung (*A Complete Book*, ed. Djang Chu, *op.cit.* p. 327) states that only suspects and convicts awaiting execution were imprisoned: witnesses were "released on bond".

41 Provincial gazetteer, *op.cit.* p. 220. The story was taken by the provincial gazetteer from a collection of stories, 世經堂集.

42 From his biography in the provincial gazetteer, *op.cit.* p. 220.

43 See the biographies of the magistrates in question, 卷10, Cheung Yat-ping, *op.cit.* pp. 411, 415, 416–417, 1819 gazetteer, 卷14, pp. 880, 884–885.

44 Provincial gazetteer, *op.cit.* p. 375.

45 See P. H. Hase, *Custom, Land and Livelihood*, *op.cit.* pp. 195–214, and *Hatred and Enmity: Settlement and Politics in Early Sai Kung, 1550–1850*, forthcoming. References to inter-personal civil disputes having been judged by the magistrate are similarly very rare in clan genealogies from the area. The Hong Kong government officials who took the New Territories area over from 1899 only mention disputes arising from the respective rights of subsoil and topsoil land-holders as occurring with any frequency, as seems also to have been the situation in Kwong Ning (see J. H. Stewart Lockhart, "Report on the New Territory During the First Year of British Administration", in *Papers Laid before the Legislative Council of Hong Kong, 1900*) (Sessional Papers, 1900), No. 15/1900, p. 257, "in the matter of land … disputes and family feuds have been general": this comment was made in the context of a discussion on subsoil and topsoil land-holdings.

46 See Philip C. C. Huang, *Civil Justice in China*, *op.cit.* Table 18.

47 For a fuller account of the administrative structure of San On, see Peter Y. L. Ng with Hugh D. R. Baker, *New Peace County: A Chinese Gazetteer of the Hong Kong Region*, Hong Kong University Press, 1983, and P. H. Hase, *Custom, Land and Livelihood in Rural South China*, *op.cit.* Introduction. For a general background to the staffing and work within the yamen, see especially Bradly Reed, *Talons and Teeth*, *op.cit.* and 任立達, 中國古代縣衙制度史 (青島出版社) (Ren Lida: History of the Structure of Ancient Chinese County yamen), and 那思陸, 清代州縣衙門番判制度 (中國政法大學出版社), 2006 (Na Silu: Legal Arrangements in County and Prefectural yamen in the Qing), among many others.

48 Cheung Yat-ping, *op.cit.* 1819 gazetteer, 卷5, p. 726.

49 See T'ung-tsu Chü, *Local Government in China under the Ch'ing*, *op.cit.* pp. 9–11.

50 Feng shui (風水), seeks to align buildings to the optimum flow of the life-forces through the site, and thus to maximize the good fortune of the institution, or family, using the building.

51 卷5, Cheung Yat-ping, *op.cit.* pp. 318–319.

52 See the description of the yamen at 卷5, Cheung Yat-ping, *op.cit.* p. 318. 譙樓 means "watchtower": a watchman was always stationed in the Drum Tower, day and night, to give warning of any fire breaking out in the City. The Drum Tower collapsed in the typhoon of 1671, and again in the flood of 1686, and was in both cases rebuilt.

53 Plates 9 and 10 are of buildings in the surviving Qing-period yamen at Yexian (葉縣, Yip Yuen) in Henan Province. None of the buildings of the San On yamen survive, but the Yexian yamen was very similar to the San On yamen, and so these Plates are included for general information.

54 Huang Liu-hung, *A Complete Book*, ed. Djang Chu, *op.cit.* p. 127, 308, 536, mentions that miscreants might be detained in the granary rather than be imprisoned in the prison when they were not suspected of crime (especially men who persistently failed to pay taxes on time). The granary office was, therefore, required to be secure, and this would fit this small courtyard in the San On yamen.

55 For descriptions of the magistrate's yamen, see 卷5, Cheung Yat-ping, *op.cit.* pp. 318–319, 1819 gazetteer, 卷7, pp. 782–783: these two descriptions are verbally substantially different, but clearly describe buildings which were much the same at the two dates. In the city of Nam Tau today there is a building which claims to be the yamen, but this is a recently constructed edifice built to satisfy local tourists who demand to see it: it is not on the original site, nor is it in any way built according to the original plan. It is, in fact, built on a feng shui site so poor that no Imperial government building would ever have been built there. Nothing survives of any of the San On civil yamen except for part of the late Qing assistant magistrate's yamen in Kowloon City.

56 For the San On magistracy staff see Ng and Baker, *New Peace County, op.cit.* pp. 50–66.

57 For magistracy clerks, see 明清胥吏的作用與歷史的進程, 劉潤和, 香港經濟學社 (IES), 1995 (Thomas Lau: History, Use, and Development of Magistracy Clerks in the Ming and Qing), and Bradly Reed, *Talons and Teeth, op.cit.*

58 卷4, Cheung Yat-ping, *op.cit.* pp. 293–294, 1819 gazetteer, 卷5, p. 718.

59 1819 gazetteer, Cheung Yat-ping, *op.cit.* 卷5, p. 718. For the Tung Kwun clerk, see the 1464 Tung Kwun Gazetteer, 卷2, Cheung Yat-ping, *op.cit.* p. 89.

60 1819 gazetteer, 卷5, Cheung Yat-ping, *op.cit.* p. 718.

61 The preface to this gazetteer, by Zhou Xiyao, survives: 卷12, Cheung Yat-ping, pp. 483–485, 1819 gazetteer, 卷23, pp. 1056–1057: the 1819 gazetteer gives the date as 1643.

62 卷4, Cheung Yat-ping, *op.cit.* p. 294.

63 See T'ung-tzu Chü, *Local Government in China under the Ch'ing, op.cit.* p. 39, and Bradly Reed, *Talons and Teeth, op.cit.*

64 "Corvée" was a labour tax: every family had to provide one fit, adult male for so many days each year, to labour without pay on government projects. By the late Ming, it had become normal for families to pay a small cash sum in lieu of corvée: in 1711, this was enforced throughout the empire, with the small cash sum being added to the land tax, although it always remained within the power of the imperial authorities to enforce corvée in extraordinary circumstances. The bao-jia was a way of enforcing local security and peace: a group of families (nominally ten) would

be grouped together, and each would be oath-sworn to inform the authorities of any improper or criminal action by any one of their members — if any crime was committed, the members of the bao-jia involved would be punished for having failed to warn the authorities beforehand. The bao-jia was also used as the base unit for a number of other local duties.

65 See 姚柯楠 (Yao Kenan), 説不盡的府衙往事:南陽知府衙門考 ("A Complex Tale of Bygone Things at the Prefectural Yamen: A Study of the Nanyang Prefectural Yamen"), 中州古籍出版社, 2008, pp. 154–156, for a detailed discussion of the duties of each clerical fong.

66 See the 1464 Tung Kwun Gazetteer, 卷2, Cheung Yat-ping, *op.cit.* pp. 88–89. The 1464 gazetteer also lists the clerks working at that date in the granaries in Tai Pang and in Nam Tau.

67 Bradly Reed (*Talons and Teeth*, *op.cit.*) notes that, in the county he studied (Ba County, 巴縣, in Szechuan) the clerks were arranged in ten fong, personnel, granary, revenue, rites, salt, military, punishments, works, receipt and transmission, and documents: "punishments" is 刑, translated above as "legal", and "revenue" is 戶, translated above as "households". In Tung Kwun, the granary clerk was seen as a separate post, and not as one of the fong. The salt clerk is the only significant difference: neither Tung Kwun nor San On had a salt clerk: the records of the salt monopoly were kept outside the purview of the magistrate. Otherwise the arrangement of the clerks in Ba County and in San On and Tung Kwun was very similar.

68 See 卷5, Cheung Yat-ping, *op.cit.* pp. 318–319.

69 See 卷5, Cheung Yat-ping, *op.cit.* pp. 318–319.

70 See 卷4, Cheung Yat-ping, *op.cit.* p. 293. Huang Liu-hung does not mention a chief clerk: in his book all the established clerks are treated as equal (*A Complete Book*, ed. Djang Chu, *op.cit. passim.*

71 These staff are often called by other English names, including "lictors", "archers" etc.

72 See T'ung-tsu Chü, *Local Government in China Under the Ch'ing*, *op.cit.* p. 57, and Bradly Reed, (*Talons and Teeth*, *op.cit.*).

73 卷5. Cheung Yat-ping, *op.cit.* pp. 330–331, 1819 gazetteer, 卷22, p. 861. The establishment of the Tung Kwun route is omitted, presumably in error, from the 1688 gazetteer. For the 25 horses, see below. The establishment of the Tai Pang route was originally 14, but this was reduced to 13 in 1621, see 1819 gazetteer, 卷11, Cheung Yat-ping, *op.cit.* p. 861; Ng and Baker, *New Peace County*, *op.cit.* p. 100.

74 See Huang Liu-hung, *A Complete Book*, ed. Djang Chu, *op.cit.* 卷25–26, pp. 525–556, for a full discussion of the courier services, and the uses of the magistracy horses for imperial messengers and high officials.

75 Details are in the 1819 gazetteer, 卷11, Cheung Yat-ping, *op.cit.* p. 853. The 1688 gazetteer mentions these mounted soldiers (馬軍) but gives no details, see 卷8, Cheung Yat-ping *op.cit.* p. 383.

76 See Ng and Baker, *New Peace County*, *op.cit.* p. 54. The figure of 60 runners in the county in 1899 is given in J. H. Stewart Lockhart, *Extracts from a Report by Mr Stewart Lockhart on the Extension of the Colony of Hong Kong*, in *Papers Laid before the Legislative Council of Hong Kong, 1899* (Sessional Papers, 1900), No 9/1899, para. "Police", p. 192.

77 Du Fengzhi notes that collecting the taxes in the villages in Kwong Ning, rather than at the yamen was "according to Kwangtung custom", 廣寧收粮在鄉, 粵省風氣如是. See Yau Tsit, 知縣與地方士紳, *op.cit.* p. 18. Huang Liu-hung states that the land tax was paid in only at the yamen in the counties he was familiar with, and in ten installments, rather than the two which were the norm in San On, see *A Complete Book*, ed. Djang Chu, *op.cit.* pp. 193–194.

78 As with the recently constructed magistrate's yamen, there is a building in Nam Tau today which claims to be the military yamen. It was built to satisfy local tourists. It is not on the original site, and does not reflect the original plan, and is on a site which does not meet the feng shui requirements for a military yamen. The original military yamen stood on a side street off the main east-west street of the city, and separated from it by a row of civilian buildings. The military yamen lay in the north-west of the city, and the magistracy in the north-east, on the other side of the main north-south street. In some other counties, where the numbers of soldiers was lower than in San On (for instance, Pingyao, 平遙, in Shanxi), the county military headquarters were within the same compound as the magistrate's yamen, but this was not the case in San On.

79 See Philip C.C. Huang, *Civil Justice in China*, *op.cit.* ch. 5.

80 Some counties had a full-time post of jail-keeper, but there does not seem to have been such a post in San On. T'ung-tsu Chü, *Local Government in China Under the Ch'ing*, *op.cit.* p. 10, says such a permanent jail warden post "existed in practically all" counties, but there does not seem to have been such a post in San On (or, indeed, in Tung Kwun).

81 T'ung-tsu Chü, *Local Government in China Under the Ch'ing*, *op.cit.* p. 180, suggests that magistrates were urged not to use their subordinates as sources of information about the county, but it seems clear that they did in fact regularly do so: Djang Chu (introduction to Huang Liu-hung, *A Complete Book*, ed. Djang Chu,

op.cit. p. 23) states that the "new magistrate was obliged to depend on [magistracy underlings] for information about the area".

82 Oral information given to the author from village elders. In Tai Wai village, one villager in the later 19th century had been given a position as clerk in the Kwun Fu assistant magistrate's yamen: according to the elders, when he returned to his village (once or twice every year), the elders would take him out to dinner and get as much information as to action in hand in the magistracy as they could.

83 Bradly Reed, (*Talons and Teeth*, *op.cit.*), states that the magistracy clerks in Ba County had to find the funds to repair the rooms they used as offices, and that the magistrate did not have to find the funds to keep these buildings in repair, but only all the other buildings.

84 Du Fengzhi was obliged to support some ten families of his relatives, between 30 and 40 people: many were employed by him as servants in the yamen.

85 Djang Chu, introduction to Huang Liu-hung, *A Complete Book*, *op.cit.* p. 43, "It was common practice for a magistrate to postpone the repair of public buildings until they were on the verge of collapse … most public buildings were in various stages of delapidation." In Canton, the yamen of the high provincial authorities were renovated and re-furnished for each new appointee: in the late Qing this was done at the expense of the magistrates of the two metropolitan counties, see Yau Tsit, 同治光緒年間廣州官紳, *op.cit.* p. 37. Du Feng Zhi had to find 3,000 taels towards the refurbishment of the yamen of the provincial governor in 1872.

86 *The Great Ming Code: Da Ming lü*, translated and introduced, Jiang Yonglin, University of Washington Press, Asian Law Series, 2004, Articles 243, 247.

87 T'ung-tsu Chü, *Local Government in China in the Ch'ing*, *op.cit.* pp. 39, 59. See also in particular Bradly Reed, (*Talons and Teeth*, *op.cit.*) for the substantial number of supernumeraries in Ba County at the very end of the Qing, and for the complex way they were arranged.

88 T'ung-tsu Chü, *Local Government in China Under the Ch'ing*, *op.cit.* pp. 76–77.

89 Huang Liu-hung, *A Complete Book*, ed. Djang Chu, *op.cit.* p. 101, 103, 107.

90 卷12, Cheung Yat-ping, op.cit. p. 452, 1819 gazetteer, 卷22, p. 1015, edict 僉段實 以杜包侵, "Eradicate embezzlement by ensuring accuracy". This was Zhou Xiyao's fourth edict. See D. Faure, *The Structure of Chinese Rural Society*, *op.cit.* pp. 128–129, including a partial translation of this edict, 卷12, Cheung Yat-ping, pp. 463–464, 1819 gazetteer, 卷22, pp. 1024–1025, edict 禁包當以清里役. This is Li Kecheng's sixth edict.

91 The author visited the county yamen at Pingyao, 平遙, (Shanxi), Neixiang, 內鄉, and Yexien, 葉縣, (both in Henan), and the prefectural yamen at Nanyang (Henan), 南陽, to look into this point.

92 Bradly Reed, *Talons and Teeth*, *op.cit.* pp. 61–69, 128–136.

93 Du Fengzhi found that many of the senior clerks in his yamen had been "recommended" by the gentry leaders of Kwong Ning County, and thus were difficult for him to control. See Yau Tsit, 知縣與地方士紳, *op.cit.*

94 Bradly Reed, *Talons and Teeth*, *op.cit.* does not mention copyists, but the need to take copies of so many documents would have made copyists an essential feature of any yamen.

95 Stewart Lockhart, *Extracts from a Report by Mr Stewart Lockhart on the Extension of the Colony of Hong Hong*, 1898, in *Papers Laid before the Legislative Council of Hong Kong, 1899* (Sessional Papers), Hong Kong Government Printer, 1900, No. 9/99, p. 192, section "Police".

96 Bradly Reed, *Talons and Teeth*, *op.cit.* p. 34. 劉鵬九 (Liu Pengjiu), 內鄉縣衙與衙門文化 ("Neixiang County Yamen and Yamen Culture"), 中州古籍出版社, 2006, p. 161.

97 Huang Liu-hung, *A Complete Book*, ed. Djang Chu, *op.cit.* p. 83.

98 Du Fengzhi employed substantial numbers of his relatives in the yamen, but mostly as servants. Some were used, not to check the work of the clerks, but as "representatives to supervise" them. The most important of these were the relatives he employed as 坐省 and 坐府; agents employed to act as his eyes and ears in the offices of his superiors, and to give bribes as necessary to keep them sweet. See Yau Tsit, 知縣與地方士紳, *op.cit.* pp. 5–6.

99 See 內鄉縣衙, *loc.cit.*

100 See 南陽知府衙門考, *op.cit.* pp. 153–156.

101 See T'ung-tsu Chü, *Local Government in China Under the Ch'ing*, *op.cit.* ch. VI, pp. 93–115.

102 Huang Liu-hung, *A Complete Book*, ed. Djang Chu, *op.cit.* p. 81.

103 Djang Chu, introduction to Huang Liu-hung, *A Complete Book*, *op.cit.* p. 14–15.

104 Ng and Baker, *New Peace County*, *op.cit.* makes no mention of any supernumerary staff, nor of any personal servants of the magistrates being used in the yamen, nor yet of any private secretaries employed there. Stewart Lockhart mentions three private secretaries as employed by the San On magistrate in 1899, advising the magistrate on "crime, revenue, and official correspondence" (but not, it would seem, on civil litigation). For the private secretaries in 1899, see Stewart Lockhart, *Extracts from a Report by Mr Stewart Lockhart on the Extension of the Colony of Hong Kong*, in *Papers Laid before the Legislative Council of Hong Kong, 1899* (Sessional Papers, 1899), Hong Kong Government Printer, 1900, No. 9/99, p. 192, "Civil Officers" section. Du Fengzhi employed a private secretary in 1866 (Yau Tsit, p. 37).

105 See P. H. Hase, *Custom, Land and Livelihood*, *op.cit.* pp. 239–243, and fn. 12, p. 452.

106 卷9, Cheung Yat-ping, *op.cit.* pp. 395–404, 1819 gazetteer, 卷15, pp. 891–899.

107 T'ung-tsu Chü, *Local Government in China Under the Ch'ing*, *op.cit.* ch. X, states that only graduates (indeed, only graduates of the rank of Kui Yan or above) would have advised the magistrate, and that only these graduates should be considered as forming part of the county elite, but this is clearly not so for San On.

108 See D. Faure, "The Structure of Chinese Rural Society: Lineage and Village in the Eastern New Territories", Hong Kong, *East Asian Historical Monographs*, Oxford University Press, Hong Kong, 1986, pp. 130–140, and "The Po Tak Temple in Sheung Shui Market" in *Journal of the Hong Kong Branch of the Royal Asiatic Society*, Vol. 22, 1983, pp. 271–79, and see also Vol. 28, 1989, pp. 262–263.

109 The Tung Ping Kuk seems to have differed from the councils set up in the early-mid 19th century to oversee the local militia, not only in its date, but also in its original aim (see Yau Tsit, 晚清廣东的公局, *op.cit.*, *passim*, for these 19th century councils), but, by the mid 19th century may well have become rather similar to these later bodies.

110 For the Tung Wo Kuk, see P. H. Hase, "The Alliance of Ten: Settlement and Politics in the Sha Tau Kok Area", *Down to Earth: the Territorial Bond in South China*, ed. D. Faure and H. F. Siu, Stanford University Press, 1995, pp. 123–160.

4   The Ming Magistrates: Zhou Xiyao and His Predecessors

1 See the Xinjian Gazetteer, 中國地方志集成, 江西府縣志輯, 同治新建縣志, 1871, photo-reproduced 江蘇古籍出版社, with 上海書店 and 巴蜀書社, Vol. 1, 卷31, p. 331.

2 See the Hoi Fung Gazetteer, op.cit. p. 21, and the Zhangping Gazetteer, *op.cit.* 卷 7, p. 223, 卷8, p. 265–266.

3 旌德人文 ("Culture of Jingde County"), 方光華 (Fang Guangwa), Hefei University of Technology Press, 2011, is of little value for the early (Ming-early Qing) cultural history of the area, as this book only deals with the last century or so (late Qing-present).

4 See the Jingde Gazetteer, *loc.cit.*

5 The reason given for the resignation is mentioned in the Jingde County Gazetteer.

6 Guo Daoxian was the leader of a group of friends from Hunan who were to refuse to surrender to the Qing. When the Qing soldiers came to arrest him, he and his daughter escaped. He became a monk, but reluctantly (he used as his monastic

name 頑石, "Reluctant Stone"), and aimed to spend the rest of his life growing flowers, practising his calligraphy, and writing poems. He found it impossible to settle, however, and he wandered from place to place, eventually dying far from home. His poems were published in two volumes, 補山堂詩集 and 紫庵難著. See 湖湘士子謠, in 藝海, Vol. 3, 2007, 李安仁, and 肇慶七星岩石刻詩文選, 廣東省肇慶星湖風景名勝區管理局, ed. 黃柏權, 1989, pp. 111–114. I am indebted to Selia Tan Jinhua of Wuyi University for drawing my attention to this latter book.

7   The poem was inscribed in the calligraphy of a Taoist recluse, presumably one living at that date in one of the hermitages at Seven Stars Crag, with an introduction stating that the poem is by Zhou Xiyao, and that Zhou Xiyao was inspired by Guo Daoxian's poem, and that the recluse had copied it for inscription on the rock. The inscription is to be found in the Lin Fa Tung Cave (蓮花洞, also known as 千詩洞, "Cave of the Thousand Poems"). I am indebted to Mr Tim Ko Tim-keung for Plates 16 and 17.

8   肇慶七星岩石刻詩文選. pp. 115–116.

9   Jingde County Gazetteer, op.cit. p. 162. No copy of this book seems to exist in any library in Hong Kong, nor in the National Library in Beijing, nor the Shanghai Library, nor yet in the libraries of the Universities of Hefei or Shenzhen. It would seem probable that this book no longer survives.

10 Biography of He Mengzhuan, 1819 gazetteer 卷14, Cheung Yat-ping, op.cit. p. 884. The titles of the books are given in the biography.

11 Biography of Li Wenzhao, 1819 gazetteer, 卷14, Cheung Yat-ping, op.cit. p. 885.

12 卷12, Cheung Yat-ping, op.cit. pp. 457–459, 1819 gazetteer, 卷22, pp. 1019–1020.

13 卷11, Cheung Yat-ping, op.cit. p. 443, 1819 gazetteer, 卷13, pp. 870–871, New Peace County, op.cit. pp. 108–109. The city of Tai Pang (大鵬, Dapeng) had also been besieged by pirates in 1571. See Table 2 in Chapter 7, below.

14 For an incident that occurred during this attack, see the biography of the daughter of Ng Yuen-ming, 吳元明, Wu Yuanming, who was murdered when she grabbed a rock and smashed the nose of a pirate who was trying to rape her, 卷10, Cheung Yat-ping, op.cit. p. 432, 1819 gazetteer, 卷20, p. 965, Ng and Baker, op.cit. p. 118.

15 1819 gazetteer, 卷19, Cheung Yat-ping, p. 961: this biography seems to have been omitted from the 1688 gazetteer, presumably in error: it would have been copied to the 1819 gazetteer from the "old gazetteer" of 1643. See Ng and Baker, New Peace County, op.cit. pp. 108–109.

16 They had sent ships to block the entrance to Victoria Harbour at Lyemun (鯉魚門, Liyumen), but had withdrawn them shortly afterwards. 卷11, Cheung Yat-ping, p. 442–443, 1819 gazetteer, 卷13, pp. 870–872, *New Peace County*, pp. 107–108. "Tamaō Island" was the name given by the Portuguese to their settlement: it is called 屯門島 ("Tuen Mun Island") in the Chinese sources.

17 In the "All the Problems" paper, 卷12, Cheung Yat-ping, *op.cit.* pp. 457–459, 1819 gazetteer, 卷22, pp. 1019.

18 卷3, Cheung Yat-ping, *op.cit.* p. 242.

19 Biography of Chen Gu, 卷10, Cheung Yat-ping, *op.cit.* p. 411, 1819 gazetteer, 卷 14, p. 881.

20 卷12, Cheung Yat-ping, *op.cit.* pp. 451–452, 1819 gazetteer, 卷22, p. 1013. This is a county edict, entitled 建臺堡以固海疆, "Build a strong fort to protect the sea-coast", issued by Zhou Xiyao, to announce the successful finalisation of this new defence-work. The edict is the first of fourteen that he issued (條議十四). The arrangement at Nam Tau was almost identical with that at Kowloon City, where the mid 19th century stone pier was similarly protected by a strong fort built between the city and the foot of the pier. See also 卷3, Cheung Yat-ping, *op.cit.* p. 243.

21 For Wu Wenming, see the entry in the "Bandits", 寇盜 section, 卷11, Cheung Yat-ping, *op.cit.* p. 443, 1819 gazetteer, 卷13, p. 871, Ng and Baker, *New Peace County*, *op.cit.* pp. 108–109. For Ma Yimao, see his biography, 卷10, Cheung Yat-ping, *op.cit.* p. 415, 1819 gazetteer, p. 883.

22 卷11, Cheung Yat-ping, *op.cit.* pp. 438–441, 1819 gazetteer, 卷13, pp. 870–871, *New Peace County*, *op.cit.* pp. 106–111.

23 卷11, Cheung Yat-ping, *op.cit.* pp. 442–443, 1819 gazetteer 卷13, pp. 870–872, *New Peace County*, pp. 107–108. Criminals could normally be executed only after the magistrate had submitted the papers to the board of punishments in the capital, who would issue approval for the execution only after they had satisfied themselves that the trial held was fairly conducted, and the evidence sufficient. However, the magistrate could execute summarily, without holding a trial or seeking approval, where the guilt of the accused was manifest, especially where bandits or rebels were caught with weapons in their hands, and actively attacking the county.

24 Biography of Zhang Wenxing, 卷10, Cheung Yat-ping, *op.cit.* pp. 414–415, 1819 gazetteer, 卷14, p. 883. This was probably the Chan Yiu bandit gang mentioned in the gazetteer, "Bandits", 寇盜 section, as having attacked the county in 1647 (卷 11, Cheung Yat-ping, *op.cit.* p. 444, 1819 gazetteer, 卷13, p. 872), but it does not mention there that the magistrate had been besieged in the county city.

25 卷11, Cheung Yat-ping, *op.cit.* p. 443, 1819 gazetteer, 卷13, p. 871, *New Peace County*, *op.cit.* p. 109. Zhou Xiyao obliquely refers to the destruction of this bandit gang in his preface to the San On Gazetteer, 卷12, Cheung Yat-ping, *op.cit.* pp. 483–484, 1819 gazetteer, 卷23, pp. 1056–1057. Zhou Xiyao rewarded the Lung Yeuk Tau elders for their assistance in the defeat of this group of pirates by petitioning that an imperial plaque be awarded to a Lung Yeuk Tau scholar (this imperial plaque no longer survives), see D. Faure, *The Structure of Chinese Rural Society: Lineage and Village in the Eastern New Territories, Hong Kong*, Oxford University Press, East Asian Historical Monographs, 1986, p. 156 and fn 29.

26 1464 Tung Kwun Gazetteer, 卷2, Cheung Yat-ping, *op.cit.* p. 89.

27 卷8, Cheung Yat-ping, *op.cit.* p. 390.

28 1819 gazetteer, 卷8, Cheung Yat-ping, *op.cit.* p. 816, 卷12, Cheung Yat-ping, *op.cit.* p. 865.

29 Exactly the same thing arose in the mid 19th century, when the patrol ship stationed at Fuk Wing was rented out to a pirate, see Ng and Baker, *op.cit.* p. 65.

30 卷12, Cheung Yat-ping, p. 454, 1819 gazetteer, 卷22, p. 1016–1017. The edict, 懲假哨以衛商漁, "Punish false patrol vessels to protect merchants and fisher-people", was the eighth to be issued.

31 In an edict in 卷12, Cheung Yat-ping, *op.cit.* pp. 455, 1819 gazetteer, 卷22, p. 1017. This edict, 肅軍令以保民生, "Bring the Army into order, in order to preserve the people's livelihood", was the ninth issued.

32 Details from an edict issued by Zhou Xiyao. 卷12, Cheung Yat-ping, *op.cit.* p. 456, 1819 gazetteer, 卷22, p. 1018, *New Peace County*, *op.cit.* pp. 122–123. This edict, 編蛋甲以塞盜源, "Register the Tanka to cut off the supply of pirates" was the twelfth issued.

33 卷12, Cheung Yat-ping, *op.cit.* pp. 456–457, 1819 gazetteer, 卷22, pp. 1018–1019. This edict, 嚴保甲以安地方, "Strictly enforce the bao-jia to pacify the area", was the thirteenth issued.

34 卷12, Cheung Yat-ping, *op.cit.* p. 455, 1819 gazetteer, 卷22, p. 1017. This edict, 驅外奸以杜內患, "Drive away outsider bandits to eradicate insider problems" was the tenth issued.

35 卷3, Cheung Yat-ping, *op.cit.* p. 272, 1819 gazetteer, 卷22, p. 699. The mention of the Yao people is under 柑坑山, which refers to these mountains. While references to the Yao living in this area were carried over into the 1819 gazetteer, it is probable that these Yao (who were still clearly present in the 1640s) disappeared at the time of the Coastal Evacuation: all the present-day inhabitants of the area are Hakka, who claim to have settled there after the Coastal Evacuation, after about 1700. There were a string of forts along the north coast of Mirs Bay in 1688: these were probably established after 1670, possibly by Li Kecheng.

36 卷12, Cheung Yat-ping, *op.cit.* p. 455–456, 1819 gazetteer, 卷22, p. 1018. This edict, 清料船以靖海氛, "Get rid of the 'outsider boats' to preserve the peace of the sea" was the eleventh to be issued.

37 From a booklet 爛頭島開發, *The Development of Lantau*, published in 1941 to look into the question of the development of Lantau, with the hope of eventually providing homes and workplaces for the huge numbers of refugees from the Japanese. Ng Hei (吳曦) wrote a report on Tai O (大澳), in which he says that Tai O had always had three to five smuggling families using such boats for smuggling salt into China, and opium, and other products, from China to Hong Kong, but that this had risen to about 50 within the year 1940–1941. Ng Hei deplored the social and economic problems dependence on smuggling with these boats brought to Tai O.

38 See *Salt: Production and Taxation*, China: Imperial Maritime Customs, V. Office Series: Customs Papers No 81, published for the Customs Archives, Shanghai, Statistical Department of the Inspectorate General of Customs, 1906, *passim*.

39 Biography of Li Xuan, 卷10, Cheung Yat-ping, *op.cit.* p. 411, 1819 gazetteer, 卷 14, p. 881, the entry in the provincial gazetteer, *op.cit.* is at p. 221.

40 Biography in the provincial gazetteer, *op.cit.* p. 375.

41 Oral history accounts, and the clan genealogies (族) from New Territories villages, have a great deal to say about how the first ancestors of the clans came to the area, and their hardships before they were able to establish a home there.

42 The first of these edicts on this subject was his second, 禁詭冒以懲奸徒, "Stop false identities to punish crafty villains", the second on this subject was his third, 禁擄詐以重人命, "Stop squeeze and venerate human life", and the third on this subject was his seventh, 戢囂爭以按民堵, "Bring an end to violence to bring peace to the people", 卷12, respectively Cheung Yat-ping, *op.cit.* pp. 452, 452, 453–454, 1819 gazetteer, 卷22, pp. 1014–1015, 1015, 1016, the last of these edicts is translated in *New Peace County*, *op.cit.* p. 122.

43 卷12, Cheung Yat-ping, *op.cit.* pp. 451, 1819 gazetteer, 卷22, pp. 1013–1014. This is the edict 黃冊之弊區可駭, "The corruption of the Yellow Books startles the district", and was Li Xuan's second. The poor condition of the Yellow Books should probably be taken as implying that already, by Li Xuan's time, the corvée in San On was commuted to a cash payment, probably as a supplement to the land tax, and so the corvée registers did not need to be kept up properly.

44 A county magistrate could write to a magistrate of another county, asking him to apprehend and return criminals fleeing from his jurisdiction, but it is clear that this practice was rarely followed in this period.

45 卷12, Cheung Yat-ping, *op.cit.* pp. 451–452, 1819 gazetteer, p. 1013. The details of the Lotus Path Fort are in the same county edict, 建臺堡以固海疆, "Build a

strong fort to protect the sea-coast", as the details of the pier-foot fort. See also 卷8, Cheung Yat-ping, *op.cit.* p. 384.

46 Huang Liu-hung faced an outbreak of exactly this sort as well: see *A Complete Book*, ed. Djang Chu, *op.cit.* p. 352.

47 The Qing code said that any man so reclaiming land had the right to register it for the land tax, and thus become the full legal owner of the land. The Ming code is silent on the issue, but it is probable that the Ming law was essentially the same as the Qing code.

48 Tang Man-wai does not comment on this edict: he was central to his clan's successful wresting of the market at Yuen Long from the control of the Ping Shan branch of the Tang clan to the Kam Tin Branch, see Chan Wing-hoi, "The Dangs of Kam Tin" *op.cit.*

49 卷5. Cheung Yat-ping, *op.cit.* pp. 326–327.

50 Biography of Zeng Kongzhi, 卷10, Cheung Yat-ping, *op.cit.* p. 411, 1819 gazetteer, 卷14, Cheung Yat-ping, *op.cit.* p. 880.

51 卷5. Cheung Yat-ping, *op.cit.* p. 326. Huang Liu-hung (*A Complete Book*, ed. Djang Chu, *op.cit.* p. 525) stresses that promotion of education was a vital part of a magistrate's duties, and that most magistrates, who ignored this need, were missing the point: Zhou Xiyao would, clearly, have agreed.

52 For the history of the county school, see 卷5, Cheung Yat-ping, *op.cit.* pp. 321–322, 1819 gazetteer, 卷7, pp. 785–786, *New Peace County*, *op.cit.* pp. 88–89.

53 Biography of Qiu Tiqian. 卷10, Cheung Yat-ping, *op.cit.* p. 410. 1819 gazetteer, 卷 14, Cheung Yat-ping, *op.cit.* p. 879.

54 From his biography in the provincial gazetteer, *op.cit.* p. 220, taken from the Fujian Provincial Gazetteer.

55 Plate 24 shows one of the wells of Nam Tau: this well served the military yamen area. Plate 25 shows one of the streets in Tai Pang: the deep stone-lined ditch was used to drain off rainwater, but was also used as an open sewer into which the household sewage was poured. The drainage of Nam Tau would have been of this character as well.

56 Feng shui is the science of geomancy, which maximizes the good fortune of a place by ensuring that all the buildings (and especially roads, wells, water courses, and doorways) are so placed that they align with the flow of the natural forces of the world through the place, so that anyone living or working in the place will enjoy optimum peace, security, and ease.

57 卷5, Cheung Yat-ping, *op.cit.* pp. 321–322 for the history of the county temple of Confucius and school.

58 Biography of Peng Yunnian, 卷10, Cheung Yat-pin, *op.cit.* p.411, 1819 gazetteer, 卷14, p. 881.

59 See Zhou Xiyao's preface to a new edition of the county gazetteer of 1643, 卷12, Cheung Yat-ping, *op.cit.* pp. 483–484, 1819 gazetteer, 卷23, pp. 1056–1057, for his views on the lack of culture in the county, and the need for education. See also his preface for the new school, 卷12, Cheung Yat-ping, *op.cit.* pp. 486–487, and his poem 鼎遷學宮, "On the Move of the County School", 卷12, Cheung Yat-ping, p. 521. Zhou Xiyao was not the first county magistrate to take this line, he refers to his predecessor, "Mr Wang" as having had similar views, in his poem on the move of the school, probably referring to Wang Tingyue (1614–1619).

60 Plate 1 is taken from the 1819 gazetteer. It is a drawing of the county school and temple of Confucius as they were in 1819. The county temple of Confucius, despite the various repairs and restorations, was still, in 1819, basically as Zhou Xiyao had built it. See 卷5, Cheung Yat-ping, *op.cit.* pp. 321–322, and 1819 gazetteer, 卷7, pp. 785–786, *New Peace County, op.cit.* pp. 88–89. No trace of the building survives today.

61 卷5, Cheung Yat-ping, *op.cit.* pp. 321–322.

62 卷5, Cheung Yat-ping, *op.cit.* pp. 326–327.

63 卷5, Cheung Yat-ping, *op.cit.* p. 326. In the Republican period, the county was formally re-named Po On (Baoan).

64 1819 gazetteer, 卷9, Cheung Yat-ping, *op.cit.* p. 827.

65 Biography of Duan Yansheng, 1819 gazetteer, 卷14, Cheung Yat-ping, *op.cit.* p. 884. The biography goes on to say that the income from the land was later "reduced" (probably implying that it was diverted to other purposes), but that that did not reduce the value of Duan Yansheng's original work.

66 Biography of He Mengzhuan, 1819 gazetteer, 卷14, Cheung Yat-ping, *op.cit.* pp. 884–885.

67 1819 gazetteer, 卷9, Cheung Yast-ping, *op.cit.* p. 827.

68 See 1819 gazetteer, Cheung Yat-ping, 卷23, *op.cit.* pp. 1067–1068, Ng and Baker, *op.cit.* pp. 124–125, also 卷8, Cheung Yat-ping, *op.cit.* p. 814.

69 Biographies of these magistrates, 卷10, Cheung Yat-ping, *op.cit.* pp. 415, 417, and 1819 gazetteer, 卷14, pp. 883, 884, 880, 885.

70 The land tax, and most other taxes, were paid by way of a fixed sum, which did not change from year to year. This fixed sum was the "tax quota". Huang Liu-hung notes that an unchangeable sum was required to be sent from each county to the province each year (*A Complete Book*, ed. Djang Chu, *op.cit.* p. 214). See below.

71 Many are duplicates — forts with more than one name — but there were at least forty of them.

72 See Zhou Xiyao's paper 詳減積穀, "Reduce Grain Stocks", 卷12, Cheung Yat-ping, *op.cit.* pp. 460–461, 1819 gazetteer, 卷22, p. 1022.

73 This is Yu Zhu's edict 革馬差之害, 卷12, Cheung Yat-ping, *op.cit.* pp. 449–450, 1819 gazetteer, 卷22, p. 1012. The summary is from the biography of Yu Zhu, 卷 10, Cheung Yat-ping, *op.cit.* p. 410, 1819 gazetteer, 卷14, p. 879.

74 卷6. Cheung Yat-ping, *op.cit.* p. 360.

75 Biography of An Yumei, 卷10, Cheung Yat-ping, *op.cit.* pp. 416–417, 1819 gazetteer, 卷14, p. 884. Huang Liu-hung (*A Complete Book*, ed. Djang Chu, *op.cit.* 卷 pp. 571–584) discusses in detail the problems he faced in getting good, usable horses in the counties he administered.

76 卷12, Cheung Yat-ping, *op.cit.* p. 457, 1819 gazetteer, 卷22, p. 1019, edict 革陋規 以豁行戶, "Eradicate evil rules to free businesses from tax". This was the 14th edict issued. Huang Liu-hung also states firmly that it was essential that the magistracy paid the full market price for everything that was bought by it (*A Complete Book*, ed. Djang Chu, *op.cit.* p. 106). It is possible that these prestations in kind were taken from hawkers wishing to sell goods from the roads within the walls, and were, at least in theory, perhaps, a sort of permit fee. Huang Liu-hung mentions (*A Complete Book*, ed. Djang Chu, *op.cit.* p. 215) a "tax on peddlars", which was levied in some, but not all, counties: he felt this was an evil tax, which should be abolished wherever it was levied, because of the poverty of the peddlars who had to pay it (see *A Complete Book*, ed. Djang Chu, *op.cit.* p. 215), so suggesting that something of this sort might underlie the San On levy.

77 From his biography in the provincial gazetteer, *op.cit.* p. 220.

78 From the biography of Yu Zhu, 卷10, Cheung Yat-ping, *op.cit.* p. 410, 1819 gazetteer, 卷14, p. 879.

79 Biographies of An Yumei and Jin Wenmo, 卷10, Cheung Yat-ping, *op.cit.* pp. 416– 417, 1819 gazetteer, 卷14, p. 884. Li Kecheng's ban on this practice is contained in his edict, "革火耗以勸輸將, Forbid meltage fee payments for silver exchange, in order that tax payments can be encouraged", 卷12, Cheung Yat-ping, *op.cit.* pp. 463–464, 1819 gazetteer, 卷22, pp. 1024–1025.

80 Respectively, 卷12, Cheung Yat-ping, *op.cit.* pp. 487, 458, 521. The last reference is from a poem by Zhou Xiyao, 署中糲食, "Eating coarse food in the office". The second reference strictly says that there was no official quota for servants at the magistracy, so no servants could be paid for from official funds. It is these references which make it clear that Zhou Xiyao had access to, at best, very little by way of private income.

81 卷12, Cheung Yat-ping, *op.cit.* pp. 452, 1819 gazetteer, 卷22, p. 1015, edict 僉段
    實以杜包侵, "Eradicate embezzlement by ensuring accuracy". This was the fourth
    edict. See D. Faure, *The Structure of Chinese Rural Society*, *op.cit.* pp. 128–129,
    including a partial translation of this edict.

82 See John R. Watt, *The District Magistrate*, *op.cit.* p. 111.

83 卷12, Cheung Yat-ping, *op.cit.* p. 458, 1819 gazetteer, 卷22, p. 1020. See Huang
    Liu-hung (*A Complete Book*, ed. Djang Chu, *op.cit.* pp. 304–305) for a discussion
    on the problems posed by people absconding.

84 This was to be made a legal requirement from 1750, but was not a requirement
    of the Ming code. See P. H. Hase, *Custom, Land and Livelihood*, *op.cit.* pp. 220–
    222.

85 The Ming code has a complete section on granaries (Jiang Yonglin, *The Great
    Ming Code*, *op.cit.* section 4, articles 125–148, especially articles 133–139). Use
    of false scales is prohibited under article 128, allowing grain to rot under article
    144, issuing fraudulent receipts under article 131 and article 138, malfeasance by
    articles 138 and 137, and embezzling grain by article 136, etc.

86 卷10, Yu Zhu biography, Cheung Yat-ping, *op.cit.* p. 410, 1819 gazetteer, 卷14, p.
    879.

87 卷10, Li Xuan biography, Cheung Yat-ping, *op.cit.* p. 411, 1819 gazetteer, 卷14, p.
    881.

88 For these residences, see the description of the yamen at 卷5, Cheung Yat-ping,
    op.cit. pp. 318–319.

89 1819 gazetteer, Cheung Yat-ping, 卷11, *op.cit.* p. 860.

90 1819 gazetteer, Cheung Yat-ping, 卷11, *op.cit.* p. 860.

91 卷4, Cheung Yat-ping, *op.cit.* p. 294.

92 Malfeasance in military granaries, especially conversion of ration grain to the
    private account of military supervisors is forbidden by article 137 of the Ming
    code, *The Great Ming Code*, Jian Yonglin, *op.cit.*

93 1819 gazetteer, 卷11, Cheung Yat-ping, *op.cit.* p. 860.

94 1819 gazetteer, 卷11, Cheung Yat-ping, *op.cit.* p. 860.

95 卷12, Cheung Yat-ping, *op.cit.* pp. 460–461; 1819 gazetteer, 卷22, pp. 1022–
    1023; Ng and Baker, *New Peace County*, *op.cit.* pp. 122–123. This is a report
    by Zhou Xiyao to his superiors in Canton, 詳減積穀, "A Proposal to Reduce Grain
    Stocks".

96 Article 131(3) of the Ming code, forbade commutation, but it was, clearly, common
    in San On, see *The Great Ming Code*, Jiang Yonglin, *op.cit.*

97 卷12. Cheung Yat-ping, *op.cit.* pp. 460–461; 1819 gazetteer, 卷22, pp. 1022–1023; Ng and Baker, *New Peace County*, *op.cit.* pp. 122–123.

98 See Stewart Lockhart, *Extracts from a Report by Mr Stewart Lockhart on the Extension of the Colony of Hong Kong, 1898*, in *Papers Laid before the Legislative Council of Hong Kong* (Sessional Papers), 1899, Hong Kong, Government Printer, 1900, No. 9/99, Appendix 6, p. 208.

99 卷12. Cheung Yat-ping, *op.cit.* p. 463, 1819 gazetteer, 卷22, p. 1024.

100 The catty is a weight equivalent to $1^1/_3$ lbs, the tael is one-sixteenth of a catty, and so equivalent to $1^1/_3$ ounces.

101 Zhou Xiyao's two reports on this demand for grain are the report 詳免軍需, "Proposal to Waive the Supplies for the Army", 卷12, Cheung Yat-ping, *op.cit.* pp. 460–461, 1819 gazetteer, 卷22, p. 1021, and 詳滅積穀, "Proposal to Reduce Grain Stocks", 卷12, Cheung Yat-ping, *op.cit.* pp. 460–461, 1819 gazetteer, 卷22, pp. 1013, *New Peace County*, *op.cit.* pp. 123–124.

102 The Ming code made it a criminal offence to delay disbursement of grain to soldiers, see *The Great Ming Code*, Jiang Yonglin, *op.cit.* Article 135(3).

103 See Appendix 1. Huang Liu-hung took much the same line on granary control as Zhou Xiyao: the granaries should never be allowed to hold stocks less than one year's expected disbursement — if demands were made by the provincial authorities for "loans" of grain, this must not be allowed to deplete the granaries below this figure. He clearly also felt that holdings of any amount well above a year's expected disbursements was unwise. (See *A Complete Book*, ed. Djang Chu, *op.cit.* p. 562).

104 卷12, Cheung Yat-ping, *op.cit.* pp. 485–486, 1819 gazetteer, 卷24, pp. 1073–1074. The text is entitled 禳疫告城隍文, "Text of Prayer to the City God, to Avert an Epidemic".

105 This prayer-text has been discussed by Puk Wing-kin (卜永堅, Bu Yongjian), in an article 抗租與迎神:從己卯年 (1999) 香港大埔林村鄉十年一度太平清醮看青代林村與龍躍頭鄧氏之關係 in 華南研究資料中心通訊 (South China Research Resource Station Newsletter), No. 18, 2000.

106 From his biography in the provincial gazetteer, *op.cit.* p. 221, taken from the Kuangxi Provincial Gazetteer.

107 卷11, Cheung Yat-ping, *op.cit.* p. 439. The 1819 gazetteer, 卷13, p. 867 gives a very much shortened version of this entry.

108 In the preface for the 1643 gazetteer (卷12, Cheung Yat-ping, *op.cit.* pp. 483–484, 1819 gazetteer, 卷23, pp. 1056–1057) he states that 地處極炎, "This place blazes extremely fiercely".

109 He wrote a poem on the experience, 颶風即事, "Experiences of a Typhoon", 卷12, Cheung Yat-ping, *op.cit.* p. 522.

110 See 卷11, Cheung Yat-ping, *op.cit.* p. 439, 1819 gazetteer, 卷13, p. 867. *New Peace County*, *op.cit.* p. 102 translates this from the 1819 gazetteer, which uses a slightly shorter form of words than the 1688 gazetteer.

111 He wrote a poem on them, 卷12, Cheung Yat-ping, p. 519, 新安春色篇, "On the New Year in San On". This has been quoted and discussed in 古代風俗詩面 ("Poems on Ancient Folk Practices"), ed. 孫民 (Sun Min), 1992, p. 14.

112 The poem is 鐘鼓石, "On the Bell-Drum Stone", 卷12, Cheung Yat-ping, *op.cit.* p. 519.

113 卷5, Cheung Yat-ping, *op.cit.* p. 328, 1819 gazetteer, 卷7, p. 788.

114 卷5, Cheung Yat-ping, *op.cit.* pp. 318–319, 1819 gazetteer, 卷7, p. 782: the gazetteer does not say where the money for this came from.

115 From the "All the Problems" paper, 卷12, Cheung Yat-ping, *op.cit.* p. 458, 1819 gazetteer, 卷22, p. 1020.

116 卷10, Cheung Yat-ping, *op.cit.* pp. 412–413, 1819 gazetteer, 卷14, p. 881, *New Peace County*, *op.cit.* p. 115. The translation at Appendix 1 is modified from that in *New Peace County*.

5   Li Kecheng and the Early Qing Magistrates

1 鐵嶺縣志, 1931, reprinted 成文出版社: 中國方志叢書:東北地方, 第五號, 1998.

2 卷4, Cheung Yat-ping, *op.cit.* p. 296, 1819 gazetteer, 卷5, p. 721.

3 For the southern Ming see *The Cambridge History of China: Vol. 7: The Ming Dynasty, Part 1*, ed, F. W. Mote and D. Twitchett, 1988, ch. 11, "The Southern Ming, 1644–1662", L.A. Struve.

4 Information in the "Officials: Magistrates", 文官表:知縣 section, 卷4, Cheung Yat-ping, *op.cit.* p. 296, not copied to the 1819 gazetteer.

5 卷11, Cheung Yat-ping, *op.cit.* p. 444, 1819 gazetteer, 卷13, p. 872, *New Peace County*, *op.cit.* pp. 109–110. See David Faure, *The Structure of Chinese Rural Society, op.cit.* pp. 156–157, Sung Hok-pang, "Legends and Stories of the New Territories: Kam Tin; Part II", in *Journal of the Hong Kong Branch of the Royal Asiatic Society*, Vol. 14, pp. 160–185, esp. pp. 172–173, and 羅香林; 一八四二年以前之香港及其對外交通, Hong Kong, 1959, p. 146, n. 17.

6 卷6, Cheung Yat-ping op.cit. p. 363. The Kwai Tak salt fields also conducted occasional censuses of their salt workers, but there the numbers of workers had

been declining steadily over the years before the Coastal Evacuation, from 2,263 in 1543, to 1,922 in 1614, and to 1,736 in 1633. Over the period of the Coastal Evacuation the numbers declined further, to 1,414 in 1688, a further 23% drop: the numbers never thereafter recovered. See gazetteer, 卷6, pp. 368–369.

7   卷6, Cheung Yat-ping, *op.cit.* p. 364.

8   卷6, Cheung Yat-ping, *op.cit.* p. 363.

9   Biography of Ma Yimao, 卷10, Cheung Yat-ping, *op.cit.* p. 415, 1819 gazetteer, 卷 14, p. 883. The wording differs significantly between the two gazetteers, here the quotation is taken mostly from the 1819 gazetteer.

10   Except for the figures for the censuses of 1603 and 1613, which look as if they merely copied the figure from the 1593 census; although, if the figure was copied, at least the salt monopoly authorities in 1603 and 1613 did not think there had been any radical change in numbers in the interval.

11   卷6, Cheung Yat-ping, *op.cit.* p. 365.

12   卷6, Cheung Yat-ping, *op.cit.* p. 367.

13   卷6, Cheung Yat-ping, *op.cit.* p. 363.

14   卷11, Cheung Yat-ping, *op.cit.* pp. 445–448. This description was not carried over into the 1819 gazetteer, which has only a very brief description of the evacuation, at 卷13, Cheung Yat-ping, op.cit. pp. 873–877, and it is this brief 1819 description which is translated at *New Peace County*, *op.cit.* pp. 111–113. *New Peace County*, *op.cit.* pp. 26–27 has a discussion of the evacuation, centring on a translation of a passage from 屈大均:廣東新話 (Qi Tajun, Wat Tai-kwan, "New Tales of Kwangtung", 1700), but this passage is clearly to a large extent taken from the 1688 San On Gazetteer. Since the full text of the description of the evacuation in San On, as given in the 1688 gazetteer, is not available in an English translation, it has been given here, at Appendix 2.

15   Respectively, from the gazetteer account of the evacuation (Appendix 2), and the biography of Li Kecheng (Appendix 3).

16   卷6, "Population", 戶口 section, 1819 gazetteer 卷8, Cheung Yat-ping, *op.cit.* pp. 334–336, 801–803. Ng and Baker, *New Peace County*, *op.cit.* pp. 27–28, 51 and 90–93.

17   Oral information from discussion with the clan elders, and from their written accounts of their history.

18   See P. H. Hase, "Beside the *Yamen*: Nga Tsin Wai Village", in *Journal of the Hong Kong Branch of the Royal Asiatic Society*, Vol. 39, 1999, pp. 1–82.

19   Oral evidence from the clan elders, and information from the clan genealogy.

20   卷3, Cheung Yat-ping, *op.cit.* p. 254.

21   卷3, Cheung Yat-ping, *op.cit.* p. 267.

22   Oral evidence from today's clan elders and their clan genealogies.

23   The comments starting "Li Kecheng, the county magistrate took up his post" in the account of the evacuation in the gazetteer (Appendix 2) are, almost certainly, either taken from something written by Li Kecheng, or record his words as spoken to Tang Man-wai, the editor of the 1688 gazetteer, and express his personal shock at what he saw.

24   卷12, Cheung Yat-ping, *op.cit.* pp. 507–510, 1819 gazetteer, 卷23, pp. 1058–1062.

25   知縣李可成條議興革事宜八條, 卷12, Cheung Yat-ping, *op.cit.* pp. 461–465, 1819 gazetteer, 卷22, pp. 1023–1026.

26   This is the edict 勸開墾以增國賦, "Encourage opening of waste land to increase the nation's resources". 卷12, Cheung Yat-ping, *op.cit.* p. 461, 1819 gazetteer, 卷22, p. 1023. It is the first of Li Kecheng's edicts.

27   Li Kecheng says something very similar in his preface to the county gazetteer 卷 12, Cheung Yat-ping, *op.cit.* pp. 507–510, 1819 gazetteer, 卷23, pp. 1058–1062, 辟萊開疆教以鳩居茅撤土蓋, "Destroy the weeds and open up the land, and build simple homes of grasses, with mud-plaster roofs".

28   卷12, Cheung Yat-ping, *op.cit.* pp. 507–510, 1819 gazetteer, 卷23, p. 1058–1062.

29   See Appendix 2 for donations of plough-equipment. The preface to the county gazetteer is at 卷12, Cheung Yat-ping, *op.cit.* pp. 507–510, 1819 gazetteer, 卷23, pp. 1058–1062.

30   Preface to the county gazetteer, 卷12, Cheung Yat-ping, *op.cit.* pp. 507–510, 1819 gazetteer, 卷23, pp. 1058–1062.

31   卷13, Cheung Yat-ping, *op.cit.* p. 532–533.

32   In the context of the takeover of the New Territories, Mr H. H. J. Gompertz, member of the New Territories Land court, in his *Some Notes on Land Tenure in the New Territories* (Appendix 1 to J.H. Stewart Lockhart *Report on the New Territories for the Year 1900*, in *Papers Laid before the Legislative Council of Hong Kong, 1901*, No 28/1901, Hong Kong, Government Printer, 1902), p. 10 states that it was believed that, in the period after the rescission of the Coastal Evacuation, "the central government made small grants of money to encourage immigration from other districts … on easy terms": this refers to these grants by Li Kecheng, although all other references make it clear that it was Li Kecheng's personal money that was thus disbursed.

33   卷6, Cheung Yat-ping, *op.cit.* p. 335.

34   See Patrick H. Hase, *Custom, Land and Livelihood in Rural South China, op.cit.* pp. 58–61.

35   Edict 端士習以興教化, "Arrange for scholarly activity, to encourage learning", 卷12, Cheung Yat-ping, *op.cit.* pp. 461–462, 1819 gazetteer, 卷22, p. 1023. This is the second of Li Kecheng's edicts.

36   卷5, Cheung Yat-ping, *op.cit.* pp. 326–327.

37   *New Peace County, op.cit.* p. 1–3 says that this typhoon occurred on 21 March 1671, but the 1688 gazetteer says 八月二十一日 which is September (卷11, Cheung Yat-ping, p. 441). The error comes from the 1819 gazetteer, which mis-transcribes the date, saying 二月十一日 (Cheung Yat-ping, 卷12, p. 868).

38   卷5, Cheung Yat-ping, *op.cit.* p. 322, 1819 gazetteer, 卷7, p. 785, *New Peace County, op.cit.* p. 89.

39   Edict 修城池以資保障, "Restore the wall and moat in order to provide protection" (the third edict), and edict 築臺寨以固邊防, "Build forts and camps in order to strengthen the borders" (the fourth edict), both at 卷12, Cheung Yat-ping, *op.cit.* p. 462, 1819 gazetteer, 卷22, pp. 1023–1024.

40   卷3, Cheung Yat-ping, *op.cit.* p. 242, 1819 gazetteer, 卷7, p. 778, *New Peace County, op.cit.* p. 87, omits all this. See also 卷11, Cheung Yat-ping, *op.cit.* p. 440, 1819 gazetteer, 卷13, p. 868 (greatly shortened: *New Peace County. op.cit.* p. 104 translates this shortened version). Three military officers also donated a total of 42.135 taels from their private funds to the work as well. Li Kecheng also mentions the importance to the province as a whole of the Nam Tau defences in his preface to the county gazetteer, as well as the destruction caused by the typhoons, and the urgent need to secure donations to get the restoration work finished, 卷12, Cheung Yat-ping, *op.cit.* pp. 507–510, 1819 gazetteer, 卷23, p. 1058–1062.

41   卷3, Cheung Yat-ping, *op.cit.* p. 242, 1819 gazetteer, 卷7, p. 778.

42   卷3, Cheung Yat-ping, *op.cit.* p. 243, 1819 gazetteer, 卷7, p. 781. *New Peace County, op.cit.* p. 87 omits all this. See also 卷11, Cheung Yat-ping, *op.cit.* p. 440, 1819 gazetteer, 卷13, p. 868 (greatly shortened: *New Peace County. op.cit.* p. 104 translates this shortened version).

43   卷12, Cheung Yat-ping, *op.cit.* pp. 507–510, 1819 gazetteer, 卷23, p. 1058–1062.

44   In the gazetteer section relating to the yamen buildings, 卷5, Cheung Yat-ping, *op.cit.* p. 319, 1819 gazetteer, 卷7, p. 782, in different wording.

45   卷12, Cheung Yat-ping, *op.cit.* p. 533, 1819 gazetteer, 卷24, p. 1084; 卷12, Cheung Yat-ping, *op.cit.* p. 508, 1819 gazetteer, 卷23, p. 1059.

46   For the flood, see 卷 11, Cheung Yat-ping, *op.cit.* pp. 440–441, 1819 gazetteer,
     卷14, p. 888, *New Peace County*, op.cit. p. 104, for the damage to the yamen,
     see 卷5, Cheung Yat-ping, *op.cit.* p. 319, 1819 gazetteer, 卷7, p. 782, in different
     wording.

47   1819 gazetteer, 卷14, Cheung Yat-ping, *op.cit.* p. 880, Ng and Baker, *New Peace
     County*, *op.cit.* pp. 114–115.

48   卷11, Cheung Yat-ping *op.cit.* pp. 440–441, 1819 gazetteer, p. 868, Ng and
     Baker, *New Peace County*, *op.cit.* pp. 104–105.

49   Biography of Jin Wenmo 卷10, Cheung Yat-ping, *op.cit.* p. 417, 1819 gazetteer,
     卷14, p. 884 (significantly shortened).

50   For the Chiu Yam Nunnery, and its foundation by Jin Qizhen, see Cheung Yat-
     ping, *op.cit.* 1819 gazetteer, 卷18, p. 943.

51   卷5, Cheung Yat-ping, *op.cit.* p. 328, 1819 gazetteer, 卷7, pp. 787–788. The
     gazetteer states that the Kwan Tai Temple was restored by Li Kecheng and a
     senior military officer: probably this implies that the funds for the restoration were
     donated by these two officers.

52   There is, in Nam Tau today, a large Kwan Tai Temple, built just outside the south
     gate of the city. This claims to be a rebuilding of the old temple, but it is an entirely
     new structure, and stands nowhere near the site of either of the two old temples.

53   卷12, Cheung Yat-ping, *op.cit.* pp. 506–507, 1819 gazetteer, 卷24, pp. 1075–
     1076.

54   In addition to the typhoons of 1671, 1673, and 1677, there had been another
     serious typhoon in 1669, just before Li Kecheng took up his post as county
     magistrate.

55   The edict is 築臺寨以固邊防, "Build forts and camps in order to strengthen the
     borders" (the fourth edict), at 卷12, Cheung Yat-ping, *op.cit.* p. 462, 1819
     gazetteer, 卷22, pp. 1023–1024; the preface is at 卷12, Cheung Yat-ping, *op.cit.*
     pp. 507–510, 1819 gazetteer, 卷23, pp. 1058–1062; the poem is 蠔涌克捷,
     "Speedy pacification at Ho Chung", 卷12, Cheung Yat-ping, *op.cit.* p. 533; for
     the biography, see Appendix 3: the entry in the "Bandits", 寇盜 section is at 卷
     11, Cheung Yat-ping, *op.cit.* p. 444, 1819 gazetteer, 卷13, p. 872, *New Peace
     County*, *op.cit.* p. 110.

56   The clan genealogy of the Wan (溫, Wen) clan of Ho Chung states that the third
     son, Yi-tsap (宜集), of the founding ancestor of the clan (善慶) was "killed by
     bandits at Pak Mong Fa, and then more than a hundred men were taken there
     and slaughtered, 因被賊擄至白芒花後招贅 [? for 聚] 其地產 [for 剷] 下有百餘人云". It
     adds that Yi-tsap's father went to look for him when the bandits took his son, but
     he never returned, "and where his remains lie is unknown, 不知踪跡". The clan

believe that this tragedy was at the hands of Lei Kei and his gang, and this must be correct. This reference, therefore, shows us how bloody the fighting at Ho Chung was.

57   The edict is 築臺寨以固邊防, "Build forts and camps in order to strengthen the borders" (the fourth edict), at 卷12, Cheung Yat-ping, *op.cit.* p. 462, 1819 gazetteer, 卷22, pp. 1023–1024.

58   卷8, Cheung Yat-ping, *op.cit.* p. 387. The other civil officials donated a year's salary.

59   卷3, Cheung Yat-ping, *op.cit.* p. 243, 1819 gazetteer, 卷7, p. 780.

60   卷11, Cheung Yat-ping, *op.cit.* p. 444, 1819 gazetteer, 卷13, p. 872, *New Peace County*, *op.cit.* p. 110. This "bandit attack" occurred at exactly the time Shang Zhixin was engaged in the Revolt of the Three Feudatories, and may, as noted above, be connected with this.

61   Oral evidence given to the author by village elders.

62   These are the edicts 革火耗以勸輸將, "Forbid meltage fee payments for silver exchange, in order that tax payments can be encouraged", and 禁包當以清里役, "Forbid substituting duties to ensure Yamen Runners are kept in order", 卷12, Cheung Yat-ping, *op.cit.* pp. 463–464, 1819 gazetteer, 卷22, pp. 1024–1025. These are Li Kecheng's fifth and sixth edicts.

63   Huang Liu-hung (*A Complete Book*, ed. Djang Chu, *op.cit.* p. 528) states that the meltage fee cannot be done without, but that magistrates should not increase the surcharge above a reasonable figure. He also notes the problems magistrates could face from unscrupulous silversmiths in the refining of silver.

64   Biographies of Chen Liangyan, Peng Yunnian, and Ding Tangfa, 卷10, Cheung Yat-ping, *op.cit.* p. 411 (Chen Liangyan, and Peng Yunnian), 1819 gazetteer, 卷14, p. 881, p.880 (Ding Tangfa).

65   See Patrick H. Hase, *Custom, Land and Livelihood in Rural South China*, *op.cit.* pp. 73–77.

66   See biographies of these magistrates, 卷10, Cheung Yat-ping, *op.cit.* pp. 411, 416, 1819 gazetteer 卷14, pp. 881, 884.

67   1819 gazetteer, 卷14, Cheung Yat-ping, *op.cit.* p. 880, *New Peace County*, *op.cit.* pp. 114–115.

68   卷6. Cheung Yat-ping, op.cit. p. 360.

69   This was the edict 戢刁訟以安善良, "Eradicate corrupt lawsuits, in order to achieve peace and security", 卷12, Cheung Yat-ping, *op.cit.* p. 464, 1819 gazetteer, 卷22, p. 1026. This was the eighth edict.

70 This is the edict 嚴保甲以稽奸宄, "Rigorously enforce the bao-jia in order to check evildoers", 卷12, Cheung Yat-ping, *op.cit.* p. 464, 1819 gazetteer, 卷22, pp. 1025–1026. This was the seventh edict.

71 John R. Watt, *The District Magistrate, op.cit.* ch. 3.

72 See 卷5, Cheung Yat-ping, *op.cit.* p. 319.

73 5,000 taels is 6,666 ounces, or 3.7 hundredweights of silver.

74 Biographies of Chen Gu and Li Zungzhu, 卷10, Cheung Yat-ping, *op.cit.* pp. 411, 415, 1819 gazetteer, 卷14, pp. 881, 883 (shortened). The episode about commander Wong Sau-tso is incomplete in the biography of Li Jungzhu in the San On Gazetteer: Li Jungzhu's biography in the provincial gazetteer, *op.cit.* p. 375, supplies some of the missing details.

75 卷12, Cheung Yat-ping, *op.cit.* pp. 529–532, 八景詩. One of the beauty spots which Li Kecheng visited was the cave of Pui To on Castle Peak at Tuen Mun: the poem he wrote on this visit is 杯渡仙踪, "Spiritual Relics of Pui To".

6 Salt and Fish

1 卷12, Cheung Yat-ping, *op.cit.* p. 450, 1819 gazetteer, 卷22, pp. 1012–1013, edict of magistrate Yu Zhu (1594–1599), 革灶鹽之害, "Stop the harm to the salt workers". 卷12, Cheung Yat-ping, *op.cit.* p. 450, 1819 gazetteer, 卷22, p. 1013, edict of magistrate Li Xuan (1635–1637), 灶丁之困已甚, 冗場之設宜釐, "The difficulties of the salt workers are great: ameliorate them by improving conditions at the salt fields", 卷12 Cheung Yat-ping, *op.cit.* p. 453, 1819 gazetteer, 卷22, pp. 1015–1016. Edict of Zhou Xiyao, 復土民以益課餉, "Revitalise the people and improve the tax income", 卷12, Cheung Yat-ping, op.cit. p. 453, 1819 gazetteer, 卷22, pp. 1015–1016 (the sixth edict). The second edict of Zhou Xiyao's is 禁豪強以惠漁蛋, "Prohibit powerful men from causing distress to the fisher-people", and is at 卷12, Cheung Yat-ping, *op.cit.* p. 453, 1819 gazetteer, 卷22, pp. 1015 (the 5th edict). See also 卷6, Cheung Yat-ping, *op.cit.* p. 374, for a discussion of Zhou Xiyao's reform of the salt fau.

2 *The Great Ming Code*, Jiang Yonglin, *op.cit.* Article 150.

3 Gazetteer, 卷6, Cheung Yat-ping, *op.cit.* p. 361.

4 Gazetteer, 卷6, Cheung Yat-ping, *op.cit.* p. 361.

5 *The Great Ming Code*, Jiang Yonglin, *op.cit.* Article 246. The only ships permitted to sail out to sea were "maritime merchants" with special licences issued by the imperial authorities.

6   See *The Cambridge History of China, Vol. 7, The Ming Dynasty, 1368–1644, Part 1*, 1988, reprinted 2013, ch. 8, "The Chia-ching reign, 1522–1566", James Geiss, p. 495.

7   1464 Tung Kwun Gazetteer, 卷2, 3, Cheung Yat-ping, *op.cit.* pp. 89, 170.

8   卷6, Cheung Yat-ping, *op.cit.* pp. 372–373.

9   卷6. Cheung Yat-ping, *op.cit.* p. 374, 集餉 ("Miscellaneous Taxes") section.

10 卷6. Cheung Yat-ping, *op.cit.* p. 373, 魚課 ("Fish Tax") section.

11 "Fish tax" section of the 1688 gazetteer, *loc.cit.*

12 Gazetteer, 卷6, Cheung Yat-ping, *op.cit.* pp. 373, 374.

13 卷6, Cheung Yat-ping, *op.cit.* p. 373.

14 粵東省例新纂, "A New Collection of Kwangtung Provincial Edicts", originally published 1846, republished with an appendix added in the late 19th century, reprinted 成文出版社, Taipei, 1968, Vol. 2, pp. 761–780.

15 1819 gazetteer, 卷8, "Salt *Fau*", 鹽埠 sub-section, Cheung Yat-ping, *op.cit.* p. 816.

16 A fau could sell salt freely, but the salt could only be sold at the fau, and could not be exported inland to compete with the salt monopoly's trade in consumption quota salt.

17 See 卷12. Cheung Yat-ping, *op.cit.* p. 450 (edict 革灶鹽之害, "Reform the Difficulties at the Salt works"), 1819 gazetteer, 卷22, pp. 1012–1013. See also gazetteer, 卷6, Cheung Yat-ping, *op.cit.* p. 374.

18 The San On salt workers had been specifically freed of corvée between 1390 and 1492, gazetteer, 卷6, Cheung Yat-ping, *op.cit.* p. 361.

19 卷6, Cheung Yat-ping, *op.cit.* p. 375.

20 This is a clear case of a speculator abusing a monopoly position, and taking far more than the tax he was forwarding, in this case to the salt monopoly: by putting the salt makers as a communal body in charge of the levy, Li Xuan was hoping that only a reasonable sum, close to the tax due, would be levied. See 卷 12, Cheung Yat-ping, *op.cit.* p. 460 (edict 灶丁之困己甚), 1819 gazetteer 卷22, p. 1013. See also 卷6. Cheung Yat-ping, *op.cit.* p. 374.

21 卷6. Cheung Yat-ping, op.cit. p. 374.

22 Zhou Xiyao's first edict on this subject is 復土民以益課餉, "Revitalise the people and improve the tax income", 卷12, Cheung Yat-ping, *op.cit.* p. 453, 1819 gazetteer, 卷22, pp. 1015–1016 (the sixth edict). The second edict of Zhou Xiyao's on this subject, 禁豪強以惠漁蛋, "Prohibit powerful men from causing distress to the fisher-people", is at 卷12, Cheung Yat-ping, *op.cit.* p. 453, 1819 gazetteer, 卷22, p. 1015 (the fifth edict). See also 卷6. Cheung Yat-ping, *op.cit.* pp. 374–375: this

states that the information is taken from another edict of Zhou Xiyao, which seems to be different from the other two.

23 This form of words, 舊有, is regularly used in the gazetteer to mean "at the start of the dynasty". The "salt making areas" are often spoken of in the gazetteer as the "Four Districts, 四鄉", and these four fau are probably one for each salt making area.

24 1819 gazetteer, 卷8, Cheung Yat-ping, *op.cit.* p. 816.

25 The edict in question is 復土民以益課餉, "Revitalise the people and improve the tax income", 卷12, Cheung Yat-ping, *op.cit.* p. 453, 1819 gazetteer, 卷22, pp. 1015–1016, see also 卷6, Cheung Yat-ping, *op.cit.* p. 374.

26 卷6. Cheung Yat-ping, *op.cit.* p. 374.

27 卷6, Cheung Yat-ping, *op.cit.* p. 375.

28 卷6, Cheung Yat-ping, *op.cit.* p. 361.

29 卷6, Cheung Yat-ping, *op.cit.* p. 375.

30 卷6, Cheung Yat-ping, *op.cit.* pp. 371–72.

31 1819 gazetteer. 卷8, Cheung Yat-ping, *op.cit.* pp. 812, 816.

32 1819 gazetteer, 卷8, Cheung Yat-ping, *op.cit.* pp. 812, 815. The weight of the Kwangtung salt bau, as it was customary at the end of the 19th century, is given in *Salt: Production and Taxation*, op.cit. It is probable that the higher-than-face-value weight of the bau dates from 1737. The increase in the weight of the bau above the face-value was achieved by enforcing the use of the "Swatow Scale", which weighed 18 standard taels to the catty, thus increasing the weight of the bau by an eighth, and by increasing allowances for spillage, ullage, and overpacking (the bau was essentially a unit of volume, a standard sack, which was assumed to weigh a given weight: the viceroy allowed pressing the volume down, so that the bau weighed much more than the volume would suggest). The salt rent paid for the furnace lands was, it would seem, a provincial levy, and could thus be altered without the Peking authorities being consulted.

33 1819 gazetteer, 卷8, Cheung Yat-ping, *op.cit.* p. 816.

34 The edict of Zhou Xiyao 復土民以益夥餉, "Revitalise the people and improve the tax income", 卷12, Cheung Yat-ping, *op.cit.* p. 453, 1819 gazetteer, 卷22, pp. 1015–1016 (the sixth edict) makes it clear that, before the establishment of the fau at Cheung Chau and Sha Yue Chung, the salt for the fisher people was mostly handled at the fau at Pak Shek, near Sai Heung.

35 1819 gazetteer, 卷8, "Salt *Fau*", 鹽埠 sub-section, Cheung Yat-ping, *op.cit.* p. 816.

36 1819 gazetteer, 卷8, Cheung Yat-ping, *op.cit.* p. 815.

37 1819 gazetteer, 卷8, Cheung Yat-ping, *op.cit.* p. 815.

38 Early 20th century Hong Kong government records give a good deal of information on the system that they found when they took over the New Territories in 1899. See in particular Hong Kong Public Records Office, documents CSO 4904/1903 Ext (HKRS No 58 D-S No 1/21 (104)), 1903, and CSO Ext. 89/1900 (HKRS No 58 D-S No 1/15/14), 1900.

39 *Salt: Production and Taxation, op.cit.*

7 Corruption

1 See John R. Watt, *The District Magistrate in Late Imperial China, op.cit.* ch. 5, for a fuller discussion of all this.

2 Huang Liu-hung (*A Complete Book*, ed. Djang Chu, *op.cit. passim*).

3 Bradly Reed, *Talons and Teeth, op.cit. passim.*

4 Djang Chu, introduction to Huang Liu-hung, *A Complete Book*, op.cit. p. 24, "Local practice and the magistrate's conscience were the only limitations on excess".

5 T'ung-tsu Chü, *Local Government in China Under the Ch'ing, op.cit.* p. 22.

6 W. F. Mayers, N. B. Dennys, C. King, *The Treaty Ports of China and Japan: A Complete Guide to the Open Ports of those Countries, together with Peking, Yedo, Hongkong and Macao, Forming a Guide Book and Vade Mecum for Travellers, Merchants, and Residents in General*, Trübner and Co. London, 1867, p. 24. Coolie wages in the 1890s are as given in the Hong Kong government statistical returns (the *Blue Book*).

7 Du Fengzhi, as magistrate of Nam Hoi, had to pay 18,500 taels a year in such routine gifts in the early 1870s, and usually 3,000–5,000 taels on such things as special gifts for incoming officials, for the annual festivities for the Empress Dowager's birthday, for the viceroy's birthday, and so forth. It is likely that he had to find at least 21,000 taels each year. While the gifts demanded from small rural counties would have been far less than this, the total sum would always have been a significant factor in the magistrate's accounts. While it is likely that the gifts demanded in the late Ming and early Qing were somewhat less, they must still have been a grave burden. See Yau Tsit, 同治光緒年間廣州的官紳民, *op.cit.* pp. 37–38.

8 For the gifts received by Du Fengzhi in Kwong Ning, see Yau Tsit, 知縣與地方士紳, *op.cit.* p. 5.

9 T'ung-tsu Chü, *Local Government in China Under the Ch'ing, op.cit.* pp. 22–26, states that, even after the Yongzheng pay increases "there is no doubt that [such

extra-legal demands from the Provinces] far exceeded the magistrate's total salary", but this seems unlikely to be true of San On: the general tenor of the gazetteer strongly suggests pressure on the county's finances were much less severe in the later 18th century than they had been a century earlier.

10 "Several times a month" in Kwong Ning in 1866, according to Du Fengzhi, see Yau Tsit, 知縣與地方士紳, *op.cit.* p. 14.

11 Huang Liu-hung (*A Complete Book*, ed. Djang Chu, *op.cit.* especially pp. 571–577) shows what problems visiting dignitaries could cause a magistrate.

12 Bradly Reed suggests that, in Ba County, the clerks had to find the money to maintain and clean the building in which they worked (*Talons and Teeth, op.cit.*), but it was the magistrate who had to find the money for the maintenance of the rest of the yamen.

13 See P. H. Hase, *Custom, Land and Livelihood, op.cit.* pp. 34–37.

14 卷6, Cheung Yat-ping, *op.cit.* pp. 372–373.

15 *Lord Macartney's Observations upon China*, in *An Embassy to China, being the Journal kept by Lord Macartney during his Embassy to the Emperor Ch'ien-lung, 1793–1794*, London, Folio Society, 2004, p. 213. Taxes began to be increased from the middle 19th century, after likin (internal customs payments) began to be collected. Likin, however, was an impost collected by and for the provincial government: central government taxes, and especially the land tax and the salt tax, remained unchanged. Taxes in Kwong Ning in 1866 were low: about 7,500 taels taken from about 208,000 mu of arable land registered for tax, or barely 40 cash a mu (about 25 Hong Kong cents an acre), see Yau Tsit, 知縣與地方士紳, op.cit. p. 17.

16 See Bradly Reed, *Talons and Teeth, op.cit.* for a discussion of the problems inadequate income for the magistracies gave rise to.

17 The Ming code has a section on "Malfeasance in Public Office" (section 6, articles 367–378) and another on "Judgement and Imprisonment" (section 11, articles 419–447) which together provide a wide-ranging set of rules on malfeasance in public office. The death penalty was imposed on any official who, for a consideration, convicted an innocent person, and let a guilty one go free, the innocent person then being executed for the crime. See *The Great Ming Code*, Jiang Yonglin, *op.cit.*

18 Yau Tsit, 知縣與地方士紳, *op.cit.* p. 4.

19 Collecting tax in excess of the quota was illegal under article 132 of the Ming Code. Tax grain had to be measured off level, without being shaken down or heaped up (article 128). Fees could not be taken (article 128). Taking donations

for public works was illegal under article 374. See *The Great Ming Code*, Jiang Yonglin, *op.cit.* The Qing code had similar strictures.

20 See Bradly Reed, *Talons and Teeth*, *op.cit.* for a valuable discussion of these points. He makes the point that the magistracy clerks held themselves up as Confucian superior men, doing work which served the people, while depending entirely on income which was strictly against the law.

21 Huang Liu-hung (*A Complete Book*, ed. Djang Chu, *op.cit.* pp. 137, 138, 141, 528).

22 T'ung-tsu Chü, *Local Government in China Under the Ch'ing*, *op.cit.* p. 133.

23 Du Fengzhi, when magistrate of Nam Hoi, collected 152,000 taels of silver annually as land tax. His quota was 90,000 taels. The excess tax was used to meet his office expenses, but these came to 72,000 taels, so the excess tax did not quite meet all the expenses (excess taxes collected on other taxes made up the difference). Nonetheless, the money received was very much above the quota sent to the provincial teasurer. See Yau Tsit, 同治光緒年間廣州的官紳民, *op.cit.* p. 39.

24 Du Fengzhi was able to collect all the taxes due on his quota in Kwong Ning also, but, until he was able to break the gentry strangle-hold over tax collection, his receipts of excess tax were less than he needed.

25 Du Fengzhi certainly used excess tax to pay off the debts he had amassed before becoming magistrate.

26 卷6, Cheung Yat-ping, *op.cit.* p. 374.

27 See P. H. Hase, *Custom, Land and Livelihood*, *op.cit.* pp. 71–93, and 44–46, and see pp. 206–214 for a case where new land tax was registered for newly reclaimed land in the 19th century.

28 Huang Liu-hung (*A Complete Book*, ed. Djang Chu, *op.cit.* pp. 217, 219, 245) states that no newly reclaimed land should be reported, for fear the tax quota would be permanently raised, but any tax from it should be held back: no surveys should be conducted, for the same reason, or, if conducted, their findings should not be reported. Clearly Huang Liu-hung felt very strongly that excess land tax should be held back and spent within the magistracy.

29 See the biographies of these magistrates, *loc.cit.*

30 Huang Liu-chung (*A Complete Book*, ed. Djang Chu, *op.cit.* p. 107) states that supernumerary clerks and "runners" received no wages.

31 T'ung-tsu Chü, *Local Government in China Under the Ch'ing*, *op.cit.* p. 45.

32 Djang Chu, introduction to Huang Liu-hung, *A Complete Book*, *op.cit.* p. 24.

33　See Bradly Reed, *Talons and Teeth*, *op.cit.* for the customary fees charged in Sichuan.

34　For other fees charged, see 內鄉縣與衙門文化, *op.cit.* p. 162.

35　Huang Liu-hung (*A Complete Book*, ed. Djang Chu, *op.cit.* p. 255) states that anyone beating the drum without a valid reason should be "punished severely".

36　In land deeds surviving from the New Territories, tax payment in silver of 0.0053 taels to 0.014 mau is given as the normal commutation for a plot which may well have been the only tax-paying land held by the taxpayer in question (less than a fiftieth of an ounce of silver). Other land deeds suggest payments of 0.1855, 0.0045, 0.0045, 0.0066. 0.0151, and 0.0195 taels at this same rate of commutation, that is, payments of between about a fiftieth of an ounce to about a quarter of an ounce. See P. H. Hase, *Custom, Land and Livelihood*, *op.cit.* pp. 216–219, 222–226, 231–236.

37　*The Great Ming Code*, Jiang Yonglin, *op.cit.* Article 143.

38　T'ung-tsu Chü, *Local Government in China Under the Ch'ing*, *op.cit.* p. 135. Huang Liu-hung (*A Complete Book*, ed. Djang Chu, *op.cit.* pp. 190–191) had a very low opinion of the honesty of the silversmiths his magistracy employed.

39　T'ung-tsu Chü, *Local Government in China Under the Ch'ing*, *op.cit.* p. 132.

40　Biography of An Yumei, 卷10, 1819 gazetteer, 卷14, much shortened, Cheung Yat-ping op.cit. pp. 416–417, 884. Li Kecheng's comments on the meltage fee are in his edict 革火耗以勸輸將, "Forbid meltage fee payments for silver exchange, in order that tax payments can be encouraged", 卷12, Cheung Yat-ping, *op.cit.* pp. 463, 1819 gazetteer, 卷22, pp. 1024.

41　See Huang Liu-hung, *A Complete Book*, ed. Djang Chu, *op.cit.* p. 257.

42　Biographies of Qiu Tiqian and Yu Zhu, 卷10, Cheung Yat-ping, *op.cit.* pp. 410, 411, 1819 gazetteer, 卷14, pp. 879, 881. See Bradly Reed, *Talons and Teeth*, *op.cit.* for a discussion of the importance of fees in criminal cases to the runners, the complex regulations which Ba County used to ensure that these plum jobs were distributed fairly, and the frequent intervention of the magistrate where accusations of improper distribution, contrary to the county rules, had taken place. Presumably there were similar rules in San On, and Qiu Tiqian and Yu Zhu were probably intervening, like the Ba County magistrates, to ensure that they were followed.

43　Biographies of these magistrates, 卷10, Cheung Yat-ping, *op.cit.* pp. 411, 415, 416–417, 1819 gazetteer, 卷14, pp. 880, 884, 885. Du Fengzhi had put a complainant of a crime into detention pending the hearing, but forgot all about him until he received a plaintive petition a month later: he was embarrassed, as he usually tried to ensure that he heard cases quickly to avoid people staying in jail for any length of time, see Cheung Yin, 清代縣級政權, *op.cit.* Table 6.5, 1, and p. 213.

44   P. H. Hase, *Custom, Land and Livelihood, op.cit.* p. 75.

45   P. H. Hase, *Custom, Land and Livelihood, op.cit.* pp. 206–214.

46   Du Fengzhi in 1866 was outraged to learn that his staff were charging him twice the amount as "gate fee" (he called this payment 門包) for getting documents into his superiors' yamen than they were actually paying. See Yau Tsit, 知縣與地方士紳, *op.cit.* p. 6.

47   Li Kecheng's comments are in his eighth edict, 戢刁訟以安善良, "Eradicate corrupt lawsuits, in order to achieve peace and security", 卷12, Cheung Yat-ping, *op.cit.* p. 464, 1819 gazetteer, 卷22, p. 1026. Huang Liu-hung (*A Complete Book*, ed. Djang Chu, *op.cit.* pp. 304–305) notes that a crime cannot be determined until any absconding suspect is apprehended.

48   From his biography in the provincial gazetteer, *op.cit.* taken from his biography in the Fujian Provincial Gazetteer.

49   For Zhou Xiyao and Li Kecheng, see above, for An Yumei and Jin Wenmo, see their biographies, *loc.cit.*

50   See the biographies of these magistrates, 卷10, Cheung Yat-ping, *op.cit.* pp. 411, 412–413, 415, 416–417, 1819 gazetteer, 卷14, pp. 880, 881, 884.

51   See the biographies of these magistrates, *loc.cit.*

52   Du Fengzhi in Kwong Ning needed this money, however, and was prepared to go to quite some lengths to get it if payment was delayed: he would send his servants to surround the defaulting clerk's desk, where they would beat gongs and clash wooden staves together, chanting, "Hand over the money", until the clerk stumped up. See Yau Tsit, 知縣與地方士紳, *op.cit.* p. 6.

53   See P. H. Hase, "Rules on the Protection of Village Trees in the New Territories and Associated Matters", in *Journal of the Hong Kong Branch of the Royal Asiatic Society*, Vol. 51, 2011, pp. 31–56.

54   Gazetteer, 卷6, Cheung Yat-ping, *op.cit.* p. 374.

55   1819 gazetteer, 卷8, Cheung Yat-ping, *op.cit.* pp. 812–813.

56   See the biographies of these magistrates, *loc.cit.*

57   See the biographies of these magistrates in the provincial gazetteer, *op.cit.* pp. 221, 375.

59   See the biographies of these magistrates, *loc.cit.* Huang Liu-hung, writing before the increase in magistrates' salaries, (*A Complete Book*, ed. Djang Chu, *op.cit.*

pp. 72, 547, and elsewhere) stresses the importance of frugality as a virtue of magistrates.

59 See the biographies of these magistrates, *loc.cit.*

60 The prefectural gazetteer biography was copied to the provincial gazetteer, *op.cit.* p. 375.

61 From his biography in the provincial gazetteer, *op.cit.* p. 221, taken from his biography in the Fujian Provincial Gazetteer.

62 Biography of Peng Yunnian, 卷10, 1819 gazetteer, 卷14, Cheung Yat-ping, *op.cit.* pp. 411, 881.

63 Biography in the provincial gazetteer, *op.cit.* p. 375.

64 Biography, 1819 gazetteer, 卷14, Cheung Yat-ping, *op.cit.* p. 885. Huang Liu-hung also includes diligence as a virtue needed by magistrates (*A Complete Book*, ed. Djang Chu, *op.cit.* p. 72, and elsewhere).

65 See the biographies of these magistrates, *loc.cit.* Also Ng and Baker, *New Peace County, op.cit.* pp. 114–116.

66 See the biographies of these magistrates, *loc.cit.*

67 Biography of Chen Gu, 卷10, Cheung Yat-ping, *op.cit.* p. 411, 1819 gazetteer, 卷 14, p. 881.

68 Huang Liu-hung (*A Complete Book*, ed. Djang Chu, *op.cit.* p. 622) states that "the magistrate has frequent social contacts with the members of the local gentry", and, clearly, found nothing undesirable in this.

69 See Yau Tsit, 同治光緒年間光州的官紳民, *op.cit.* pp. 41–47, and 晚清廣東的公局, *op.cit.* and also Cheung Yin, 清代縣級政權, *op.cit. passim.*

70 See Yau Tsit, 同治光緒年間光州的官紳民, *op.cit.* p. 36: 太平天國被平定以後，各大城市滿州駐防官員的地位進一步下隆, "After the pacification of the Tai Ping Kingdom, the position of Manchu military officers in every large city decreased step by step." See also Yau Tsit, 關于康有為祖輩的一些新史料 ("New Historical Material on the Ancestors of Kang Yu-wei"), reprinted in 晚清民國初年, *op.cit.* p. 62.

71 See P. H. Hase, "A Village War in Sham Chun", in *Journal of the Hong Kong Branch of the Royal Asiatic Society*, Vol. 30, 1990, pp. 265–281.

72 Stewart Lockhart, *Extracts from a Report by Mr Stewart Lockhart on the Extension of the Colony of Hong Kong, 1898*, in *Papers Laid before the Legislative Council of Hong Kong, 1899* (Sessional Papers), Government Printer, Hong Kong, 1900, No. 9/99, pp. 192–193, "Local Government in the Villages" section. See also Yau Tsit, 晚清廣東的公局, *op.cit.* pp. 84–85, and Cheung Yin, 清代縣級政權, *op.cit. passim.*

73 Tax collection was being supervised by a gentry committee, the 倉局, and it was the gentry militia which was the only force available to collect taxes from the less willing: see Yau Tsit, 知縣與地方士紳, *op.cit.*

74 Despite his problems, however, Du Fungzhi said that the position in Kwong Ning was nowhere near as bad as that in Shun Tak (Shunde, 順德) County, where the gentry were so powerful that few men wanted to be posted there as magistrate. Yau Tsit makes it clear that the magistracy of Du Fengzhi was a "turning-point" in the developing relationship between the magistrate and the elite in Kwong Ning: Du Fengzhi effectively managing to stop the drift towards elite control (See Yau Tsit, 知縣與地方士紳, *op.cit.* pp. 31–33).

75 Huang Liu-hung, *A Complete Book*, ed. Djang Chu, *op.cit.* p. 529 and elsewhere. For anonymous denunciations, see P. H. Hase, "Village Literacy and Scholarship: Village Scholars and their Documents", in *Journal of the Hong Kong Branch of the Royal Asiatic Society*, Vol. 52, 2012, pp. 77–138, at pp. 89–92.

76 Translated (not quite completely) by Herbert A. Giles, 4th revised Ed. Reprinted Kelly and Walsh, Hong Kong, 1968.

77 Translated by Yang Hsien-yi and Gladys Yang, Foreign Languages Press, Peking, 1957.

78 See P. H. Hase, *Custom, Land and Livelihood*, op.cit. pp. 202–206.

79 Cheung Yin, 清代縣級政權, *op.cit.* p. 231, 192, and elsewhere. Liu Pangjiu, 內鄉縣 衙與衙門文化, *op.cit.* p. 162.

8 Conclusions

1 The biography of Ma Yimao differs in the 1688 gazetteer and the 1819 gazetteer, and elements of both versions are included here. See 卷10, Cheung Yat-ping, *op.cit.* p. 415, 1819 gazetteer, 卷14, p. 883.

Appendices

1 1688 gazetteer, 卷10, Cheung Yat-ping, *op.cit.* pp. 412–413, 1819 gazetteer, 卷 14, p. 881, *New Peace County*, op.cit. p. 115.

2 1688 gazetteer, 卷11, Cheung Yat-ping, *op.cit.* pp. 445–448.

3 1688 gazetteer, 卷10, Cheung Yat-ping, *op.cit.* p. 415, 1819 gazetteer, p. 884, partially translated in *New Peace County*, op.cit. p. 115. A brief note on Li Kecheng is also to be found in *Dictionary of National Biography*, ed. M. Holdsworth and C. Munn, Hong Kong University Press, 2012, p. 255–256, but it is not altogether accurate.

Bibliography

Baker, Hugh D. R, see Peter Y. L. Ng.

Board of Civil Appointments, Records, 中國第一歷史檔案館藏清代官員履歷檔案全編.

Breitschneider, E. *On the Knowledge Possessed by the Ancient Chinese of the Arabs and Arabian Colonies, and also Western Countries, Mentioned in Chinese Books*, Trübner, London, 1871.

The Cambridge History of China, gen. ed. J. K. Fairbank, Vol. 3, *The Sui and Tang Dynasties, Part 1*, ed. D. C. Twitchett; Vol. 7, *The Ming Dynasty, 1368–1644, Part 1*, ed. F. W. Mote and D. Twitchett; Vol. 9, *The Ch'ing Dynasty to 1800, Part 1*, ed. W. J. Peterson; Vol. 10, *The Late Ch'ing, 1800–1911, Part 1*, ed, J. K. Fairbank; Vol. 11, *The Late Ch'ing 1800–1911, Part 2*, ed. J. K. Fairbank and Liu Kwang-ching.

Chan Wing-hoi, "The Dangs of Kam Tin and their Jiu Festival", in *Journal of the Hong Kong Branch of the Royal Asiatic Society*, Vol. 29.

Cheung Yat-ping (張一兵, Zhang Yibing), 深圳舊志三種 ("Three Ancient Gazetteers of Shenzhen"), 海天出版社, Shenzhen, 2006.

Cheung Yat-ping, (張一兵, Zhang Yibing) 深圳古代簡史 ("A Brief History of Shenzhen in Ancient Times"), 深圳博物館, 文物出版社, 1997.

Cheung Yin (Zhang Yan, 張研), 清代縣級政權控制鄉村的具體考察: 以同治年間廣寧知縣杜鳳治日記為中心 ("A Study of Qing County Authority and the Villages: Centred on the Tongzhi Period Diary of Kwong Ning Magistrate Du Fengzhi"), 大象出版社, 2010.

China: Imperial Maritime Customs, see *Salt: Production and Taxation*.

Chü T'ung-tsu, *Law and Society in Traditional China*, Paris, Mouton, 1961.

Chü T'ung-tsu, *Local Government in China under the Ch'ing*, Harvard University Press, 1962.

Chung Li-chang, *The Chinese Gentry: Studies on their Role in Nineteenth Century Chinese Society*, Washington Paperbacks on Russia and Asia, University of Washington Press, 1955.

Dennys, N. B, see Mayers, W. F.

Dictionary of National Biography, ed. M. Holdsworth and C. Munn, Hong Kong University Press, 2012.

Djang Chu (章楚), ed., and trans., *A Complete Book Concerning Happiness and Benevolence: A Manual for Local Magistrates in Seventeenth-Century China (福惠全書)*, Huang Liu-hung (黃六鴻), University of Arizona Press, 1984.

Elman, Benjamin A. *A Cultural History of Civil Examinations in Late Imperial China*, University of California Press, 2000.

Elman, Benjamin A. *Civil Examinations and Meritocracy in Late Imperial China*, Harvard University, 2013.

Great Ming Code: Da Ming lü, trans. and introduced, Jiang Yonglin, University of Washington Press, Asian Law Series, 2004.

Fairbank, J. K. see *The Cambridge History of China*.

Fang Guangwa, (方光華) 旌德人文 ("Culture of Jingde County"), Hefei University of Technology Press, 2011.

Faure, David, *The Structure of Chinese Rural Society: Lineage and Village in the Eastern New Territories, Hong Kong*, East Asian Historical Monographs, Oxford University Press, Hong Kong, 1986.

Faure, David, "The Po Tak Temple in Sheung Shui Market" in *Journal of the Hong Kong Branch of the Royal Asiatic Society*, Vol. 22, 1983.

Faure David, see Hase P. H.

Gardiner, C. S, *Chinese Traditional Historiography*, Harvard University Press, 1938, as reprinted 1961.

Gazetteer, see Cheung Yat-ping, Ng, Peter Y. L, Guangdong Provincial, Hoi Fung, Jiashin, Jingde, Jinxian, Kaizhou, Linzhou, Qizhou, Shenzhen City, Shiqian, Tieling, Tong'an, Xinjian, Yihuang, Zhangping.

Giles H., trans. 聊齊誌異 (translated as *Strange Stories from a Chinese Studio* 4th revised edition. Reprinted Kelly and Walsh, Hong Kong, 1968).

Gompertz, H. H. J, *Some Notes on Land Tenure in the New Territories* (Appendix No. 1 to J.H. Stewart Lockhart *Report on the New Territories for the Year 1900*, in *Papers Laid before the Legislative Council of Hong Kong, 1901*, No 28/1901 (Sessional Papers), Hong Kong, 1902.

Guangdong Provincial Gazetteer, [道光]廣東通志, (photoreproduction of the 1934 reprint of the 1822 original), 續修四庫全書, 史部地理彙, Vol. 674, 上海古籍出版社, 1995.

Haifeng, see Hoi Fung.

Hase P. H. "A Village War in Sham Chun", in *Journal of the Hong Kong Branch of the Royal Asiatic Society*, Vol. 30, 1990.

Hase, P. H. "The Alliance of Ten: Settlement and Politics in the Sha Tau Kok Area", in *Down to Earth: the Territorial Bond in South China*, ed. D. Faure and H.F. Siu, Stanford University Press, 1995.

Hase, P. H. "Beside the Yamen: Nga Tsin Wai Village", *Journal of the Hong Kong Branch of the Royal Asiatic Society*, Vol. 39, 1999.

Hase, P. H, "Rules on the Protection of Village Trees in the New Territories and Associated Matters", in *Journal of the Hong Kong Branch of the Royal Asiatic Society*, Vol. 51, 2011.

Hase, P. H, "Village Literacy and Scholarship: Village Scholars and their Documents", in *Journal of the Hong Kong Branch of the Royal Asiatic Society*, Vol. 52, 2012.

Hase, P. H, *Custom, Land and Livelihood in Rural South China: The Traditional Land Law of Hong Kong's New Territories*, Hong Kong University Press with the Royal Asiatic Society, Hong Kong Branch (Hong Kong Studies Series), 2013.

Hayes, J. W. "Purchase of Degrees, Rank, and Appointment in Late Qing China: Some Impressions from Contemporary Sources", *Journal of the Hong Kong Branch of the Royal Asiatic Society*, Vol. 53, 2013.

Ho, Ping-ti, *The Ladder of Success in Imperial China: Aspects of Social Mobility, 1368-1911*, Columbia University Press, 1962.

Hoi Fung Gazetteer (Haifeng), 廣東省海豐縣志, 1750, photo-reproduced, 中國方志叢書, 第十號, 成文出版社, Taipei, 1966.

Huang, Baiquan (黃柏權), ed. 肇慶七星岩石刻詩文選 ("Poems inscribed on stone at the Tsat Shing Yam, Shiu Hing"), 廣東省肇慶星湖風景名勝區管理局, 1989.

Huang, Liu-hung (黃六鴻), see Djang Chu.

Huang, Philip C. C, *Civil Justice in China: Representation and Practice in the Qing*, Stanford University Press, Stanford, 1996.

Huang, Philip C. C, *Chinese Civil Justice, Past and Present*, Bowman and Littlefield, 2010.

Huang, Ray, *1587, A Year of No Significance: Ming China in Decline*, Yale University Press, 1982.

Jiang, Yonglin, see *The Great Ming Code*.

Jiashin Gazetteer, 中國地方志集成, 浙江府縣志輯, Vol. 19, 乾隆桐盧縣志, 光緒重修嘉善縣志, 校勘光緒嘉善縣志劄記; 江蘇古籍出版社, 上海書店, 巴蜀書店, 1993.

Jingde Gazetteer, 旌德縣志, 1808, reprinted 1925. 成文出版社:中國方志叢書, no. 227, reprinted 1998. 南京:江蘇古籍出版社:中國地方志集成, Vol. 53.

Jinxian Gazetteer, 中國地方志集成, 浙江府縣志輯, Vol. 59, 同治進賢縣志, 同治十年,江蘇古籍出版社, 上海書店, 巴蜀書店, 1996.

Johnson, R. *Confucianism and Modern China*, Victor Gollancz, 1934.

Johnson, R. *Confucian Personalities*, ed. A. F. Wright and D. C. Twitchett, Stanford University Press, 1962.

Kaizhou Gazetteer, 清光緒開州縣志, 濮陽縣地方史志辦公室校注, 中州古籍出版社, 1995.

King C, see Mayers, W. F.

Lam, Tin-wai (林天蔚, Lin, Tianwei) and Siu, Anthony K. K. 香港前代論集 ("Notes on Hong Kong History"), 臺灣商務印書館, 1985.

Lau, Thomas Y. W. (劉潤和) 明清胥吏的作用與歷史的進程, ("History and Duties of Magistracy Clerks in the Ming-Qing Period"), 香港經濟學社 (IES), 1995.

Li, Anren, (李安仁), 湖湘士子謠, in 藝海, Vol. 3, 2007.

Liang, Linxia, *Delivering Justice in Qing China: Civil Trials in the Magistrate's Court*, Oxford University Press, for the British Academy, 2007.

Linzhou Gazetteer, 中國地方志集成, 江西府縣志輯, Vol. 48, 同治臨州縣志, 江蘇古籍出版社, 上海書店, 巴蜀書社, photoreproduction of 同治九年 (1870) original, 1996.

Liu, Kwang-ching, see *The Cambridge History of China*.

Liu, Pengjiu, (劉鵬九), 內鄉縣衙與衙門文化 ("Neixiang County Yamen and Yamen Culture"), 中州古籍出版社, 2006.

Lo, Hsiang-lin (羅香林), 一八四二年以前之香港及其對外交通 ("Hong Kong and its External Communications before 1842: The History of Hong Kong Prior to British Colonisation"), Hong Kong, 1959 (Partial English Translation, Institute of Chinese Culture, Hong Kong 1963).

Lo, Hsiang-lin, see Law Heung-lam.

Lockhart, J. H. Stewart, *Report on the New Territory during the First Year of British Adninistration*, in *Papers Laid before the Legislative Council of Hong Kong, 1900* (Sessional Papers, 1900), Hong Kong, Government Printer, 1901, No. 15/1900.

Lockhart, J. H. Stewart, *Extracts from a Report by Mr. Stewart Lockhart on the Extension of the Colony of Hong Kong*, in *Papers Laid before the Legislative Council of Hong Kong, 1899* (Sessional Papers, 1899), No. 9/99, Hong Kong Government Printer, 1900

Lockhart, J. H. Stewart, *Report on the New Territories for the Year 1900*, see Gompertz, H. H. J.

Macartney, Lord, *Lord Macartney's Observations upon China*, in *An Embassy to China, being the Journal kept by Lord Macartney during his Embassy to the Emperor Ch'ien-lung, 1793–1794*, London, Folio Society, 2004, p. 213.

Mayers, W. F. Dennys, N. B. King, C. *The Treaty Ports of China and Japan: A Complete Guide to the Open Ports of those Countries, Together with Peking, Yedo, Hong Kong and Macao, Forming a Guide Book and Vade Mecum for Travellers, Merchants, and Residents in General*, Trübner and Co. London, 1867.

Mote, F. *Imperial China, 900–1800*, Harvard University Press, 1999.

Mote, F. see *The Cambridge History of China*.

Na, Silu, (那思陸), 清代州縣衙門番判制度, 中國政法大學出版社, 2006 ("Legal Arrangements in County and Prefectural yamen in the Qing")

"*A New Collection of Kwangtung Provincial Edicts*", 粵東省例新纂, originally published 1846, republished with an appendix added in the late nineteenth century, reprinted 成文出版社, Taipei, 1968.

Ng, Hei (吳曦) in *Lantau, The Development of*, 爛頭島開發, 1941.

Ng, Peter Y. L. and Baker, Hugh D. R. *New Peace County: A Chinese Gazetteer of the Hong Kong Region*, Hong Kong University Press.

Nivison, D. S. *Confucianism in Action*, Stanford University Press, 1959.

Nivison, D. S. *The Ways of Confucianism: Investigations in Chinese Philosophy*, Open Court Publishing, 1996.

Norton, F. W, see Spence, Jonathan.

Nylan, M. see Wilson, T. A.

Palmer, Michael J. E. "The Surface-Subsoil Form of Divided Ownership in Late Imperial China: Some Examples from the New Territories of Hong Kong", in *Hong Kong Law Journal*, Vol. 21.1, 1991.

Peterson, W. J. see *The Cambridge History of China*.

Puk, Wing-kin, (卜永堅, Bu Yongjian), 抗租與迎神:從己卯年(1999)香港大埔林村鄉十年一度太平清醮看青代林村與龍躍頭鄧氏之關係 ("Notes from the *Ta Tsiu* in Lam Tsuen and Lung Yeuk Tau") in 華南研究資料中心通訊 (South China Research Resource Station Newsletter), No. 18, 2000.

Qi, Tajun, (屈大均): 廣東新話 ("New Tales of Kwangtung"), 1700.

Reed, Bradly, *Talons and Teeth: County Clerks and Runners in the Qing Dynasty*, Stanford University Press, 2000.

Qizhou Gazetteer, 中國地方志集成,湖北府縣志輯, Vol. 23, 光緒蘄州志, 光緒八年, photoreproduction, 江蘇古籍出版社,上海書店,巴蜀書社, 1996.

Ren, Lida (任立達), 中國古代縣衙制度史 (青島出版社) ("History of the Structure of Ancient Chinese County yamen").

Salt: Production and Taxation, China: Imperial Maritime Customs, V. Office Series: Customs Papers No 81, published for the Customs Archives, Shanghai, Statistical Department of the Inspectorate General of Customs, 1906.

Sessional Papers, see Lockhart, J. H. Stewart, and see Gompertz, H. H. J.

Shenzhen City Gazetteer, 深圳市志,社會風俗卷 ("*Shenzhen City Gazetteer*, Society and Customs Volume"), 深圳市地方志編纂委員會, 方志出版社, 2014.

Shiqian Gazetteer, 中國地方志集成, 貴州府縣志, Vol. 47, 石阡縣志, 江蘇古籍出版社, 上海書店, 巴蜀書社, photoreproduction of 1922 original, 1965, 1996.

Siu, Anthony K. K. (蕭國健, Xiao Guojian), *Forts and Fortlets: Coastal Defence in Guangdong During the Ming and Qing Dynasties*, 關城與炮台:明清兩代廣東海防, Urban Council, Hong Kong, 1997.

Siu, Anthony K. K. (蕭國健, Xiao Guojian), 香港之海防歷史與軍事遺蹟 ("The History of Coastal Defences in the Hong Kong Area, and Military Relics"), 中華文教交流服務中心, 2006.

Siu, Anthony K.K. see Lam, Tin-wai.

Siu, Helen F, see Hase P. H.

Spence, Jonathan, *The Search for Modern China*, 2nd edition, ed. F.W. Norton, 1999.

Sun, Min, (孫民), ed. 古代風俗詩面 ("Poems on Ancient Folk Practices"), 1992.

Sung, Hok-pang, "Legends and Stories of the New Territories: Kam Tin; Part II", in *Journal of the Hong Kong Branch of the Royal Asiatic Society*, Vol. 14.

Tieling Gazetteer, 鐵嶺縣志, 1931, reprinted 成文出版社:中國方志叢書:東北地方,第五號, 1998.

Tong'an Gazetteer, 中華民國拾捌年刊, 同安縣志, 廈門市同安區方志編纂委員會辦公室整理, 方志出版社, 吳錫璜著, 2007.

Tu, Wei-ming, *Way, Learning and Politics: Essays on the Confucian Intellectual*, State University of New York Press, 1993.

Tu, Wei-ming, *Confucian Thought*, State University of New York Press, 1985.

Tu, Wei-ming, *Humanity and Self-Cultivation: Essays in Confucian Thought*, Berkeley, Asian Humanities Press, 1985.

Twitchett, D. C, see *The Cambridge History of China*.

Wang Gungwu, *The Nanhai Trade: The Early History of Trade in the South China Sea*, Journal of the Malayan Branch of the Royal Asiatic Society, Vol. 31, No. 2, 1958, reprinted 2003.

Watt, John R, *The District Magistrate in Late Imperial China*, Columbia University Press, 1972.

Wilson, T. A, *On Sacred Ground: Culture, Society, Politics, and the Formation of the Cult of Confucius*, Harvard University Press, 2002.

Wilson, T. A. and Nylan, M. *Confucius through the Ages: The Many Lives of Civilizations Greatest Sage*, Doubleday, New York, 2010.

Xinjian Gazetteer, 中國地方志集成,江西府縣志輯,同治新建縣志, 1871, photo-reproduced 江蘇古籍出版社, with 上海書店 and 巴蜀書社, Vol. 1.

Yao, Kenan, (姚柯楠), 説不盡的府衙往事: 南陽知府衙門考 ("A Complex Tale of Bygone Things at the Prefectural Yamen: A Study of the Nanyang Prefectural Yamen"), 中州古籍出版社, 2008.

Yang, Gladys, see Yang, Hsien-yi.

Yang, Hsien-yi and Gladys Yang, 儒林外史 (translated into English as *The Scholars*, Foreign Languages Press, Peking, 1957).

Yau, Tsit, (邱捷, Qiu Jie), 晚清民國初年:廣東的士神與商人 ("Kwangtung gentry and merchants in the late Qing and early Republic"), Guangxi Normal University Press, 2012.

Yihuang Gazetteer, 中國地方志集成,湖北府縣志輯, Vol. 51,同治宜黃縣志, 同治十年, photoreproduction, 江蘇古籍出版社, 上海書店, 巴蜀書社, 1996.

Yongxin Gazetteer, 中國地方志集成, 江西縣志輯, Vol. 71, 同治永新縣志, 江蘇古籍出版社, 1996.

Qiu Jie, see Yau Tsit.

Zhangping Gazetteer, 中國方志叢書,第九十三號,福建省漳平縣志, 1935, photoreproduced 成文出版社, Taipei, 1967.

Zhang, Yan, see Cheung Yin.

Zhang, Yibing, see Cheung Yat-ping.

卜永堅, see Puk Wing-kin.

中國第一歷史檔案館藏清代官員履歷檔案全編, see Board of Civil Appointments.

方光華, see Fang, Guangwa.

永新縣志, see Yongxin Gazetteer.

石阡縣志, see Shiqian Gazetteer.

同安縣志, see Tong'an Gazetteer.

任立達, see Ren, Lida.

吳曦, see Ng, Hei.

那思陸, see Na, Silu.

邱捷, see Yau, Tsit.

林天蔚, see Lam, Tin-wai.

李安仁, see Li, Anren.

屈大均, see Qi, Tajun.

宜黃縣志, see Yihuang Gazetteer.

姚柯楠, see Yao, Kenan.

海豐縣志, see Hoi Fung Gazetteer.

孫民, see Sun, Min.

清代稿抄本 ("Ching Hand-written Texts"), 廣東省立中山圖書館, Canton, 廣東人民出版社, 2007.

張研, see Cheung Yin.

張一兵, see Cheung Yat-ping.

深圳市志,社會風俗卷, see Shenzhen City Gazetteer.

旌德縣志, see Jingde Gazetteer.

聊齊誌異, see Giles, H.

開州縣志, see Kaizhou Gazetteer.

進賢縣志, see Jinxian Gazetteer.

黃六鴻 (Huang Liu-hung), see Djang, Chu.

新建縣志, see Xinjian Gazetteer.

粵東省例新纂, see *"A New Collection of Kwangtung Provincial Edicts"*.

嘉善縣志, see Jiashin Gazetteer.

漳平縣志, see Zhangping Gazetteer.

劉潤和, see Lau, Thomas Y. W.

劉鵬九, see Liu, Penjiu.

廣東通志, see Guangdong Provincial Gazetteer.

蕭國健, see Siu, Anthony K. K.

儒林外史, see Yang, Hsien-yi.

臨州縣志, see Linzhou Gazetteer.

蘄州志, see Qizhou Gazetteer.

關城與炮台, Siu, Anthony K.K.

爛頭島開發, see Ng, Hei.

鐵嶺縣志, see Tieling Gazetteer.

Index

G

H

I

Illustrious Officials, *see* Shrine of
  Illustrious Officials
imperial clan *see* emperor
inscription against four evils 67

J

jiansheng degrees 42
Jiashan County 43
Jiayi *see* Kap Yat
Jingde County 111
Jingjidao 50
Jinning prefecture 12, 49
Jin Qizhen, magistrate 23, 44–45,
  48, 56, 59, 170, 242, 245
  appointment (bannerman:
    possible member of imperial
    clan) 42–43
  cancels need for guarantors in
    tax payments 179–180
  dredges river 169, 171, 182,
    231
  founds Chiu Yam
    Nunnery171–172
  founds Shan Chuen Tan Temple
    171–172
Jinshi *see* Tsun Sz
Jintian *see* Kam Tin
Jin Wenmo, magistrate 22, 44, 50,
  53, 56, 224, 230, 245–246
  appeals for donations to county
    projects 170–171
  diligence 229
  discusses the classics with
    county scholars 137
  donates to county projects 170,
    182
  expeditious in hearing criminal
    cases 79
  frugality 228

place of origin 43
possible writer of petition
  against high salt taxes 201
promoted to censor, then to head
  of Fujian Salt Monopoly 51
rebuilds city walls 167
rejects zero-fee provision of
  daily necessities 140
repeals evil customs 225
writings 58
Jiulong *see* Kowloon
Jiulong River 110
Judge Bao 238
Judge Dee 238

K

Kaizhou County 51
Kam Tin 11, 23,
Kang Shoubai *see* Hong Sau-pak
Kaozhou *see* Ko Chau
Kap Yat *see* Nam Tau
Ke Chen *see* Ho Chan
Ko Chau 48
Kowloon 4, 8, 12, 16, 88–89, 120,
  161
Koxinga 20, 38, 159
Kui Yan degree 39, 153
Kunming 48
Kunyang 48
Kuiyong *see* Kwai Chung
Kwai Chung 161–162
Kwai Shin, County 252
Kwai Tak salt fields 194–195, 198,
  291
Kwangtung Province 18
  early history of 18
  impotence of military forces of
    in mid 19th century